William Shakespeare's

King Lear

With notes by
Hugh Holmes

Ordinary and Higher Level

Mentor Books Ltd.,
43 Furze Road
Sandyford Industrial Estate
Dublin 18
Republic of Ireland

Tel: +353 1 295 2112/2
Fax: +353 1 295 2114
e-mail: admin@mentorbooks.ie
www.mentorbooks.ie

ISBN: 978–1–909417–24–3

Editor: Daniel McCarthy
Cover, typesetting and design: Mary Byrne

King Lear

Act 4

Act 5

Character List

LEAR:	King of Britain
GONERIL:	Lear's eldest daughter
REGAN:	Lear's second daughter
CORDELIA:	Lear's youngest daughter
DUKE OF ALBANY:	Goneril's husband
DUKE OF CORNWALL:	Regan's husband
FRANCE:	King of France
BURGUNDY:	Duke of Burgundy
GLOUCESTER:	Earl of Gloucester
EDGAR:	Gloucester's eldest son
EDMUND:	Gloucester's illegitimate son
KENT:	Earl of Kent
THE FOOL:	Lear's jester
OSWALD:	Servant to Goneril
CURAN:	A follower of Gloucester
OLD MAN:	Gloucester's tenant

A Herald, a Captain, an Officer, a Doctor, Knights, Gentlemen, Attendants, Servants, Soldiers, Messengers

Setting
King Lear is set in Britain in the 8th Century BCE

Act 1 / Scene 1

Scene Summary

- The play opens with Kent and Gloucester talking about the pending abdication (stepping down) of King Lear.
- They also discuss Gloucester's son, Edmund, who was born out of marriage, and Gloucester's 'legitimate' son Edgar. Their conversation is playful and shows that Gloucester is fond of both his sons.
- Lear and his subjects arrive. Lear announces his intention to relinquish his crown and divide his kingdom between his three daughters (Goneril, Regan and Cordelia) and their husbands.
- Firstly he asks for his daughters to prove their love for him by encouraging them to flatter him.
- Goneril and Regan are quick to do so. However, Cordelia refuses.
- Lear is enraged and disowns her as his daughter.
- Kent asks Lear to show some restraint. Lear punishes him by banishing him from the kingdom.
- Lear then offers Cordelia as a wife to the Kings of France and Burgundy. However, he withdraws the previous promise of a dowry.
- Burgundy declines to marry her. However, despite these new terms, France agrees to the marriage as he sees her as a person of virtue and an 'unprized precious maid'.
- After Lear and his subjects leave, Goneril and Regan discuss Lear's rash behaviour. Together they discuss ways of protecting themselves from Lear's whims.

King Lear's Palace.
Enter KENT, GLOUCESTER and EDMUND

KENT
I thought the King had more affected[1] the Duke of Albany than Cornwall.

[1] **had more affected:** had more affection for i.e. favoured

GLOUCESTER
It did always seem so to us: but now, in the division of the kingdom,[2] it appears not which of the Dukes he values most; for equalities are so weighed, that curiosity in neither can make choice of either's moiety.[3]

[2] **division of the kingdom:** King Lear intends to divide his kingdom

[3] **for equalities...moiety:** as their shares are so even, no examination by either man could decide that the other's share ('moiety') of the kingdom was preferable

KENT
Is not this your son, my Lord?

GLOUCESTER
His breeding, sir, hath been at my charge.[4] I have so often blushed to acknowledge him, that now I am brazed to it.[5]

[4] **His breeding...charge:** 1 It is said that I am his father 2 I have paid for his upbringing

[5] **brazed to it:** used to it / no longer embarrassed by it

5

KENT

10 I cannot conceive[6] you.

GLOUCESTER

Sir, this young fellow's mother could;[7] whereupon she grew round-wombed, and had, indeed, sir, a son for her cradle ere[8] she had a husband for her bed. Do you smell a fault?[9]

KENT

I cannot wish the fault undone, the issue of it being so proper.[10]

GLOUCESTER

But I have, sir, a son by order of law,[11] some year elder than this, who yet is no dearer in my account;[12] though this knave came something saucily into the world[13] before he was sent for, yet was his mother fair; there was good sport at his

20 making,[14] and the whoreson[15] must be acknowledged. Do you know this noble gentleman, Edmund?

EDMUND

No, my Lord.

GLOUCESTER

My Lord of Kent: remember him hereafter as my honourable friend.

EDMUND

My services to your Lordship.

KENT

I must love you, and sue[16] to know you better.

EDMUND

Sir, I shall study deserving.[17]

GLOUCESTER

He hath been out[18] nine years, and away he shall again. The King is coming.

[Sennet.[19] Enter LEAR, CORNWALL, ALBANY, GONERIL, REGAN, CORDELIA and Attendants]

LEAR

30 Attend the Lords of France and Burgundy, Gloucester.

---

6 **conceive:** understand ('conceive' also means to become pregnant, which picks up on the idea of the illegitimacy of Gloucester's son)

7 **could:** i.e. could conceive (become pregnant)

8 **ere:** before

9 **fault:** sin

10 **the issue...proper:** the outcome/offspring ('issue') being so fine ('proper')

11 **by order of law:** 'legitimate'

12 **no dearer...account:** I don't value any higher i.e. both sons are held in equal esteem

13 **this knave...the world:** this rogue's birth was somewhat impertinent

14 **yet his mother...making:** yet his mother was pretty and it was good fun making him

15 **whoreson:** son of a whore. Despite his coarse sounding language, Gloucester is being affectionate and playful

16 **sue:** ask

17 **I shall study deserving:** I will try to deserve your good opinion

18 **out:** abroad

19 **Sennet:** Trumpet calls

GLOUCESTER

I shall, my Lord.

[Exeunt GLOUCESTER and EDMUND]

LEAR

Meantime we[20] shall express our darker purpose.[21]

Give me the map there. Know that we have divided

In three our kingdom: and 'tis our fast intent

To shake all cares and business from our age,[22]

Conferring them on younger strengths, while we

Unburthened crawl toward death.[23] Our son of Cornwall,

And you, our no less loving son of Albany,

We have this hour a constant will to publish

Our daughters' several dowers,[24] that future strife[25]

May be prevented now. The Princes, France and Burgundy,

Great rivals in our youngest daughter's love,

Long in our court have made their amorous sojourn,[26]

And here are to be answered. Tell me, my daughters, –

Since now we will divest us both of rule,[27]

Interest of territory, cares of state –

Which of you shall we say doth love us most?

That we our largest bounty[28] may extend

Where nature doth with merit challenge.[29] Goneril,

Our eldest-born, speak first.

GONERIL

Sir, I love you more than words can wield the matter,[30]

Dearer than eye-sight, space and liberty,[31]

Beyond what can be valued, rich or rare,

No less than life, with grace,[32] health, beauty, honour,

As much as child e'er loved, or father found;

A love that makes breath poor, and speech unable;

Beyond all manner of so much I love you.

CORDELIA

[Aside] What shall Cordelia speak? Love, and be silent.

LEAR

Of all these bounds, even from this line to this,

With shadowy[33] forests and with champains riched,[34]

With plenteous[35] rivers and wide-skirted meads,[36]

We make thee Lady. To thine and Albany's issues

Be this perpetual.[37] What says our second daughter,

Our dearest Regan, wife to Cornwall? Speak.

[20] **we:** I. Lear uses the 'royal plural'

[21] **darker purpose:** secret intention

[22] **'tis our fast intent...age:** it is my firm intention to rid myself of all worries in my old age

[23] **Conferring...toward death:** giving them to the strength of younger people as I move towards death without any burdens

[24] **a constant will...dowers:** a firm intention to make known my daughters' dowries

[25] **strife:** disagreement

[26] **Long...sojourn:** have stayed a long time in their courtship of (Cordelia). 'amorous': romantic. 'sojourn': stay/visit

[27] **we will divest...rule:** I will relinquish my power

[28] **largest bounty:** largest portion (of the kingdom)

[29] **nature doth...challenge:** where affection ('nature') deserves ('with merit') to claim ('challenge') this portion

[30] **more than words...matter:** more than words can say

[31] **space and liberty:** freedom and the space to enjoy it

[32] **grace:** happiness / favour

[33] **shadowy:** shady

[34] **champains riched:** rich, fertile land

[35] **plenteous:** fruitful / abundant

[36] **wide-skirted meads:** extensive meadows

[37] **perpetual:** in perpetuity i.e. forever

REGAN
I am made of the self-same mettle[38] that my sister is,
And prize me at her worth.[39] In my true heart
I find she names my very deed of love;[40]
Only she comes too short:[41] that I profess
Myself an enemy to all other joys,
70 Which the most precious square of sense[42] possesses
And find I am alone felicitate[43]
In your dear Highness' love.

CORDELIA
[Aside] Then poor Cordelia![44]
And yet not so, since, I am sure, my love's
More ponderous than my tongue.[45]

LEAR
[To REGAN] To thee and thine hereditary ever[46]
Remain this ample third of our fair kingdom,
No less in space, validity[47] and pleasure,
Than that conferred on Goneril. Now, our joy,
80 Although our last and least, to whose young love
The vines[48] of France and milk[49] of Burgundy
Strive to be interested,[50] what can you say to draw
A third more opulent[51] than your sisters? Speak.

CORDELIA
Nothing, my Lord.

LEAR
Nothing!

CORDELIA
Nothing.

LEAR
Nothing will come of nothing.[52] Speak again.

CORDELIA
Unhappy that I am, I cannot heave
My heart into my mouth. I love your Majesty
90 According to my bond;[53] no more nor less.

LEAR
How, how, Cordelia! Mend your speech a little,
Lest it may mar your fortunes.

---

[38] **self-same mettle:** 1 same substance (as in 'metal') 2 same spirit (as in 'mettle')
[39] **prize me at her worth:** value myself as highly
[40] **she names...of love:** she describes my love (as though she presented the same legal document: 'deed')
[41] **Only...too short:** but she doesn't go far enough
[42] **most precious square of sense:** the most perfectly formed sensibility
[43] **alone felicitate:** only joyful
[44] **poor Cordelia:** 'poor' in the sense that she may miss out on a portion of the kingdom, but not 'poor' in the sense that her love for Lear is genuine
[45] **my love's/More...tongue:** my love is weightier than can be expressed
[46] **hereditary ever:** inheritance to be kept forever
[47] **validity:** value

[48] **vines:** vineyards
[49] **milk:** pastureland
[50] **be interested:** lay claim
[51] **opulent:** richer

[52] **Nothing will come of nothing:** a Latin saying: *Ex nihilo nihil fit*

[53] **bond:** duty

CORDELIA

          Good my Lord,
You have begot[54] me, bred me, loved me: I
Return those duties back as are right fit,
Obey you, love you, and most honour you.
Why have my sisters husbands, if they say
They love you all? Haply,[55] when I shall wed,
That lord whose hand must take my plight[56] shall carry
Half my love with him, half my care and duty.
Sure, I shall never marry like my sisters,
To love my father all.[57]

LEAR
But goes thy heart with this?[58]

CORDELIA

         Ay, good my Lord.

LEAR
So young, and so untender?[59]

CORDELIA
So young, my Lord, and true.

LEAR
Let it be so; thy truth, then, be thy dower:[60]
For, by the sacred radiance of the sun,
The mysteries of Hecate,[61] and the night;
By all the operation of the orbs[62]
From whom we do exist, and cease to be;[63]
Here I disclaim all my paternal care,[64]
Propinquity and property of blood,[65]
And as a stranger to my heart and me
Hold thee, from this, for ever. The barbarous Scythian,[66]
Or he that makes his generation messes[67]
To gorge his appetite, shall to my bosom
Be as well neighboured, pitied and relieved,
As thou my sometime daughter.[68]

KENT

         Good my Liege, –

LEAR
Peace, Kent!
Come not between the dragon and his wrath![69]
I loved her most, and thought to set my rest[70]
On her kind nursery.[71] [To CORDELIA] Hence, and avoid my sight!

[54] **begot:** fathered

[55] **Haply:** Perhaps
[56] **plight:** marriage pledge

[57] **all:** exclusively

[58] **But goes thy heart with this?:** Do you really mean this?

[59] **untender:** unkind

[60] **thy truth...dower:** let truth be your only dowry
[61] **Hecate:** Goddess of Witchcraft
[62] **orbs:** planets and stars. These were thought to influence human fate
[63] **From whom...to be:** which governs our lives and deaths
[64] **Here I disclaim...care:** I give up my duty to you as a father
[65] **Propinquity...blood:** blood relationship and family obligations
[66] **barbarous Scythian:** savage inhabitants of Scythia (modern day Russia)
[67] **makes his...messes:** makes his meals from his own children
[68] **shall to my bosom...sometime daughter:** will be as close to my heart, helped, pitied and aided, as you my former daughter. Lear is saying that Cordelia will be as close to him as a savage cannibal
[69] **Come not...wrath!:** Don't come between a dragon and the object of his anger!
[70] **set my rest:** 1 live permanently with 2 stake all (a gambler's phrase)
[71] **nursery:** loving care

9

So be my grave my peace,[72] as here I give
Her father's heart from her![73] – Call France. Who stirs?[74]
Call Burgundy. Cornwall and Albany,
With my two daughters' dowers digest this third.[75]
Let pride, which she calls plainness, marry her.[76]
I do invest you jointly with my power,[77]
Pre-eminence, and all the large effects
That troop with majesty.[78] Ourself, by monthly course,
130 With reservation of an hundred knights,[79]
By you to be sustained, shall our abode
Make with you by due turns.[80] Only we still retain
The name, and all th' addition to a king;[81]
The sway, revenue, execution of the rest,
Beloved sons, be yours;[82] which to confirm,
This coronet[83] part betwixt you.
[Giving the crown]

KENT

                    Royal Lear,
Whom I have ever honoured as my king,
Loved as my father, as my master followed,
As my great patron[84] thought on in my prayers –

LEAR
140 The bow is bent and drawn, make from the shaft.[85]

KENT
Let it fall rather, though the fork[86] invade
The region of my heart. Be Kent unmannerly,
When Lear is mad.[87] What wilt thou[88] do, old man?
Think'st thou that duty shall have dread to speak,
When power to flattery bows?[89] To plainness honour's
bound,
When majesty stoops to folly.[90] Reserve thy state,[91]
And, in thy best consideration check[92]
This hideous rashness. Answer my life my judgement,[93]
Thy youngest daughter does not love thee least;
150 Nor are those empty-hearted whose low sound
Reverbs no hollowness.[94]

LEAR

                    Kent, on thy life, no more!

KENT
My life I never held but as a pawn[95]
To wage against thy enemies, nor fear to lose it,
Thy safety being the motive.[96]

[72] **So be...peace:** May I only find peace in my grave i.e. when I die
[73] **I give...from her!:** I take away her father's love from her
[74] **Who stirs?:** Who will do what I have asked?
[75] **digest this third:** i.e. add Cordelia's share of the kingdom to Goneril's and Regan's dowries
[76] **Let pride...marry her:** Let pride, which she calls plain-speaking, be her marriage dowry
[77] **I do invest...power:** I give my power to Cornwall and Albany together
[78] **Pre-eminence...majesty:** superiority and all of the magnificence that accompanies kingship
[79] **With reservation...knights:** I reserve control over a troop of 100 knights
[80] **our abode...due turns:** I will take turns to live with each of you
[81] **Only we still...king:** I will only keep the title 'King' and the honour that comes with it
[82] **The sway...be yours:** the control, money and the rest of the power, beloved sons-in-law, are yours
[83] **coronet:** small crown (perhaps the one intended for Cordelia)
[84] **patron:** protector / benefactor
[85] **make from the shaft:** avoid the arrow
[86] **fork:** arrow head
[87] **mad:** 1 rash / foolish 2 'mad' also pre-empts Lear's eventual madness later in the play
[88] **thou:** you. Used for an equal or an inferior, not used to address a king
[89] **Think'st thou...flattery bows?:** Do you think that I'll be afraid to do duty and speak out, when power gives way to flattery?
[90] **To plainness...to folly:** I am honour bound to speak bluntly, when the King acts foolishly
[91] **Reserve thy state:** 1 Keep your kingdom 2 Retain your status as ruler
[92] **check:** restrain
[93] **Answer my life...judgement:** I bet my life on this opinion
[94] **Nor are those empty...hollowness:** Neither are those who keep silent insincere/empty (hollow). Kent recalls the proverb, 'Empty vessels make the most sound' – in this sense Goneril and Regan are the empty vessels
[95] **pawn:** 1 pledge 2 the least valuable chess piece
[96] **the motive:** the reason

LEAR

Out of my sight!

KENT

See better, Lear, and let me still remain
The true blank[97] of thine eye.

97 **blank:** white spot at the centre of a target

LEAR

Now, by Apollo, –[98]

98 **Apollo:** Roman god of the sun

KENT

Now, by Apollo, King,

Thou swear'st thy gods in vain.

LEAR

O, vassal! Miscreant![99]

99 **O, vassal! Miscreant!:** O, slave! Heretic!

ALBANY and **CORNWALL**

0 Dear sir, forbear.

KENT

Kill thy physician, and the fee bestow
Upon thy foul disease.[100] Revoke thy gift,
Or, whilst I can vent clamour[101] from my throat,
I'll tell thee thou dost evil.

100 **Kill the physician...disease:** In this metaphor, Kent is 'the physician' as he offers good advice, while Goneril and Regan are the 'foul disease' whom Lear is about to pay a 'fee' to i.e. his power and kingdom

LEAR

Hear me, recreant![102]

On thine allegiance, hear me!
That thou hast sought to make us break our vow,
Which we durst never yet, and with strained[103] pride
To come betwixt our sentence[104] and our power,
Which nor our nature nor our place can bear,[105]

70 Our potency made good, take thy reward.[106]
Five days we do allot thee, for provision[107]
To shield thee from diseases of the world;
And on the sixth to turn thy hated back
Upon our kingdom. If, on the tenth day following
Thy banished trunk[108] be found in our dominions,[109]
The moment is thy death. Away! By Jupiter,[110]
This shall not be revoked.

101 **vent clamour:** utter noise
102 **recreant:** traitor

103 **strained:** forced
104 **sentence:** pronouncement / decision
105 **Which nor...bear:** which neither my personality nor my status as King can tolerate
106 **Our potency...reward:** since my power is absolute, you will take what 'reward' I give you
107 **provision:** to gather necessities
108 **trunk:** body
109 **dominions:** lands
110 **Jupiter:** King of the Roman gods

KENT

Fare thee well, King; sith[111] thus thou wilt appear,
Freedom lives hence, and banishment is here.

80 *[To CORDELIA]* The gods to their dear shelter take thee, maid,
That justly think'st, and hast most rightly said!

111 **sith:** since

[To REGAN and GONERIL] And your large speeches may
your deeds approve,[112]
That good effects[113] may spring from words of love.
Thus Kent, O Princes, bids you all adieu;[114]
He'll shape his old course in a country new.[115]
[Exit]

*[Flourish.[116] Re-enter GLOUCESTER, with FRANCE,
BURGUNDY and Attendants]*

GLOUCESTER
Here's France and Burgundy, my noble Lord.

LEAR
My Lord of Burgundy.
We first address towards you, who with this King
Hath rivalled for our daughter.[117] What, in the least,
190 Will you require in present dower with her,
Or cease your quest of love?

BURGUNDY
                  Most royal Majesty,
I crave no more than what your highness offered,
Nor will you tender[118] less.

LEAR
                  Right noble Burgundy,
When she was dear to us, we did hold her so,
But now her price is fallen. Sir, there she stands.
If aught within that little seeming substance,[119]
Or all of it, with our displeasure pieced,[120]
And nothing more, may fitly like[121] your Grace,
She's there, and she is yours.

BURGUNDY
                  I know no answer.

LEAR
200 Will you, with those infirmities she owes,[122]
Unfriended, new-adopted to our hate,
Dowered with our curse, and strangered[123] with our oath,
Take her, or leave her?

BURGUNDY
                Pardon me, royal sir,
Election[124] makes not up on such conditions.

[112] **And your large...approve:** may your grand speeches be reflected in your deeds
[113] **effects:** actions
[114] **adieu:** goodbye
[115] **He'll shape...new:** He'll carry on in his old manner (i.e. speaking bluntly) in another country
[116] **Flourish:** Trumpet call

[117] **rivalled for our daughter:** acted as a romantic rival (with the King of France) for my daughter (Cordelia)

[118] **tender:** offer

[119] **little seeming substance:** 1 worthless thing 2 person who flatters little (to 'seem' means to flatter)
[120] **pieced:** added to
[121] **may fitly like:** please and appear suitable

[122] **infirmities she owes:** flaws that she has

[123] **strangered:** disowned

[124] **Election:** decisions

LEAR
Then leave her, sir; for, by the power that made me,
I tell you all her wealth.
[To FRANCE] For you, great King,
I would not from your love make such a stray
To match you where I hate;[125] therefore beseech you
T'avert your liking a more worthier way[126]
Than on a wretch whom Nature is ashamed
Almost t'acknowledge hers.

FRANCE
                              This is most strange,
That she, whom even but now was your best object,
The argument[127] of your praise, balm[128] of your age,
Most best, most dearest, should in this trice of time[129]
Commit a thing so monstrous, to dismantle
So many folds[130] of favour. Sure, her offence
Must be of such unnatural degree
That monsters it,[131] or your fore-vouched affection
Fall into taint;[132] which to believe of her,
Must be a faith that reason without miracle
Could never plant in me.[133]

CORDELIA
                              I yet beseech your Majesty, –
If for I want[134] that glib and oily art,[135]
To speak and purpose not, since what I well intend
I'll do't before I speak – that you make known
It is no vicious blot,[136] murder or foulness,
No unchaste action, or dishonoured step,
That hath deprived me of your grace and favour,
But even for want of that for which I am richer –
A still-soliciting[137] eye, and such a tongue
As I am glad I have not, though not to have it
Hath lost me in your liking.

LEAR
                              Better thou
Hadst not been born than not t'have pleased me better.

FRANCE
Is it but this? A tardiness in nature[138]
Which often leaves the history unspoke[139]
That it intends to do? My Lord of Burgundy,
What say you to the Lady? Love's not love
When it is mingled with regards that stand

---

[125] **make such a stray…I hate:** stray so far as to expect you to marry a person I hate
[126] **T'avert…worthier way:** look elsewhere for a worthier woman

[127] **argument:** subject
[128] **balm:** comfort
[129] **trice of time:** moment in time / instant
[130] **folds:** layers
[131] **monsters it:** makes it monstrous
[132] **your fore-vouched…into taint:** the affection you swore previously has been discredited
[133] **which to believe…plant in me:** to believe this of her, would require great faith, that without a miracle, my reason could never accept

[134] **want:** lack
[135] **glib and oily art:** smooth talking

[136] **vicious blot:** moral flaw / vice

[137] **A still-soliciting:** ever searching

[138] **tardiness in nature:** natural hesitancy
[139] **leaves the history unspoke:** does not reveal the full story

Aloof from the entire point.[140] Will you have her?
She is herself a dowry.

BURGUNDY

                      Royal King,
240 Give but that portion which yourself proposed,
And here I take Cordelia by the hand,
Duchess of Burgundy.

LEAR
Nothing: I have sworn; I am firm.

BURGUNDY
I am sorry, then, you have so lost a father
That you must lose a husband.

CORDELIA

                    Peace be with Burgundy!
Since that respect and fortune are his love,[141]
I shall not be his wife.

FRANCE
Fairest Cordelia, that art most rich, being poor;
Most choice, forsaken; and most loved, despised!
250 Thee and thy virtues here I seize upon:
Be it lawful I take up what's cast away.
Gods, gods! 'Tis strange that from their cold'st neglect
My love should kindle to inflamed respect.[142]
Thy dowerless daughter King, thrown to my chance,[143]
Is Queen of us, of ours, and our fair France.
Not all the dukes of waterish Burgundy[144]
Can buy this unprized[145] precious maid of me.
Bid them farewell, Cordelia, though unkind,
Thou losest here, a better where to find.[146]

LEAR
260 Thou hast her, France. Let her be thine, for we
Have no such daughter, nor shall ever see
That face of hers again. Therefore be gone
Without our grace, our love, our benison.[147]
Come, noble Burgundy.
[*Flourish. Exeunt LEAR, BURGUNDY, CORNWALL,
ALBANY and GLOUCESTER*]

FRANCE

                Bid farewell to your sisters.

[140]**When it is mingled...entire point:** when it is mixed with something that has nothing to do with the real issue

[141]**Since that respect...love:** Since status and money are his true loves

[142]**'Tis strange...inflamed respect:** It is strange, that from the cold neglect of the gods comes my passionate regard
[143]**thrown to my chance:** cast (as with a dice in gambling)
[144]**waterish Burgundy:** 1 Burgundy: a land with many rivers 2 weak Lord Burgundy
[145]**unprized:** unappreciated / undervalued
[146]**Thou losest...to find:** you lose this place to find somewhere better

[147]**benison:** blessing

CORDELIA

The jewels of our father, with washed eyes[148]
Cordelia leaves you. I know you what you are
And, like a sister, am most loath to call
Your faults as they are named.[149] Use well our father.
To your professed bosoms I commit him
But yet, alas, stood I within his grace,
I would prefer him to a better place.
So, farewell to you both.

REGAN

Prescribe not us our duty.[150]

GONERIL

             Let your study[151]
Be to content your Lord, who hath received you
At Fortune's alms.[152] You have obedience scanted,
And well are worth the want that you have wanted.[153]

CORDELIA

Time shall unfold what plighted cunning hides;[154]
Who covers faults, at last with shame derides.[155]
Well may you prosper!

FRANCE

             Come, my fair Cordelia.
[Exeunt FRANCE and CORDELIA]

GONERIL

Sister, it is not a little I have to say of what most nearly
appertains[156] to us both. I think our father will hence[157] tonight.

REGAN

That's most certain, and with you; next month with us.

GONERIL

You see how full of changes his age is; the observation we have
made of it hath not been little. He always loved our sister most;
and with what poor judgement he hath now cast her off appears
too grossly.[158]

REGAN

'Tis the infirmity of his age: yet he hath ever but slenderly
known himself.[159]

GONERIL

The best and soundest of his time hath been but rash;[160] then
must we look to receive from his age, not alone the

---

[148] **washed eyes:** 1 washed with tears 2 clearer vision

[149] **am most loath...are named:** am reluctant to proclaim your faults for what they are

[150] **Prescribe...duty:** Don't tell us our duty

[151] **study:** effort

[152] **Fortune's alms:** the charity of fate
[153] **You have obedience...have wanted:** You have failed to be obedient and deserve to lose what you both lacked and desired; 'wanted' can mean both 'lack' and 'desire'. Goneril may be referring to Cordelia's dowry and/or her father's love
[154] **Time shall...hides:** Time will uncover what concealed cunning hides
[155] **Who covers...derides:** Whoever covers their faults will eventually but shamed and mocked

[156] **nearly appertains:** closely relates
[157] **will hence:** will go from here

[158] **appears too grossly:** is so obviously apparent

[159] **he hath...known himself:** however, he never really knew himself
[160] **rash:** impetuous

imperfections of long-engraffed condition,[161] but therewithal
the unruly waywardness[162] that infirm and choleric years[163]
bring with them.

REGAN
Such unconstant starts[164] are we like to have from him as this
of Kent's banishment.

GONERIL
There is further compliment of leave-taking between France
and him.[165] Pray you, let us sit together, if our father carry
authority with such dispositions as he bears, this last
surrender of his will but offend us.[166]

REGAN
300 We shall further think of it.

GONERIL
We must do something, and i' the heat.[167]
[Exeunt]

[161] **long-engraffed condition:** a
disposition that has been long
implanted
[162] **unruly waywardness:**
unmanageable obstinacy/
stubbornness
[163] **infirm and choleric years:** sickness
and anger that come with old age
[164] **unconstant starts:** sudden
outbursts
[165] **There is further...and him:** There
is a further formal farewell ceremony
between France and him

[166] **if our father...as he bears:** if our
father continues to act with such
rash authority as he has done, his
abdication may harm us. Goneril is
afraid that Lear may forget that he
has relinquished power

[167] **i' the heat:** immediately / strike
while the iron is hot

Key Quotations

CORDELIA   *I am sure, my love's / More ponderous than my tongue.*

LEAR   *Nothing will come of nothing.*

CORDELIA   *I cannot heave / My heart into my mouth. I love your Majesty / According to my
bond; no more nor less.*

LEAR   *Come not between the dragon and his wrath!*

LEAR   *The bow is bent and drawn, make from the shaft*

KENT   *Be Kent unmannerly,
When Lear is mad. What wilt thou do, old man?
Think'st thou that duty shall have dread to speak,
When power to flattery bows?*

KENT   *Thy youngest daughter does not love thee least; / Nor are those empty-hearted
whose low sound / Reverbs no hollowness.*

KENT   *My life I never held but as a pawn / To wage against thy enemies, nor fear to lose
it, / Thy safety being the motive.*

REGAN   *'Tis the infirmity of his age: yet he hath ever but slenderly known himself.*

Commentary

- **Lear's 'love-test' illustrates his excessive pride.** By inviting the flattery of his daughters, Lear reveals how inflated his ego is. His pride urges him to seek public validation from those around him. It is also the reason why he seeks to retain the title of King, despite relinquishing his power.

- Despite Kent's advice to 'See better', **Lear is blinded by his pride and left unable to judge the true natures of those around him.** Lear's ego and need to be publicly admired means that he fails to see Goneril and Regan for who they are. Instead, he is won over by their empty praise of him. Similarly, Lear doesn't recognise that Kent and Cordelia truly love him: he perceives their behaviours as impudent, banishing Kent and disowning Cordelia.

- **This scene illustrates Lear's foolishness.** Lear's stated motivation in abdicating is to ensure 'that future strife / May be prevented'. There is an irony here as Lear's decision to divide his kingdom is the very thing that leads to war. Furthermore, the manner in which he plans to divide his kingdom (i.e. the love-test) is a foolish one. Lear believes that he can measure his daughters' affections by their words. Such a way of proceeding is unwise and potentially disastrous. Again, it is his pride that misleads Lear.

- **Lear fails to understand the true nature of love.** He believes that it is something that can be quantified and measured in words. He therefore cannot understand Cordelia's refusal to take part in the love-test and misunderstands her words in this scene.

- **Lear's 'hideous rashness' grows out of his excessive pride.** His overreaction to Cordelia's refusal to flatter her father and to Kent's protestation reveals a character led by ego and lacking sound judgement. The manner in which he threatens Kent: 'The bow is bent and drawn, make from the shaft' and the violent imagery of cannibalism that he uses while addressing Cordelia points to a man led by violent passion rather than unclouded reason.

- **Ironically, Lear accuses Cordelia and Kent of being prideful.** He believes it is this that prevents Cordelia from flattering him: 'Let pride, which she calls plainness, marry her.' Similarly, Lear blames Kent's outspokenness on 'strained pride'. Lear however, fails to recognise his own proud nature.

- **However, despite these flaws, Kent points to Lear's former nobility and greatness as a king.** Although he banishes Kent for his behaviour, the audience understand that Lear has inspired great respect and love in Kent. Kent is horrified to see Lear's power undermined by flattery and urges Lear to restrain himself. Kent's behaviour is motivated by love for Lear and an unwavering loyalty: 'Royal Lear, / Whom I have ever honoured as my king, / Loved as my father, as my master followed, / As my great patron'. Cordelia's great love for her father is revealed in her asides. She decides to 'Love, and be silent' and her thoughts are with her father rather than her potential inheritance. The attitudes of both Kent and Cordelia suggest that Lear was once a great man, a man still deserving of loyalty and love.

- **Lear's sanity is called into question.** Later in the play, Lear is presented as mad. Whether this is the result of his suffering or is perhaps a tendency that was always there is debatable. In this first scene, Goneril and Regan, point to Lear's 'unconstant starts', 'rash' behaviour and 'poor judgement'. However, Regan suggests that this may be more than just the senility that sometimes comes with age, but rather a character trait of Lear's: ''Tis the infirmity of his age: yet he hath ever but slenderly known himself.'

--- **Commentary** (continued) ---

- **This scene introduces the idea of nothingness,** which occurs throughout King Lear. Here Cordelia says that she is unable to put a price on her love for her father, and so says 'nothing'. However, Lear is appalled and responds with the proverb 'Nothing will come of nothing.' Lear rashly decides to leave Cordelia with nothing from his kingdom. This decision subsequently leaves Lear himself with nothing as he ends up with nowhere to stay, and no one to care for him.

- **Goneril and Regan are presented as conniving and false.** Both women eagerly take part in the love-test and seek to outdo each other to secure a greater portion of the kingdom. Their gushing declarations of love are contrived and disingenuous, yet Lear fails to recognise them as such. It is Kent who suggests the falseness of Goneril's and Regan's sentiments: 'Nor are those empty-hearted whose low sound / Reverbs no hollowness'. At the end of the scene Goneril and Regan are seen conspiring against their father. They are utterly lacking in gratitude for their inheritance and instead see their father as a liability, somebody whom they have to 'do something' about.

- **Cordelia is presented as a courageous and idealistic woman.** Her refusal to take part in the love-test suggests a woman disenchanted by the pomp and pride that come with royalty. Her integrity leaves her unwilling to employ the 'glib and oily art' favoured by her sisters. Instead she vows to 'Love, and be silent'; recognising the weight of her love she says, 'I cannot heave / My heart into my mouth.' **However, some may criticise Cordelia for her stubborn refusal to humour an old man at the end of his reign.** Perhaps a more flexible and generous response to Lear's request may have averted the division within the family.

- **Kent's unwavering loyalty and love for his king is made clear in this scene.** He sees his role to serve a king whom he loves deeply, valuing Lear's life over his own: 'My life I never held but as a pawn / To wage against thy enemies, nor fear to lose it, / Thy safety being the motive.'

- **Kent is presented as brave and forthright.** He boldly speaks up for Cordelia, drawing Lear's attention to the injustice of disowning her. He bravely faces Lear's fiery temper. Even when Lear threatens Kent: 'Come not between the dragon and his wrath!', Kent persists in highlighting the terrible mistake Lear is making.

--- **Questions** ---

1. What do you think is Gloucester's attitude to his son Edmund?
2. (a) Explain how King Lear intends to decide what portion of his kingdom to give to his daughters and their husbands?
   (b) Do you think this is a sensible way of dividing the kingdom? Why / why not?
3. Lear explains that after he relinquishes all power he still plans to 'retain / The name, and all th' addition to a king'. Do you think this may pose a problem in the future? Explain your answer.
4. Do you think Cordelia was right not to take part in the love-test? Why / why not?
5. What is your impression of Goneril and Regan from this scene?
6. (a) How does Kent behave in this first scene of the play?
   (b) What is Lear's reaction to Kent's behaviour?
7. Imagine you are Cordelia. Write a diary entry reporting on the events of this scene. Explain your feelings about what has happened and your thoughts about your father.

Scene Summary

- The scene opens with Edmund's soliloquy. He expresses his bitterness for the way 'bastards' are treated by society. He expresses his intention to cheat his brother Edgar out of the land that he is due to inherit.
- Edmund produces a forged letter that lays out a plan to kill Gloucester. Edmund has signed it with his brother's name.
- As Gloucester enters the room, Edmund makes a show of hiding the letter. This arouses Gloucester's curiosity. Gloucester reads the letter and believes that Edgar wrote it. He is appalled.
- Edmund then meets with Edgar and tells him that Gloucester is angry with him. He advises Edgar to avoid their father and to carry a sword with him for protection.
- The scene ends with Edmund gloating about his scheme. He mocks his father's gullibility and his brother's naïvety.

The Earl of Gloucester's Castle.
Enter EDMUND, with a letter

EDMUND

Thou, Nature,¹ art my goddess; to thy law
My services are bound. Wherefore should I
Stand in the plague of custom, and permit
The curiosity of nations to deprive me,²
For that I am some twelve or fourteen moonshines
Lag of a brother?³ Why bastard? Wherefore base?⁴
When my dimensions are as well compact,
My mind as generous, and my shape as true,
As honest madam's issue?⁵ Why brand⁶ they us
With base? With baseness? Bastardy? Base, base?
Who, in the lusty stealth of nature,⁷ take
More composition and fierce quality⁸
Than doth, within a dull, stale, tired bed,
Go to the creating a whole tribe of fops,⁹
Got 'tween asleep and wake? Well, then,
Legitimate Edgar, I must have your land.
Our father's love is to the bastard Edmund
As to the legitimate. Fine word, 'legitimate'!
Well, my legitimate, if this letter speed
And my invention thrive,¹⁰ Edmund the base
Shall top the legitimate. I grow; I prosper;
Now, gods, stand up for bastards!

Soliquy (speaking to the audience)

[Enter GLOUCESTER]

¹ **Thou Nature...bound:** Edmund seems to be rejecting the constraints of society, civilization and morality. Instead he appeals to the 'law of the jungle' here
² **Wherefore...deprive me:** Why should I let social customs deprive me
³ **For that...a brother?:** just because I am twelve or fourteen months younger than my brother?
⁴ **base:** 1 illegitimate 2 inferior
⁵ **When my dimensions...issue?:** When my body is as well formed, my mind as noble and my appearance as similar to my father's, as any chaste woman's legitimate son?
⁶ **brand:** label
⁷ **lusty stealth of nature:** lustful, secretive passion
⁸ **More composition and fierce quality:** a better mixture and energetic qualities
⁹ **fops:** wimps/weaklings

¹⁰ **if this letter...thrive:** if this letter and my plan bring success

GLOUCESTER
Kent banished thus! And France in choler parted![11]
And the King gone tonight! Prescribed his power![12]
Confined to exhibition![13] All this done
Upon the gad![14] – Edmund, how now! What news?

EDMUND
So please your Lordship, none.
[Putting up the letter]

GLOUCESTER
Why so earnestly seek you to put up[15] that letter?

EDMUND
I know no news, my Lord.

GLOUCESTER
30 What paper were you reading?

EDMUND
Nothing, my Lord.

GLOUCESTER
No? What needed, then, that terrible dispatch[16] of it into your
pocket? The quality of nothing hath not such need to hide
itself. Let's see: come, if it be nothing, I shall not need
spectacles.[17]

EDMUND
I beseech you, sir, pardon me. It is a letter from my brother
that I have not all o'er-read, and for so much as I have
perused,[18] I find it not fit for your o'er-looking.

GLOUCESTER
Give me the letter, sir.

EDMUND
40 I shall offend, either to detain[19] or give it. The contents, as in
part I understand them, are to blame.[20]

GLOUCESTER
Let's see, let's see.

EDMUND
I hope, for my brother's justification, he wrote this but as an
essay or taste of my virtue.[21]

[11] **choler parted:** departed in anger
[12] **Prescribed his power!:** limited his own power voluntarily
[13] **Confined to exhibition!:** Reduced to having a small allowance
[14] **Upon the gad!:** On the spur of the moment!

[15] **put up:** put away

[16] **terrible dispatch:** great haste

[17] **spectacles:** glasses

[18] **perused:** read

[19] **detain:** keep
[20] **are to blame:** are offensive / are blameworthy

[21] **essay or taste of my virtue:** trial or test of my goodness / morality

GLOUCESTER

[Reads] 'This policy and reverence of age²² makes the world
bitter to the best of our times, keeps our fortunes from us till our
oldness cannot relish²³ them. I begin to find an idle and fond
bondage in the oppression of aged tyranny,²⁴ who sways, not as
it hath power, but as it is suffered.²⁵ Come to me, that of this I
may speak more. If our father would sleep till I waked him,²⁶
you should enjoy half his revenue forever, and live the beloved
of your brother – Edgar.'
– Hum! Conspiracy! – 'Sleep till I waked him, you
should enjoy half his revenue,' – My son Edgar! Had he a hand
to write this? A heart and brain to breed it in? – When came this
to you? Who brought it?

EDMUND

It was not brought me, my Lord; there's the cunning of it; I
found it thrown in at the casement of my closet.²⁷

GLOUCESTER

You know the character²⁸ to be your brother's?

EDMUND

If the matter were good, my Lord, I durst²⁹ swear it were his;
but, in respect of that, I would fain³⁰ think it were not.

GLOUCESTER

It is his.

EDMUND

It is his hand, my Lord; but I hope his heart is not in the
contents.

GLOUCESTER

Hath he never heretofore sounded you³¹ in this business?

EDMUND

Never, my Lord: but I have heard him oft maintain it to be fit,
that, sons at perfect age, and fathers declining, the father should
be as ward³² to the son, and the son manage his revenue.³³

GLOUCESTER

O villain, villain! His very opinion in the letter! Abhorred³⁴
villain! Unnatural, detested, brutish villain! Worse than brutish!
Go, sirrah, seek him. I'll apprehend him. Abominable villain!
Where is he?

---

22 policy and reverence of age: trick of respecting old age

23 relish: enjoy

24 I begin to find...tyranny: I am starting to find we are kept under useless and foolish bonds by the tyranny of our father's old age

25 who sways...suffered: who retains authority not because he is powerful but because we put up with it

26 If our father...waked him: If I had the power of life and death over our father

27 casement of my closet: window of my study

28 character: handwriting

29 durst: dare to

30 fain: gladly

31 sounded you: sounded you out

32 as ward: under guardianship

33 revenue: finances

34 Abhorred: Hated / Despised

Clear parallel between Gloucester's gullibility and ~~Edward's~~ Lear.

EDMUND

I do not well know, my Lord. If it shall please you to suspend your indignation against my brother till you can derive from him better testimony of his intent, you shall run a certain course;[35] where, if you violently proceed against him, mistaking his purpose, it would make a great gap[36] in your own honour, and shake in pieces the heart of his obedience. I dare pawn down[37] my life for him, that he hath wrote this to
80 feel[38] my affection to your honour, and to no other pretence of danger.[39]

GLOUCESTER

Think you so?

EDMUND

If your honour judge it meet,[40] I will place you where you shall hear us confer of this, and by an auricular assurance[41] have your satisfaction; and that without any further delay than this very evening.

GLOUCESTER

He cannot be such a monster –

EDMUND

Nor is not, sure.

GLOUCESTER

To his father, that so tenderly and entirely loves him. Heaven
90 and earth! Edmund, seek him out; wind me into him,[42] I pray you. Frame[43] the business after your own wisdom. I would unstate myself, to be in a due resolution.[44]

EDMUND

I will seek him, sir, presently,[45] convey[46] the business as I shall find means and acquaint you withal.[47]

GLOUCESTER

These late eclipses in the sun and moon portend no good to us;[48] though the wisdom of Nature can reason it thus and thus, yet nature finds itself scourged by the sequent effects.[49] Love cools, friendship falls off, brothers divide; in cities, mutinies;[50] in countries, discord; in palaces, treason; and the
100 bond cracked 'twixt[51] son and father. This villain of mine[52] comes under the prediction; there's son against father. The King falls from bias of nature; there's father against child.

---

[35] **run a certain course**: take the safest path

[36] **gap**: breach

[37] **pawn down**: stake

[38] **feel**: test

[39] **pretence of danger**: dangerous intention

[40] **meet**: fitting

[41] **auricular assurance**: made certain by hearing

[42] **wind me into him**: earn his confidence for my sake

[43] **Frame**: Arrange/Organise

[44] **I would unstate...resolution**: I would give everything ('unstate myself') to have this situation resolved

[45] **presently**: immediately

[46] **convey**: discreetly deal with

[47] **acquaint you withal**: inform you following that

[48] **These late...good to us**: late=recent. Gloucester sees the influence of the stars upon the lives of people. An audience in Shakespeare's time may have had in mind the 1605 eclipses of the sun and moon

[49] **though the wisdom...sequent effects**: although natural phenomena can be explained by learning, human nature is still affected by the disasters that follow (such phenomena)

[50] **mutinies**: riots

[51] **'twixt**: between

[52] **villain of mine**: i.e. Edgar

We have seen the best of our time: machinations,[53] hollowness,[54] treachery and all ruinous disorders follow us disquietly to our graves. Find out this villain, Edmund; it shall lose thee nothing. Do it carefully. And the noble and true-hearted Kent banished! His offence: honesty! 'Tis strange.
[Exit]

EDMUND
This is the excellent foppery[55] of the world, that when we are sick in fortune[56] – often the surfeit[57] of our own behaviour – we make guilty of our disasters the sun, the moon, and the stars, as if we were villains by necessity, fools by heavenly compulsion,[58] knaves, thieves, and treachers,[59] by spherical predominance,[60] drunkards, liars and adulterers, by an enforced obedience of planetary influence; and all that we are evil in, by a divine thrusting on.[61] An admirable evasion of whoremaster man, to lay his goatish disposition to the charge of a star![62] My father compounded with my mother under the dragon's tail,[63] and my nativity[64] was under Ursa Major,[65] so that it follows I am rough and lecherous. Fut![66] I should have been that I am, had the maidenliest star in the firmament[67] twinkled on my bastardising. Edgar –

[Enter EDGAR]

And pat[68] he comes like the catastrophe of the old comedy.[69] My cue is villainous melancholy[70], with a sigh like Tom o' Bedlam.[71] O, these eclipses do portend these divisions![72] Fa, sol, la, mi.[73]

EDGAR
How now, brother Edmund! What serious contemplation are you in?

EDMUND
I am thinking, brother, of a prediction I read this other day, what should follow these eclipses.

EDGAR
Do you busy yourself about that?

EDMUND
I promise you, the effects[74] he writes of succeed unhappily,[75] as of unnaturalness between the child and the parent; death, dearth,[76] dissolutions of ancient amities,[77] divisions in state, menaces and maledictions[78] against king and nobles; needless diffidences,[79] banishment of friends, dissipation of cohorts,[80] nuptial breaches,[81] and I know not what.

[53] **machinations:** plots/schemes
[54] **hollowness:** falsehood/deception
[55] **excellent foppery:** utter stupidity
[56] **sick in fortune:** misfortunate
[57] **surfeit:** excesses
[58] **by heavenly compulsion:** by the direct influence of the stars
[59] **treachers:** traitors/cheats
[60] **spherical predominance:** planetary influence
[61] **a divine thrusting on:** urged on by the heavens
[62] **An admirable...charge of a star!:** A brilliant way for a lecherous man to avoid responsibility, to blame his lustful nature on the influence of the stars!
[63] **dragon's tail:** Draco (a constellation)
[64] **nativity:** birth
[65] **Ursa Major:** the Great Bear (a constellation)
[66] **Fut!:** By God's foot!
[67] **firmament:** heavens/sky
[68] **pat:** just like that
[69] **like the catastrophe...comedy:** like the ending of a traditional comedy
[70] **My cue...melancholy:** Here is my cue to play the part of the melancholy villain
[71] **Tom o' Bedlam:** Tom the mad beggar. A nickname given to those discharged from London's Bethlehem Hospital for the insane
[72] **O, these eclipses...divisions!:** O these eclipses foreshadow this discord! Edmund is sarcastically echoing Gloucester's superstitions
[73] **Fa, sol, la, mi:** Edmund sings, perhaps to appear that he is unaware of Edgar's approach. The notes he sings are discordant and their sequence has been associated with the devil
[74] **effects:** consequences
[75] **succeed unhappily:** follow with great unhappiness
[76] **dearth:** famine
[77] **dissolutions...amities:** the endings of long held friendships
[78] **maledictions:** curses
[79] **diffidences:** doubts
[80] **dissipation of cohorts:** the breaking up of armies
[81] **nuptial breaches:** broken marriages

EDGAR
How long have you been a sectary astronomical?[82]

EDMUND
Come, come, when saw you my father last?

EDGAR
The night gone by.

EDMUND
140 Spake you with him?

EDGAR
Ay, two hours together.

EDMUND
Parted you in good terms? Found you no displeasure in him
by word or countenance?[83]

EDGAR
None at all.

EDMUND
Bethink yourself wherein you may have offended him, and at
my entreaty[84] forbear his presence till some little time hath
qualified the heat of his displeasure,[85] which at this instant so
rageth in him, that with the mischief of your person it would
scarcely allay.[86]

EDGAR
150 Some villain hath done me wrong.

EDMUND
That's my fear. I pray you, have a continent forbearance[87] till
the speed of his rage goes slower, and, as I say, retire with
me to my lodging, from whence I will fitly[88] bring you to
hear my Lord speak. Pray ye, go; there's my key. If you do
stir abroad,[89] go armed.

EDGAR
Armed, brother!

EDMUND
Brother, I advise you to the best: go armed. I am no honest
man if there be any good meaning toward you. I have told
you what I have seen and heard; but faintly,[90] nothing like
160 the image and horror[91] of it. Pray you, away.

---

[82] **sectary astronomical:** disciple of astrologers. In Shakespeare's time, the words 'astrology' and 'astronomy' meant the same thing

[83] **countenance:** appearance

[84] **entreaty:** request
[85] **forebear...displeasure:** avoid him for a while until time cools the heat of his annoyance
[86] **with the mischief...scarcely allay:** your death or injury would hardly abate

[87] **continent forbearance:** control your emotions and avoid him
[88] **fitly:** at an appropriate time
[89] **stir abroad:** go out

[90] **faintly:** hintingly
[91] **image and horror:** horrifying picture

EDGAR
Shall I hear from you anon?[92]

EDMUND
I do serve you in this business.

[Exit EDGAR]

A credulous[93] father, and a brother noble,
Whose nature is so far from doing harms,
That he suspects none; on whose foolish honesty
My practices ride easy![94] I see the business.
Let me, if not by birth, have lands by wit;[95]
All with me's meet that I can fashion fit.[96]

[Exit]

[92] **anon:** soon

[93] **credulous:** trusting/gullible
[94] **practices ride easy:** deceptions easily work
[95] **wit:** intelligence
[96] **All with...fashion fit:** Everything is acceptable to me that suits my purposes i.e. the ends justify the means

---

Key Quotations

EDMUND	*Why bastard? Wherefore base?* *When my dimensions are as well compact,* *My mind as generous, and my shape as true,* *As honest madam's issue? Why brand they us* *With base? With baseness? Bastardy? Base, base?*
EDMUND	*Edmund the base / Shall top the legitimate. I grow; I prosper; / Now, gods, stand up for bastards!*
GLOUCESTER	*This villain of mine comes under the prediction; there's son against father. The King falls from bias of nature; there's father against child.*
EDMUND	*Let me, if not by birth, have lands by wit; / All with me's meet that I can fashion fit.*

Commentary

- **This scene establishes the play's sub-plot,** i.e. Edmund's scheme to frame his brother and in the process take Gloucester's land. Clear parallels can be drawn with the main storyline: both Lear and Gloucester are blind to the insincerity of their children. However, there are differences between the plot and sub-plot. Lear effectively stage manages his own downfall whereas Gloucester is put upon by Edmund.

- **Edmund reveals his sinister nature.** His cunning is evident as he convincingly makes a show of putting away the forged letter. He believably feigns concern for both Edgar and Gloucester, earning the trust of both in the process. Edmund's soliloquies are both thrilling and shocking for the audience as we watch him celebrate his villainy. He presents his plotting as a sign of intelligence: 'Let me, if not by birth, have lands by wit' and he unrepentantly sees all means available to him: 'All with me's meet that I can fashion fit.'

- **Edmund is clearly embittered by the idea that he is looked down upon as an 'illegitimate' son.** He questions this social prejudice:

'Why bastard? Wherefore base?
When my dimensions are as well compact,
My mind as generous, and my shape as true,
As honest madam's issue? Why brand they us
With base? With baseness? Bastardy? Base, base?'

- **Edmund's bitterness fuels his treachery and, to his mind, offers justification for his actions.** He sees himself as a capable man who should be judged on his merits rather than the circumstances of his birth. He proudly asserts his right to take what he can for himself: 'Edmund the base / Shall top the legitimate. I grow; I prosper; / Now, gods, stand up for bastards!'

- **Gloucester's gullibility is readily apparent.** Just as Lear fails to see his daughters' true natures, Gloucester is blind to Edmund's cunning. Edmund himself points to this, labelling Gloucester a 'credulous father'. Gloucester is presented as a superstitious man who sees great significance in the recent eclipses, believing that they have influenced human lives. In soliloquy, Edmund caustically mocks his father for this. However, an audience in Shakespeare's time would have appreciated the importance of destiny in human affairs.

- **Edgar's honesty and trusting nature is made clear here.** Without question he gullibly believes his brother that Gloucester is displeased and takes the advice to stay out of sight and arm himself. Edmund seizes upon this aspect of Edgar's personality, characterising Edgar as: 'a brother noble, / Whose nature is so far from doing harms, / That he suspects none; on whose foolish honesty / My practices ride easy!' As with Cordelia and Kent, honesty comes at a price.

Questions

1. Basing your answer on Scenes 1 and 2, how is Gloucester's situation similar to Lear's?
2. How does Edmund create division between Edgar and Gloucester?
3. What is your impression of Edmund from this scene? Think about his flaws and his strengths.
4. How, in this scene, does Edmund justify his behaviour?

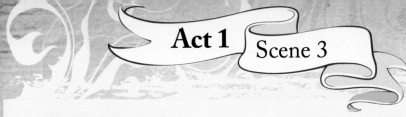
Scene Summary

- Goneril is fulfilling her duty set out by Lear that he will stay with her from time to time. However, she is clearly unhappy about this arrangement. She complains that Lear reprimands her for little reason, and that he and his knights act in an unruly manner. It is not clear if this is true or not as only Goneril makes this claim.
- Goneril instructs her servant Oswald to be rude to Lear in an effort to make her home less hospitable and to provoke Lear.
- She writes to Regan advising her to take similar action.

The Duke of Albany's Palace
Enter GONERIL, and OSWALD, her steward

GONERIL
Did my father strike my gentleman for chiding[1] of his fool?

> [1] **chiding:** scolding

OSWALD
Ay, madam.

GONERIL
By day and night he wrongs me; every hour
He flashes into[2] one gross crime[3] or other,
That sets us all at odds. I'll not endure it.
His knights grow riotous, and himself upbraids us
On every trifle.[4] When he returns from hunting,
I will not speak with him; say I am sick.
If you come slack[5] of former services
You shall do well; the fault of it I'll answer.[6]

> [2] **flashes into:** explodes/outbursts
> [3] **crime:** offence
>
> [4] **upbraids us...trifle:** reprimands us for every little thing
>
> [5] **come slack:** fall short
> [6] **answer:** take responsibility

OSWALD
He's coming, madam; I hear him.
[Horns within]

GONERIL
Put on what weary negligence[7] you please,
You and your fellows. I'll have it come to question.[8]
If he distaste it, let him to our sister,[9]
Whose mind and mine, I know, in that are one,
Not to be over-ruled. Idle[10] old man,
That still would manage those authorities
That he hath given away! Now, by my life,
Old fools are babes again, and must be used
With checks as flatteries,[11] when they are seen abused.[12]
Remember what I have said.

> [7] **weary negligence:** lax attitude
> [8] **I'll have...question:** I'd like it to provoke an argument
> [9] **If he distaste...sister:** If he doesn't like it he can go to my sister's home
> [10] **Idle:** Worthless / Foolish
>
> [11] **With checks as flatteries:** with telling-off and praise
> [12] **seen abused:** misguided

OSWALD

Well, madam.

GONERIL

And let his knights have colder looks among you;
What grows of it, no matter; advise your fellows so.
I would breed from hence occasions,[13] and I shall,
That I may speak. I'll write straight to my sister,
To hold my very course.[14] Prepare for dinner.
[Exeunt]

[13] **I would breed...occasions:** I wish to create opportunities from this
[14] **hold my very course:** do the same as me

Commentary

- **Goneril is clearly resentful of Lear's presence in her home.** She says, that like Regan, she does not wish to be 'over-ruled' suggesting she may feel that Lear undermines the new power that she and Albany have acquired. **However, although Goneril may be disgruntled about Lear's high-handed manner, her intention to deliberately provoke Lear points to a more sinister agenda.** She looks to bring about a confrontation with Lear by instructing Oswald to be rude to the former king by adopting a 'weary negligence'.

- **At this point of the play, Goneril and Regan are united.** This is evident by Goneril's willingness to write to Regan instructing her to adopt a similar strategy with Lear. The sisters' opposition to Lear brings them together but this alliance is not set to last.

- **Oswald's readiness to follow Goneril's immoral instructions shows him to be a distasteful character.** He raises no objection to Goneril's order to be disrespectful to Lear and is instead more than willing to follow her commands.

Scene Summary
- Kent disguises himself so that he can act as a servant to Lear.
- Following Goneril's instructions from the last scene, Oswald is rude to Lear. Kent is shocked to see Lear treated so disrespectfully and trips Oswald up.
- The Fool teases Lear for giving away his kingdom, labelling him the 'fool'.
- Goneril scolds Lear for the behaviour of his 'disordered' and 'deboshed' knights. She tells Lear that she is reducing his number of knights to fifty.
- Lear is outraged. He speaks sharply to his daughter comparing her to an animal. Lear then criticises himself for his own poor judgement and starts to question his own identity.
- Lear leaves for Regan's castle.

A Hall in the Duke of Albany's Palace.
Enter KENT, disguised

KENT
If but as well I other accents borrow,
That can my speech defuse, my good intent
May carry through itself to that full issue
For which I razed my likeness.[1] Now, banished Kent,
If thou canst serve where thou dost stand condemned,
So may it come, thy master, whom thou lov'st,
Shall find thee full of labours.[2]

[Horns within. Enter LEAR, Knights and Attendants]

LEAR
Let me not stay a jot[3] for dinner; go get it ready.

[Exit an Attendant]

How now! What art thou?

KENT
A man, sir.

LEAR
What dost thou profess?[4] What wouldst thou with us?

KENT
I do profess[5] to be no less than I seem: to serve him truly that will put me in trust; to love him that is honest; to converse with him that is wise, and says little; to fear judgement; to fight when I cannot choose; and to eat no fish.[6]

---

[1] **If but as well…likeness:** If, on top of my disguise, I can adopt a different accent to disguise my voice, I may achieve my good intention; this is why I have erased ('razed') my appearance

[2] **So may it…full of labours:** So, may it come to pass, Lear, whom you love, will find Kent eager to be of service

[3] **stay a jot:** wait one minute

[4] **What…profess?:** What is your profession?

[5] **profess:** proclaim

[6] **eat no fish:** The meaning is unclear. Possibly: 1 I only eat meat i.e. Kent declares himself a 'proper man' with a real appetite 2 I avoid fish as it's a food associated with Catholicism i.e. Kent proclaims that he is a Protestant. The play is set in a pre-Christian age, but Shakespeare's audience may have appreciated the reference

LEAR

What art thou?

KENT

A very honest-hearted fellow, and as poor as the King.[7]

> [7] **poor as the King:** Kent is making a joke here

LEAR

If thou be as poor for a subject as he is for a king, thou art poor enough. What wouldst thou?

KENT

20 Service.

LEAR

Who wouldst thou serve?

KENT

You.

LEAR

Dost thou know me, fellow?

KENT

No, sir, but you have that in your countenance[8] which I would fain[9] call master.

> [8] **countenance:** expression/manner
> [9] **fain:** gladly

LEAR

What's that?

KENT

Authority.

LEAR

What services canst thou do?

KENT   *Ironic (cordelia said something similiar)*

I can keep honest counsel,[10] ride, run, mar a curious tale[11] in
30 telling it, and deliver a plain message bluntly; that which ordinary men are fit for, I am qualified in, and the best of me is diligence.

> [10] **keep honest counsel:** keep matters of honour secret
> [11] **mar a curious tale:** shorten a complicated story

LEAR

How old art thou?

KENT

Not so young, sir, to love a woman for singing, nor so old to dote on her for anything. I have years on my back forty-eight.

LEAR
Follow me; thou shalt serve me. If I like thee no worse after dinner, I will not part from thee yet. Dinner, ho, dinner! Where's my knave?[12] My fool? Go you, and call my fool hither.

[Exit an Attendant]

[Enter OSWALD]

You, you, sirrah, where's my daughter?

OSWALD
So please you, – [13]
[Exit]

LEAR
What says the fellow there? Call the clotpoll[14] back.

[Exit a Knight]

Where's my fool, ho? I think the world's asleep.

[Re-enter Knight]

How now! Where's that mongrel?

KNIGHT
He says, my Lord, your daughter is not well.

LEAR
Why came not the slave back to me when I called him?

KNIGHT
Sir, he answered me in the roundest[15] manner, he would not.

LEAR
He would not!

KNIGHT
My Lord, I know not what the matter is; but, to my judgement, your Highness is not entertained with that ceremonious affection as you were wont;[16] there's a great abatement of kindness[17] appears as well in the general dependants[18] as in the Duke himself also and your daughter.

LEAR
Ha! Sayest thou so?

---

[12] **knave:** servant

[13] **So please you:** Sorry, I'm busy. Oswald is following Goneril's instruction to adopt 'weary negligence' (1.3)

[14] **clotpoll:** blockhead / fool

[15] **roundest:** rudest

[16] **your Highness is not...were wont:** your Highness is not treated with the kind of regal ceremony and fatherly affection that you are accustomed to

[17] **abatement of kindness:** lessening of goodwill

[18] **dependants:** servants

KNIGHT
I beseech you, pardon me, my Lord, if I be mistaken; for my
duty cannot be silent when I think your Highness wronged.

LEAR
Thou but rememberest me of mine own conception.[19] I have
perceived a most faint[20] neglect of late, which I have rather
blamed as mine own jealous curiosity[21] than as a very
pretence[22] and purpose of unkindness. I will look further
60 into't. But where's my fool? I have not seen him this two
days.

KNIGHT
Since my young Lady's[23] going into France, sir, the Fool hath
much pined away.[24]

LEAR
No more of that; I have noted it well. Go you, and tell my
daughter I would speak with her.

[Exit an Attendant]

Go you, call hither my fool.

[Exit an Attendant]

[Re-enter OSWALD]

O, you sir, you, come you hither, sir. Who am I, sir?

OSWALD
My Lady's father.

LEAR
'My Lady's father'! My Lord's knave. You whoreson dog!
70 You slave! You cur!

OSWALD
I am none of these, my Lord; I beseech your pardon.

LEAR
Do you bandy[25] looks with me, you rascal?
[Striking him]

OSWALD
I'll not be struck, my Lord.

Sporting Metaphors

19 **Thou but...conception:** You are onl
  reminding me of what I thought myse
20 **faint:** subtle
21 **jealous curiosity:** suspicions
22 **very pretence:** actual intention

23 **young Lady:** i.e. Cordelia
24 **pined away:** 1 fretted 2 yearned for

25 **bandy:** exchange. The term is taken
  from tennis where players 'bandy' the
  ball back and forth

Sporting metaphor. ✓

KENT
Nor tripped neither, you base football player.[26]
[Tripping up his heels]

[26] **base football player:** lowly football player. Kent is continuing the sporting metaphor from 'bandy' above

LEAR
I thank thee, fellow; thou servest me, and I'll love thee.

KENT
[To OSWALD] Come, sir, arise, away! I'll teach you differences:[27] away, away! If you will measure your lubber's length again, tarry;[28] but away! Go to! Have you wisdom? So.
[Pushes OSWALD out]

[27] **differences:** the importance of rank
[28] **If you will...tarry:** If you would like to have your loutish body measured again, hang around

LEAR
Now, my friendly knave, I thank thee: there's earnest of thy service.
[Giving KENT money]

[Enter FOOL]

FOOL
Let me hire him too: here's my coxcomb.[29]
[Offering KENT his cap]

[29] **coxcomb:** fool's cap

LEAR
How now, my pretty knave! How dost thou?

FOOL
Sirrah,[30] you were best[31] take my coxcomb.[32]

[30] **Sirrah:** a form of 'sir' usually reserved for inferiors
[31] **you were best:** you had better
[32] **take my coxcomb:** the Fool is suggesting that Kent should act the fool if he serves Lear

KENT
Why, Fool?

FOOL
Why? For taking one's part that's out of favour. Nay, and thou canst not smile as the wind sits, thou'lt catch cold shortly.[33] There, take my coxcomb. Why, this fellow has banished two on's[34] daughters, and did the third a blessing against his will. If thou follow him, thou must needs wear my coxcomb. How now, nuncle![35] Would I had two coxcombs and two daughters!

[33] **thou canst not smile...shortly:** you cannot side with those in power, you will soon suffer for it
[34] **on's:** of his
[35] **nuncle:** my uncle. A term of affection

LEAR
Why, my boy?

FOOL
If I gave them all my living,[36] I'd keep my coxcombs myself. There's mine; beg another of thy daughters.

[36] **living:** lands / wealth

LEAR

Take heed, sirrah: the whip![37]

FOOL

Truth's a dog must to kennel; he must be whipped out, when the Lady Brach may stand by the fire and stink.[38]

LEAR

A pestilent gall to me![39]

FOOL

Sirrah, I'll teach thee a speech.

LEAR

Do.

FOOL

100 Mark it, nuncle:

Have more than thou showest,
Speak less than thou knowest,
Lend less than thou owest,[40]
Ride more than thou goest,
Learn more than thou trowest,[41]
Set less than thou throwest;[42]
Leave thy drink and thy whore,
And keep in-a-door,[43]
And thou shalt have more
110 *Than two tens to a score.[44]*

KENT

This is nothing, Fool.

FOOL

Then 'tis like the breath of an unfee'd lawyer:[45] you gave me nothing for't. Can you make no use of nothing, nuncle?

LEAR

Why, no, boy; nothing can be made out of nothing.

FOOL

[To KENT] Prithee, tell him, so much the rent of his land comes to.[46] He will not believe a fool.

LEAR

A bitter[47] fool!

[37] **Take heed...whip!:** Be careful or you will be whipped! Fools were sometimes whipped if their comments went too far

[38] **Truth's a dog...stink:** Truth is like a dog sent out to its kennel; it has to be whipped while the pet bitch (Lady Brach) stays by the fire even though it stinks

[39] **A pestilent gall to me!:** That's like a bothersome sore to me!

[40] **owest:** own

[41] **trowest:** believe

[42] **Set less...throwest:** Bet less than everything on a single throw (of the dice)

[43] **keep in-a-door:** stay indoors

[44] **two tens to a score:** your score (twenty) shall be worth more than just two tens i.e. you will prosper

[45] **Then...lawyer:** Then it's worth as much as the breath of an unpaid lawyer i.e. nothing

[46] **so much...comes to:** i.e. nothing, as Lear has no land

[47] **bitter:** sarcastic

FOOL
Dost thou know the difference, my boy, between a bitter fool and a sweet fool?

LEAR
No, lad. Teach me.

FOOL
That lord that counselled thee
To give away thy land,
Come place him here by me,
Do thou for him stand:[48]
The sweet and bitter fool
Will presently appear;
The one in motley[49] *here,*
The other found out[50] *there.*[51]

LEAR
Dost thou call me fool, boy?

FOOL
All thy other titles thou hast given away; that thou wast born with.

KENT
This is not altogether fool,[52] my Lord.

FOOL
No, faith, lords and great men will not let me. If I had a monopoly[53] out, they would have part on't, and ladies too; they will not let me have all fool to myself: they'll be snatching. Give me an egg, nuncle, and I'll give thee two crowns.

LEAR
What two crowns shall they be?

FOOL
Why, after I have cut the egg i' the middle, and eat up the meat,[54] the two crowns of the egg. When thou clovest[55] thy crown i' the middle, and gavest away both parts, thou borest thy ass on thy back o'er the dirt.[56] Thou hadst little wit in thy bald crown, when thou gavest thy golden one away. If I speak like myself in this, let him be whipped that first finds it so.
[Singing] Fools had ne'er less grace in a year;
*   For wise men are grown foppish,*
*   They know not how their wits to wear,*
*   Their manners are so apish.*[57]

---

[48] **thou for him stand:** take his place. This is because there was no 'lord' that counselled Lear

[49] **motley:** a multi-coloured garment worn by fools

[50] **found out:** revealed to be (a fool)

[51] **there:** the Fool points at Lear here

[52] **altogether fool:** completely foolish

[53] **monopoly:** total control. The Fool deliberately misinterprets Kent's words above to mean total ownership of foolishness. The word 'monopoly' also refers to James I's controversial custom of awarding monopolies to favoured courtiers over certain industries

[54] **meat:** i.e. yolk

[55] **clovest:** split/divided

[56] **thou borest...the dirt:** you carried the donkey on your back over the dirt. This is a reference to one of Aesop's fables where a man carried his donkey to market for fear of overburdening the animal

[57] **Fools had ne'er...apish:** Fools have never been less popular than they are now, just because wise men have become foolish ('foppish'); they don't know how to use their heads, instead their behaviour is an imitation of fools' ('apish')

LEAR
When were you wont to be so full of songs, sirrah?

FOOL
I have used it, nuncle, ever since thou madest thy daughters
150 thy mothers; for when thou gavest them the rod,⁵⁸ and put'st
down thine own breeches,⁵⁹
[Singing] Then they for sudden joy did weep,
       And I for sorrow sung,
       That such a king should play bo-peep,⁶⁰
       And go the fools among.
Prithee,⁶¹ nuncle, keep a schoolmaster that can teach thy fool
to lie: I would fain⁶² learn to lie.

58 rod: cane (for punishment)	
59 breeches: trousers	

60 bo-peep: 'peekaboo'

61 Prithee: Pray you/Please
62 fain: gladly

LEAR
An⁶³ you lie, sirrah, we'll have you whipped.

63 An: If

FOOL
I marvel what kin⁶⁴ thou and thy daughters are: they'll have
160 me whipped for speaking true, thou'lt have me whipped for
lying; and sometimes I am whipped for holding my peace. I
had rather be any kind o' thing than a fool; and yet I would
not be thee, nuncle. Thou hast pared⁶⁵ thy wit o' both sides,
and left nothing i' the middle. Here comes one o' the parings.

64 kin: relatives

65 pared: 1 shaved (as in a pencil)
2 divided in two

[Enter GONERIL]

LEAR
How now, daughter! What makes that frontlet on?⁶⁶
Methinks you are too much of late i' the frown.

66 What…frontlet on?: Why do you
wear that frown? A 'frontlet' was an
ornament worn on the forehead.

FOOL
Thou wast a pretty fellow when thou hadst no need to care
for her frowning. Now thou art an O without a figure.⁶⁷ I am
better than thou art now: I am a fool, thou art nothing. *[To*
170 *GONERIL]* Yes, forsooth,⁶⁸ I will hold my tongue; so your
face bids me, though you say nothing.
       Mum, mum!
       He that keeps nor crust nor crum,
       Weary of all, shall want some.⁶⁹
[Pointing to LEAR] That's a shealed peascod.⁷⁰

67 an O…figure: a zero without another
number before it to give it value i.e.
nothing
68 forsooth: for truth / truly

69 Mum…want some: Hush, hush. He
that gives everything away because it
tires him, will be in need
70 shealed peascod: shelled peapod
i.e. hollow/nothing

GONERIL
Not only, sir, this your all-licensed⁷¹ fool,
But other of your insolent retinue⁷²
Do hourly carp⁷³ and quarrel, breaking forth
In rank⁷⁴ and not-to-be endured riots. Sir,

71 all-licensed: free to say what he
pleases
72 insolent retinue: rude followers
73 carp: moan / complain
74 rank: violent / gross

I had thought, by making this well known unto you,
To have found a safe redress, but now grow fearful,
By what yourself too late have spoke and done,
That you protect this course, and put it on[75]
By your allowance; which if you should, the fault
Would not 'scape censure,[76] nor the redresses[77] sleep,
Which, in the tender of a wholesome weal,[78]
Might in their working do you that offence,
Which else were shame, that then necessity
Will call discreet proceeding[79].

FOOL
For, you know, nuncle,
                    The hedge-sparrow fed the cuckoo so long,
                    That it had it head bit off by it young.
So, out went the candle, and we were left darkling.[80]

LEAR
Are you our daughter?

GONERIL
I would you would make use of that good wisdom,
Whereof I know you are fraught,[81] and put away
These dispositions,[82] that of late transform you
From what you rightly are.

FOOL
May not an ass know when the cart draws the horse?
Whoop, Jug![83] I love thee.[84]

LEAR
Doth any here know me? This is not Lear:
Doth Lear walk thus? Speak thus? Where are his eyes?
Either his notion weakens,[85] his discernings
Are lethargied[86] – Ha! Waking? 'Tis not so.[87]
Who is it that can tell me who I am?

Learn First + Last Line

FOOL
Lear's shadow.[88]

LEAR
I would learn that; for, by the marks of sovereignty, knowledge
and reason, I should be false persuaded[89] I had daughters.

FOOL
Which they will make an obedient father.

---

75 **put it on:** encourage
76 **'scape censure:** escape disapproval
77 **redresses:** corrections
78 **tender of a wholesome weal:** tender concern for a healthy society

79 **Might...proceeding:** (The necessary measures to fix this situation) may displease you, and would – if this was another time – cause me shame, but their necessity will mean my actions will be seen as sensible

80 **darkling:** in the dark

81 **are fraught:** have plenty
82 **dispositions:** moods/inclinations

83 **Jug:** Joan
84 **Whoop...love thee:** Possibly: 1 a refrain from an old song 2 a response to a look of reproach from Goneril

85 **notion weakens:** mind weakens
86 **his discernings / Are lethargied:** his understanding is dulled
87 **Waking...not so:** Am I awake? I can't be.

88 **Lear's shadow:** 1 Lear is a shadow of his former self 2 Lear is like the one who shadows him i.e. the Fool

89 **false persuaded:** fooled/tricked

LEAR

210 Your name, fair gentlewoman?

GONERIL

This admiration, sir, is much o' the savour
Of other your new pranks.[90] I do beseech[91] you
To understand my purposes aright:
As you are old and reverend,[92] should be wise.
Here do you keep a hundred knights and squires,
Men so disordered, so deboshed[93] and bold,
That this our court, infected with their manners,
Shows[94] like a riotous inn; epicurism[95] and lust
Makes it more like a tavern or a brothel
220 Than a graced palace. The shame itself doth speak
For instant remedy. Be then desired
By her, that else will take the thing she begs,
A little to disquantity your train;[96]
And the remainders, that shall still depend,
To be such men as may besort[97] your age,
And know themselves and you.[98]

LEAR

                          Darkness and devils!
Saddle my horses! Call my train together!
Degenerate bastard![99] I'll not trouble thee.
Yet have I left a daughter.

GONERIL

230 You strike my people; and your disordered rabble
Make servants of their betters.

[Enter ALBANY]

LEAR

Woe, that too late repents –
[To ALBANY] O, sir, are you come?
Is it your will? Speak, sir. – Prepare my horses.
Ingratitude, thou marble-hearted fiend,[100]
More hideous when thou show'st thee in a child
Than the sea-monster![101]

ALBANY

                          Pray, sir, be patient.

LEAR

[To GONERIL] Detested kite![102] Thou liest!
My train are men of choice and rarest parts,[103]

[90] **This admiration...new pranks:** This astonishment ('admiration') is the same type ('savour') as your other new games
[91] **beseech:** beg / implore
[92] **reverend:** revered/respected
[93] **deboshed:** debauched/undutiful
[94] **Shows:** appears / looks
[95] **epicurism:** gluttony

[96] **disquantity your train:** reduce the number of your followers
[97] **besort:** befit / be appropriate
[98] **know themselves and you:** who know how they and you should behave

[99] **bastard:** Lear starts to imagine Goneril (and later Regan) as illegitimate because of her treatment of him

[100] **marble-hearted fiend:** hard-hearted devil
[101] **More hideous...sea-monster:** (Ingratitude) is more hideous when it appears in one's child rather than a sea-monster

[102] **kite:** a bird of prey
[103] **men...rarest parts:** men chosen for their personal qualities

That all particulars of duty know,[104]
And in the most exact regard support
The worships of their name.[105] O most small fault,
How ugly didst thou in Cordelia show!
Which, like an engine, wrenched my frame of nature
From the fixed place,[106] drew from heart all love,
And added to the gall.[107] O Lear, Lear, Lear!
Beat at this gate, that let thy folly in, *[Striking his head]*
And thy dear judgement out! Go, go, my people![108]

ALBANY
My Lord, I am guiltless, as I am ignorant
Of what hath moved you.[109]

LEAR
                    It may be so, my Lord.
Hear, Nature, hear; dear Goddess, hear!
Suspend thy purpose, if thou didst intend
To make this creature fruitful!
Into her womb convey sterility!
Dry up in her the organs of increase,
And from her derogate[110] body never spring
A babe to honour her! If she must teem,[111]
Create her child of spleen,[112] that it may live,
And be a thwart disnatured[113] torment to her!
Let it stamp wrinkles in her brow of youth;
With cadent[114] tears fret[115] channels in her cheeks;
Turn all her mother's pains and benefits
To laughter and contempt, that she may feel
How sharper than a serpent's tooth it is
To have a thankless child! Away, away!
[Exit]

ALBANY
Now, gods that we adore, whereof comes this?

GONERIL
Never afflict yourself to know the cause,[116]
But let his disposition have that scope
That dotage gives it.[117]

[Re-enter LEAR]

LEAR
What, fifty of my followers at a clap?[118]
Within a fortnight![119]

---

[104] **That all...duty know:** who know all aspects of their duty
[105] **And in...their name:** and carefully ensure that their good names are upheld
[106] **like an engine...fixed place:** like a lever, tore my natural affection from its foundations
[107] **gall:** bitterness
[108] **Go, go, my people!:** Lear may be sending his knights and attendants off stage

[109] **moved:** upset

[110] **derogate:** degenerate/debased
[111] **teem:** give birth
[112] **spleen:** violent temper
[113] **thwart disnatured:** defiant and unnatural
[114] **cadent:** falling
[115] **fret:** wear away

[116] **Never...cause:** Never bother yourself by trying to find the reason
[117] **But let...gives it:** But let his mood have the freedom that old age allows it

[118] **at a clap:** in one stroke
[119] **Within a fortnight:** 'fortnight' may refer to: 1 the amount of time allowed for the knights' dismissal 2 the amount of time Lear has stayed with Goneril so far

ALBANY

What's the matter, sir?

LEAR

I'll tell thee: *[To GONERIL]* Life and death! I am ashamed
That thou hast power to shake my manhood thus;
That these hot tears, which break from me perforce,[120]
Should make thee worth them. Blasts and fogs[121] upon thee!
The untented woundings[122] of a father's curse
Pierce every sense about thee! Old fond[123] eyes,
Beweep[124] this cause again, I'll pluck ye out,
And cast you, with the waters that you loose,[125]
280 To temper clay.[126] Yea, is't come to this?
Ha! Let it be so; I have another daughter,
Who, I am sure, is kind and comfortable.[127]
When she shall hear this of thee, with her nails
She'll flay thy wolvish visage.[128] Thou shalt find
That I'll resume the shape[129] which thou dost think
I have cast off for ever. Thou shalt, I warrant thee.[130]

[Exeunt LEAR, KENT and Attendants]

GONERIL

Do you mark[131] that?

ALBANY

I cannot be so partial, Goneril,
To the great love I bear you, –

GONERIL

290 Pray you, content. – What, Oswald, ho! –
[To the FOOL] You, sir, more knave[132] than fool, after your
master.

FOOL

Nuncle Lear, Nuncle Lear, tarry[133] and take the Fool with
thee.
> *A fox, when one has caught her,*
> *And such a daughter,*
> *Should sure to the slaughter,*
> *If my cap would buy a halter.[134]*
> *So the Fool follows after.*

[Exit]

GONERIL

300 This man hath had good counsel![135] A hundred knights!
'Tis politic[136] and safe to let him keep

[120] **perforce:** unavoidably / involuntarily
[121] **Blasts and fogs:** foul, disease ridden air
[122] **untented woundings:** wounds too deep to be treated with a roll of lint ('tent')
[123] **fond:** foolish
[124] **Beweep:** if you weep for
[125] **loose:** let fall
[126] **temper clay:** soften the ground
[127] **comfortable:** comforting
[128] **flay thy wolvish visage:** strip the skin from your wolf-like face
[129] **shape:** appearance / status (as king)
[130] **warrant thee:** guarantee you

[131] **mark:** note

[132] **knave:** servant

[133] **tarry:** wait

[134] **halter:** 1 rope to lead a beast
2 hangman's noose

[135] **This man...counsel:** This man has good judgement. Goneril is being sarcastic in these lines
[136] **politic:** prudent

At point[137] a hundred knights. Yes, that, on every dream,
Each buzz,[138] each fancy, each complaint, dislike,
He may enguard[139] his dotage with their powers
And hold our lives in mercy.[140] Oswald, I say!

ALBANY
Well, you may fear too far.

GONERIL
                              Safer than trust too far:
Let me still[141] take away the harms I fear,
Not fear still to be taken. I know his heart.
What he hath uttered, I have writ my sister;
0 If she sustain him and his hundred knights
When I have showed the unfitness, –

[Re-enter OSWALD]
                              How now, Oswald!
What, have you writ that letter to my sister?

OSWALD
Ay, madam.

GONERIL
Take you some company, and away to horse.
Inform her full of my particular fear,
And thereto add such reasons of your own
As may compact[142] it more. Get you gone,
And hasten your return.

[Exit OSWALD]
                              No, no, my Lord,
This milky gentleness and course of yours[143]
20 Though I condemn not, yet, under pardon,
You are much more ataxed for want of wisdom[144]
Than praised for harmful mildness.

ALBANY
How far your eyes may pierce I cannot tell:
Striving to better, oft we mar[145] what's well.

GONERIL
Nay, then –

ALBANY
Well, well; the event.[146]
[Exeunt]

[137] **At point:** armed	
[138] **buzz:** rumour	
[139] **enguard:** protect	
[140] **in mercy:** at his mercy	

[141] **still:** continue to

[142] **compact:** strengthen / consolidate

[143] **milky...of yours:** mild mannered course of action
[144] **ataxed for want of wisdom:** accused of lacking wisdom

[145] **mar:** damage / spoil / harm

[146] **the event:** we'll see what happens

Key Quotations

THE FOOL   *'When thou clovest thy crown i' the middle, and gavest away both parts, thou borest thy ass on thy back o'er the dirt. Thou hadst little wit in thy bald crown, when thou gavest thy golden one away.'*

LEAR   *Doth any here know me? This is not Lear: / Doth Lear walk thus? Speak thus? Where are his eyes? / ...Who is it that can tell me who I am?*

LEAR   *O Lear, Lear, Lear!*
Beat at this gate, that let thy folly in,
And thy dear judgement out!

LEAR   *I am ashamed*
That thou hast power to shake my manhood thus;
That these hot tears, which break from me perforce,
Should make thee worth them.

LEAR   *Old fond eyes,*
Beweep this cause again, I'll pluck ye out,
And cast you, with the waters that you loose,
To temper clay.

LEAR   *Thou shalt find / That I'll resume the shape which thou dost think / I have cast off for ever. Thou shalt, I warrant thee.*

Commentary

- **Kent's loyalty is readily apparent as he disguises himself so as to remain close to Lear.** In doing so, Kent takes a great risk as Lear has banished him and threatened him with death if he is found in the kingdom. Kent explains that he is motivated by love for his king and is eager to serve in any capacity he can: 'Now, banished Kent, / If thou canst serve where thou dost stand condemned, / So may it come, thy master, whom thou lov'st, / Shall find thee full of labours.'

- **This scene marks a significant step in the reversal of Lear's fortune.** As the play progresses, Lear's emotional, mental and physical wellbeing steadily deteriorate. His treatment at the hands of Goneril begins a pattern that sees Lear become an increasingly marginalised figure. However, the audience should never forget that this downfall is set in motion by Lear himself, whose pride and foolishness in the first scene created the situation he now finds himself in.

- **Lear's manner in this scene suggests that he has yet to accept the loss of his power and privileges.** He adopts the poise of a powerful ruler, issuing commands and acting in a high-handed manner. He tells an attendant that he will not wait 'a jot' for his dinner and he is later outraged by Oswald's insolence. When he asks Oswald to recognise him as the King, Oswald refers to him as 'my Lady's father'. Lear is appalled by the casual way in which he is addressed but also upset by the idea that his identity is now dependent upon his much more powerful daughter. Towards the end of the scene Lear tells Goneril, 'Thou shalt find / That I'll resume the shape which thou dost think / I have cast off for ever.

Thou shalt, I warrant thee'. Lear mistakenly believes that he can abdicate his responsibilities but retain his power.

- **As he suffers, Lear starts to recognise his own flaws and mistakes.** He sees how his mistreatment of Cordelia was grossly disproportionate to her 'most small fault' and he berates himself for his own poor judgement: 'O Lear, Lear, Lear! / Beat at this gate, that let thy folly in, / And thy dear judgement out!' Lear is coming to see himself as a flawed man whose pride has driven him to make some terrible, rash decisions. As he himself suffers he comes to understand the suffering of others. **However, Lear still has much to learn;** he still sees Cordelia as being at 'fault'. Recognition of his own flaws will prove to be a slow process.

- **However, Lear still exhibits the kind of fiery rashness that was seen in Scene 1.** He bitterly curses Goneril with sterility: 'Dry up in her the organs of increase, / And from her derogate body never spring / A babe to honour her!' This hateful passion of his words is compounded by the use of ugly, animal imagery as he calls Goneril a 'Detested kite!' and describes her face as a 'wolvish visage'.

- **Lear's suffering creates great anxiety and confusion for him.** He questions his own identity, asking 'Doth any here know me? This is not Lear: / Doth Lear walk thus? Speak thus? Where are his eyes? /…Who is it that can tell me who I am?' Without the power that he has enjoyed for so long, he no longer recognises himself, nor his place in the world. **Lear is starting to forge a new identity for himself. Only by becoming nothing can he gain wisdom and insight.**

- **Despite his growing recognition and self-awareness, Lear still lacks the insight to see Regan for who she is.** He naïvely believes that she will offer him comfort after the way Goneril has treated him. The truth about Regan is perhaps too much for Lear to cope with at this stage of his development.

- **The Fool mocks Lear for his folly.** He tells Lear: 'When thou clovest thy crown i' the middle, and gavest away both parts, thou borest thy ass on thy back o'er the dirt. Thou hadst little wit in thy bald crown, when thou gavest thy golden one away.' The Fool ridicules Lear for dividing his kingdom in two. The word 'crown' represents both Lear's power as king but also Lear's common sense: both have been split in two.

- **The Fool's function is to help Lear to see the reality of his situation.** The Fool enjoys a privileged position and doesn't hesitate to criticise Lear for his folly. He mocks Lear for the mistakes he has made and points to the fact that Lear has put himself at the mercy of Goneril and Regan: 'thou madest thy daughters thy mothers'. The Fool takes a delight in the ironic idea that Lear is a bigger fool than he; he jests that Lear himself should wear a fool's hat (coxcomb). **It is the Fool's role to help Lear along the path to self-discovery by forcing him to face his own flaws.**

- **Goneril's ingratitude and cruelty is illustrated by her readiness to limit her father's power and reduce his company of knights by half.** She suggests that she feels threatened by Lear and looks to consolidate her power by eroding his: 'Each buzz, each fancy, each complaint, dislike, / He may enguard his dotage with their powers / And hold our lives in mercy'. However, this may simply be an effort to justify her mistreatment of her father.

- **Albany's mild manners present him as a man dominated by his wife.** He appears not to know the reason for Lear's outrage, probably because Goneril has not consulted with him. He offers a weak defence of Lear to his wife, suggesting that Goneril's fear of Lear is excessive: 'you may fear too far.' Goneril however disregards Albany as a man characterised by 'milky gentleness'. Seen against some of the stronger characters such as Kent, Albany at this point of the play is quite a weak individual.

Questions

1. Why does Kent adopt a disguise and offer himself as a servant to Lear? Quote from the text in your answer.
2. (a) What does Goneril do to reduce Lear's power in this scene?
   (b) What reason does she give for doing this?
3. Earlier in the play Goneril instructs Oswald to adopt a 'weary negligence' when around Lear. What evidence in this scene shows that Oswald is obeying his mistress?
4. What in this scene suggests that Lear is starting to recognise his own flaws and mistakes? Refer to the text in your answer.
5. 'Although this scene shows that Lear is beginning to see his own flaws and mistakes, he is still a poor judge of others and a prideful man.' Do you agree with this statement? Explain your answer.
6. What is the Fool's view of Lear's predicament?
7. Describe the relationship between Albany and Goneril as you understand it from this scene.

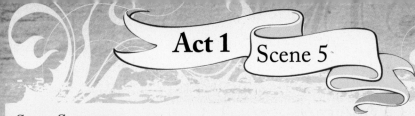
Scene Summary
- Lear sends Kent ahead with letters for Regan giving his version of the dispute with Goneril.
- The Fool warns Lear that Regan will treat him the same way that Goneril did.
- Lear expresses concerns about his own sanity.

Courtyard before Albany's Palace.
Enter LEAR, KENT and FOOL

LEAR
Go you before to Gloucester[1] with these letters.[2] Acquaint my daughter no further with anything you know than comes from her demand out of the letter.[3] If your diligence be not speedy, I shall be there afore you.

KENT
I will not sleep, my Lord, till I have delivered your letter.
[Exit]

FOOL
If a man's brains were in's heels, were't not in danger of kibes?[4]

LEAR
Ay, boy.

FOOL
Then, I prithee, be merry; thy wit shall ne'er go slip-shod.[5]

LEAR
Ha, ha, ha!

FOOL
Shalt see, thy other daughter will use thee kindly;[6] for though she's as like this as a crab's[7] like an apple, yet I can tell what I can tell.

LEAR
What canst tell, boy?

FOOL
She will taste as like this as a crab does to a crab.[8] Thou canst tell why one's nose stands i' the middle on's face?

---

[1] **before to Gloucester:** ahead to the town of Gloucester. This is a reference to the town of Gloucester near where Regan lives. It is not a reference to the Earl of Gloucester

[2] **these letters:** this letter

[3] **Acquaint...the letter:** Don't tell her anything more that you know other than questions she may have arising from the letter

[4] **kibes:** chilblains

[5] **thy wit...slip-shod:** your brains will not need slippers. The Fool is suggesting that Lear is brainless

[6] **kindly:** 1 with kindness
2 according to her nature, her 'kind' i.e. with cruelty

[7] **crab:** i.e. a crab-apple. A sour tasting apple

[8] **She will taste...crab:** i.e. Regan will be as sour as Goneril has been

LEAR
No.

FOOL
Why, to keep one's eyes of either side's nose; that what a
man cannot smell out, he may spy[9] into.

9 **spy:** look

LEAR
I did her wrong —[10]

10 **I did her wrong:** Lear is likely
referring to Cordelia here but
some critics argue that he is
referring to Goneril

FOOL
20 Canst tell how an oyster makes his shell?

LEAR
No.

FOOL
Nor I neither; but I can tell why a snail has a house.

LEAR
Why?

FOOL
Why, to put's head in; not to give it away to his daughters,
and leave his horns without a case.

LEAR
I will forget my nature.[11] So kind a father! Be my horses
ready?

11 **nature:** natural affection /
kindness as a father

FOOL
Thy asses[12] are gone about 'em. The reason why the seven
stars[13] are no more than seven is a pretty reason.

12 **asses:** foolish servants
13 **seven stars:** either the
constellation of Pleiades or The
Great Bear. The latter was
referred to by Edmund in 1.2

LEAR
30 Because they are not eight?

FOOL
Yes, indeed: thou wouldst make a good fool.

LEAR
To take't again perforce![14] Monster ingratitude!

14 **To take't...perforce!:** To take it
back by force. Lear is either
contemplating regaining his power
by force or reflecting on the
manner in which Goneril withdrew
his privileges

FOOL
If thou wert my fool, nuncle, I'd have thee beaten for being
old before thy time.

LEAR
How's that?

FOOL
Thou shouldst not have been old till thou hadst been wise.[15]

[15] **wise:** 1 sane 2 'wise' in the modern sense

LEAR
O, let me not be mad, not mad, sweet heaven!
Keep me in temper;[16] I would not be mad!

[16] **in temper:** sane

[Enter a Gentleman]

How now! Are the horses ready?

GENTLEMAN
Ready, my Lord.

LEAR
Come, boy.

[17] **She that's a maid...cut shorter:** i.e. She who laughs at me now does not truly appreciate the tragedy that is to come and therefore doesn't have the wisdom to preserve her virginity. This line is addressed directly to the audience.

FOOL
She that's a maid now, and laughs at my departure,
Shall not be a maid long, unless things be cut shorter.[17]
[Exeunt]

Commentary

- **Lear's concern for his sanity continues to grow.** The trauma of being mistreated by Goneril and his increasing recognition of his own mistakes have taken a psychological toll on Lear. He worries that his hold on reality may be slipping: 'O, let me not be mad, not mad, sweet heaven! / Keep me in temper; I would not be mad!'

- **Lear's comment 'I did her wrong' shows that he is coming to recognise his own flaws.** Lear's personal growth is an uneven process; it takes him almost until the end of the play before he truly recognises his own mistakes. However, this admission early in the play is an important step towards self-discovery.

- **Lear is still outraged by the manner in which he was treated by Goneril.** He refers to her 'Monster ingratitude!' Later in the play this focus on the 'ingratitude' of Goneril and Regan becomes a preoccupation of his mad ramblings. However, in doing so **Lear is making a victim of himself as he is still unable to face up to the reality that his actions are largely to blame for his current situation.**

- **Through his caustic remarks, the Fool continues to remind Lear of his foolishness.** He tells Lear that even a lowly snail has a house 'to put's head in; not to give it away to his daughters, and leave his horns without a case' and that Lear would 'make a good fool.' **The Fool offers the audience a moral standard which deepens our understanding of Lear.** He acts like a mirror reflecting all of Lear's flaws and mistakes, an echo of Lear's conscience.

- **The Fool's cryptic predictions foreshadow what awaits Lear under Regan's 'care'.** Displaying the kind of foresight that Lear lacks, the Fool anticipates the cool welcome Lear is soon to receive and Regan's eventual mistreatment of her father. The Fool says that Regan will prove as bitter as her sister: 'She will taste as like this as a crab does to a crab'. Ominous warnings such as this help to increase the tension within the play.

Questions

1. Lear is going to Regan in the hope that he will be better received there. Does the Fool share this hope? Explain your answer.
2. What do you think Lear means by his exclamation, 'I did her wrong'?
3. Describe Lear's worries and concerns in this scene.
4. At the start of this scene Lear give Kent a letter for Regan. Write this letter as you imagine it. How would Lear recount his argument with Goneril? How would he present his thoughts and feelings?

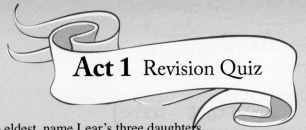

Act 1 Revision Quiz

1. Starting with the eldest, name Lear's three daughters.
2. Who does King Lear banish from his kingdom?
3. Which of Cordelia's suitors refuses to marry her after she is disinherited?
4. Which of Gloucester's sons was born out of wedlock?
5. Gloucester is fooled into believing that Edgar is plotting against him. Describe how Edmund deceives him.
6. Goneril complains about the inconvenience of having Lear stay with her. Which of the following things does she complain of?
   (a) Lear keeps spending her money (b) Lear's train of knights are unruly (c) Lear is insane
   (d) Lear is upset because he misses Cordelia
7. Why does Goneril instruct Oswald to be rude to Lear?
8. What disguise does Kent adopt to allow him to stay with Lear?
   (a) A servant (b) A knight (c) A fool (d) A soldier
9. Who says each of the following?
   (a) *I cannot heave*
      My heart into my mouth. I love your Majesty
      According to my bond; no more nor less
   (b) *My life I never held but as a pawn*
      To wage against thy enemies, nor fear to lose it,
      Thy safety being the motive
   (c) *Come not between the dragon and his wrath!*
   (d) *Let me, if not by birth, have lands by wit;*
      All with me's meet that I can fashion fit.
   (e) *Why bastard? Wherefore base?*
      When my dimensions are as well compact,
      My mind as generous, and my shape as true,
      As honest madam's issue? Why brand they us
      With base? With baseness? Bastardy? Base, base?
10. Rewrite these quotations. In each case, write the speaker's name and fill in the blanks.
   (a) *Thy youngest _____ does not love thee least;*
      Nor are those empty-hearted whose low sound
      Reverbs no _____
   (b) *I am sure, my love's*
      More _____ than my tongue
   (c) *Nothing will come of _____*
   (d) *Edmund the base*
      Shall top the legitimate. I _____; I prosper;
      Now, gods, stand up for _____!
   (e) *O Lear, Lear, Lear!*
      Beat at this gate, that let thy _____ in,
      And thy dear _____ out!

Scene Summary (Important Scene)

- Edmund is told by a courtier, Curan, that there is tension between Cornwall and Albany that may lead to war.
- Later, Edmund tricks Edgar by telling him that his hiding place has been discovered and that he needs to leave under cover of darkness. Edmund then wounds himself, telling Gloucester that Edgar did it after first trying to include him in a plot to kill Gloucester.
- Gloucester sends men to search for Edgar. He says that he will see to it that Edmund is the beneficiary of his will.
- Regan suggests that Edgar kept company with Lear's 'riotous knights'. Edmund confirms this.
- Cornwall expresses his support for Edmund.

A Courtyard within Gloucester's Castle.
Enter EDMUND and CURAN, meeting.

EDMUND
Save thee,[1] Curan.

[1] **Save thee:** God save thee

CURAN
And you, sir. I have been with your father, and given him notice that the Duke of Cornwall and Regan, his Duchess, will be here with him this night.

EDMUND
How comes that?

CURAN
Nay, I know not. You have heard of the news abroad —[2] I mean the whispered ones, for they are yet but ear-bussing arguments?[3]

[2] **news abroad:** gossip

[3] **ear-bussing arguments:** ear-kissing / whispered topics

EDMUND
Not I. Pray you, what are they?

CURAN
10 Have you heard of no likely wars toward,[4] 'twixt the Dukes of Cornwall and Albany?

[4] **toward:** impending

EDMUND
Not a word.

CURAN
You may do then, in time. Fare you well, sir.
[Exit]

EDMUND
The Duke be here tonight? The better! Best!
This weaves itself perforce into my business.⁵
My father hath set guard to take my brother;
And I have one thing, of a queasy question,
Which I must act.⁶ Briefness and fortune, work!⁷
Brother, a word; descend. Brother, I say!

[Enter EDGAR]

My father watches!⁸ O sir, fly this place!
Intelligence⁹ is given where you are hid!
You have now the good advantage of the night.
Have you not spoken 'gainst the Duke of Cornwall?
He's coming hither, now, i' th' night, i' th' haste,
And Regan with him! Have you nothing said
Upon his party 'gainst the Duke of Albany?
Advise yourself.

EDGAR
                    I am sure on't, not a word.

EDMUND
I hear my father coming. Pardon me;
In cunning¹⁰ I must draw my sword upon you.
Draw. Seem to defend yourself! Now quit you well.¹¹
[Shouting] Yield! Come before my father. Light, ho, here!
[To EDGAR] Fly, brother. *[Shouting]* Torches, torches!
[To EDGAR] So, farewell.

[Exit EDGAR]

Some blood drawn on me would beget opinion
Of my more fierce endeavour.¹²
[Wounds his arm]
                              I have seen drunkards
Do more than this in sport.¹³ Father, father!
Stop, stop! No help?

[Enter GLOUCESTER and Servants with torches]

GLOUCESTER
                    Now, Edmund, where's the villain?

---

⁵ **This weaves...business:** This will by necessity mean I'll have to involve him (Cornwall) in my scheme

⁶ **I have...must act:** I have one thing, of a sensitive nature ('queasy question') which I have to do

⁷ **Briefness...work!:** Let quick action and good luck work together!

⁸ **watches:** 1 is still awake 2 is on the look out

⁹ **Intelligence:** Information

¹⁰ **In cunning:** in trickery

¹¹ **quit you well:** acquit yourself well i.e. pretend to fight well

¹² **Some blood...endeavour:** If I had some blood on me it would give the impression that I had been involved in a fierce fight

¹³ **in sport:** for fun. This is a reference to the practice of young gallants who would cut their arms and mix the blood with wine to drink the health of their mistresses

EDMUND
Here stood he in the dark, his sharp sword out,
Mumbling of wicked charms, conjuring the moon
40 To stand auspicious mistress –[14]

GLOUCESTER
                                    But where is he?

EDMUND
Look, sir, I bleed!

GLOUCESTER
                        Where is the villain, Edmund?

EDMUND
Fled this way, sir. When by no means he could –

GLOUCESTER
Pursue him, ho! Go after.

[Exeunt some Servants]

                                    By no means what?

EDMUND
Persuade me to the murder of your Lordship;
But that I told him, the revenging gods
'Gainst parricides[15] did all their thunders bend;[16]
Spoke, with how manifold[17] and strong a bond
The child was bound to the father – sir, in fine,[18]
Seeing how loathly opposite[19] I stood
50 To his unnatural purpose, in fell motion,[20]
With his prepared[21] sword, he charges home
My unprovided[22] body, lanced mine arm;
But when he saw my best alarumed spirits,[23]
Bold in the quarrel's right,[24] roused to the encounter,
Or whether gasted[25] by the noise I made,
Full suddenly he fled.

GLOUCESTER
                                    Let him fly far,
Not in this land shall he remain uncaught;
And found – dispatch![26] The noble Duke: my master,
My worthy arch and patron,[27] comes tonight.
60 By his authority I will proclaim it,
That he which finds him shall deserve our thanks,
Bringing the murderous coward to the stake;[28]
He that conceals[29] him, death.

---

14 **To stand auspicious mistress:** to act in his favour as his patroness

15 **parricides:** murder of one's parents
16 **all their thunders bend:** aim their thunderbolts
17 **manifold:** having many forms
18 **in fine:** to be brief
19 **loathly opposite:** bitterly opposed
20 **in fell motion:** fierce thrust
21 **prepared:** unsheathed
22 **unprovided:** unprotected
23 **alarumed spirits:** my energies stirred (to fight)
24 **Bold in the quarrel's right:** given courage by how just the cause was
25 **gasted:** frightened (as if by a ghost)
26 **And found – dispatch!:** and when he is found – kill him!
27 **arch and patron:** overlord / chief patron
28 **the stake:** place of execution. Some critics argue that Gloucester has a stake to burn witches in mind, others argue that 'stake' does not refer to any specific form of execution
29 **conceals:** hides

EDMUND

When I dissuaded him from his intent,
And found him pight[30] to do it, with curst speech[31]
I threatened to discover[32] him. He replied:
'Thou unpossessing[33] bastard! Dost thou think,
If I would stand against thee, would the reposal
Of any trust, virtue, or worth in thee[34]
Make thy words faithed?[35] No, what I should deny –
As this I would, ay, though thou didst produce
My very character[36] – I'd turn it all
To thy suggestion,[37] plot, and damned practice;[38]
And thou must make a dullard of the world,[39]
If they not thought the profits of my death
Were very pregnant and potential spurs[40]
To make thee seek it.'

GLOUCESTER

         O strange and fastened[41] villain!
Would he deny his letter, said he? I never got him.[42]

[Tucket[43] within]

Hark, the Duke's trumpets! I know not why he comes.
All ports I'll bar;[44] the villain shall not 'scape;
The Duke must grant me that. Besides, his picture[45]
I will send far and near, that all the kingdom
May have the due note of him; and of my land,
Loyal and natural[46] boy, I'll work the means
To make thee capable.[47]

[Enter CORNWALL, REGAN and Attendants]

CORNWALL

How now, my noble friend! Since I came hither,
Which I can call but now,[48] I have heard strange news.

REGAN

If it be true, all vengeance comes too short[49]
Which can pursue the offender. How dost, my Lord?

GLOUCESTER

O, madam, my old heart is cracked, it's cracked!

REGAN

What, did my father's godson seek your life?
He whom my father named?[50] Your Edgar?

---

30 **pight:** determined
31 **curst speech:** angry words
32 **discover:** reveal (Edgar's supposed plot)
33 **unpossessing:** owning nothing. 'Bastards' could not inherit property
34 **the reposal...in thee:** the presence of any trust, virtue or merit in you
35 **faithed:** believed
36 **though thou...character:** even though you produced evidence against me in my own handwriting
37 **suggestion:** temptation
38 **practice:** scheming
39 **thou must...of the world:** you must think people are stupid
40 **pregnant and potential spurs:** significant and powerful incentives
41 **strange and fastened:** unnatural and determined
42 **I never got him:** I never begot (fathered) him
43 **Tucket:** Trumpet call
44 **All ports I'll bar:** I'll close all the ports / gates
45 **picture:** description
46 **natural:** 1 loyal to his father 2 'illegitimate,' born out of wedlock
47 **capable:** able to inherit
48 **Which I can call but now:** which was only just now
49 **comes too short:** is insufficient
50 **named:** In Christianity, a godparent may announce the name of the child during baptism. However, *King Lear* is set in a pre-Christian world

GLOUCESTER
O, Lady, Lady, shame would have it hid!

REGAN
Was he not companion with the riotous knights
That tended[51] upon my father?

> 51 **tended:** served / looked after

GLOUCESTER
I know not, madam: 'tis too bad, too bad.

EDMUND
Yes, madam, he was of that consort.[52]

> 52 **consort:** company

REGAN
No marvel, then, though he were ill affected.[53]
'Tis they have put him on the old man's death,
100 To have the expense and waste of his revenues.[54]
I have this present evening from my sister
Been well informed of them, and with such cautions,
That if they come to sojourn[54] at my house,
I'll not be there.

> 53 **though...ill affected:** if he was disloyal
> 54 **'Tis they...revenues:** It is they who have encouraged him to kill his father so that he can spend and waste his father's money
> 54 **sojourn:** stay

CORNWALL
                    Nor I, assure thee, Regan.
Edmund, I hear that you have shown your father
A child-like office.[55]

> 55 **child-like office:** acted as a loyal son

EDMUND
                    It was my duty, sir.

GLOUCESTER
He did bewray his practice;[56] and received
This hurt you see, striving to apprehend him.

> 56 **bewray his practice:** expose his (Edgar's) scheme

CORNWALL
Is he pursued?

GLOUCESTER
                    Ay, my good lord.

CORNWALL
110 If he be taken, he shall never more
Be feared of doing harm. Make your own purpose,
How in my strength you please.[57] For you, Edmund,
Whose virtue and obedience doth this instant
So much commend itself, you shall be ours.[58]

> 57 **Make your own...you please:** Do what you think is necessary by using my authority
> 58 **ours:** in my service

Natures of such deep trust[59] we shall much need;
You we first seize on.

EDMUND

                I shall serve you, sir,
Truly, however else.

GLOUCESTER
For him I thank your Grace.

CORNWALL
You know not why we came to visit you –

REGAN
Thus out of season,[60] threading dark-eyed night:[61]
Occasions,[62] noble Gloucester, of some poise,[63]
Wherein we must have use of your advice:
Our father he hath writ, so hath our sister,
Of differences,[64] which I least thought it fit
To answer from our home; the several messengers
From hence attend dispatch.[65] Our good old friend,
Lay comforts to your bosom; and bestow
Your needful counsel[66] to our business,
Which craves the instant use.[67]

GLOUCESTER

                I serve you, madam,
Your Graces are right welcome.
[*Exeunt. Flourish.*]

---

59 **Natures...deep trust:** Such trustworthy people

60 **out of season:** at an unexpected / inconvenient time
61 **threading...night:** making a difficult way through the dark night
62 **Occasions:** matters
63 **poise:** importance / weight
64 **differences:** disagreements

65 **attend dispatch:** wait to be sent
66 **needful counsel:** needed advice
67 **craves...use:** demands to be done immediately

Commentary

- **The start of this scene underlines the foolish manner in which Lear divided his kingdom.** Lear's original intention was to avoid disharmony within the kingdom, but Curan warns of mounting tension between Albany and Cornwall that may lead to war: 'Have you heard of no likely wars toward, 'twixt the Dukes of Cornwall and Albany?'
- **This scene further illustrates Edmund's cunning and opportunism.** Edmund tricks Edgar into a fake sword-fight and then wounds himself to help blacken Edgar's image. Edmund then skilfully dupes Gloucester into believing that Edgar is a 'murderous coward' and successfully encourages his father to write him into the will. Upon the arrival of Regan, Edmund seizes an opportunity to further tarnish Edgar's reputation by confirming Regan's suggestion that Edgar was friendly with Lear's so-called 'riotous knights'.
- **The parallel between Lear and Gloucester is made clear in this scene as the plot and sub-plot converge.** Both men are easily fooled by thankless and cruel children: just as Lear rewards the hollow flattery of Goneril and Regan, Gloucester is easily tricked into

seeing Edmund as a loyal son. Both men rashly mistreat their loyal and loving children: Lear disowns, disinherits and exiles Cordelia, while Gloucester makes Edgar a fugitive, giving his inheritance to the devious Edmund. Finally, both men create a situation where their children gain power and authority over them. At this point Lear is starting to suffer as Goneril and Regan gain power; Gloucester will soon experience a similar fate at the hands of Edmund. **In the play's first scene, Lear's excessive pride, passion and moral blindness are made clear. Gloucester, although a victim of Edmund's trickery, is also morally blind. He reacts impetuously from hurt pride and is driven by a passionate rage to exact revenge on Edgar.**

- **Edmund aligns himself with the other evil characters: Regan and Cornwall.** As the play continues, clear divisions between the good and evil characters open up. In this scene it is made very clear which side Edmund is on. He is quick to agree with Regan that Edgar was allied with Lear's knights and is warmly taken into the service of Cornwall ('you shall be ours. / Natures of such deep trust we shall much need; / You we first seize on') and sees this alliance as the best way of fulfilling his ambitions.

Questions

1. In Act 1, Scene 1, Lear explains that he wished to divide his kingdom so 'that future strife / May be prevented now'. What in this scene suggests that Lear's plans have failed in this regard?
2. How does Edmund successfully blacken the other characters' view of Edgar?
3. (a) What similarities do you notice between the situations of Lear and Gloucester?
   (b) What differences are there?
4. In what ways does Gloucester act rashly in this scene?
5. What is your impression of Edmund from this scene?

Act 2 Scene 2

Scene Summary

- Oswald and Kent arrive separately at Gloucester's castle.
- Kent is rude to Oswald before using colourful language to harshly criticise him.
- Kent draws his sword on Oswald and attacks him. Oswald cries out in fear. They are parted by Edmund.
- Cornwall, Regan and Gloucester arrive. Kent is blunt and disrespectful to Cornwall.
- Cornwall orders Kent to be placed in the stocks as punishment.
- Gloucester argues on Kent's behalf but is not listened to.
- Kent has been contacted by Cordelia, and while in the stocks, reads a letter from her.

Before Gloucester's Castle.
Enter KENT and OSWALD, severally

OSWALD
Good dawning[1] to thee, friend. Art of this house?

KENT
Ay.

OSWALD
Where may we set our horses?

KENT
I' the mire.[2]

OSWALD
Prithee, if thou lovest me, tell me.

KENT
I love thee not.

OSWALD
Why, then, I care not for thee.

KENT
If I had thee in Lipsbury pinfold,[3] I would make thee care for me.

OSWALD
0 Why dost thou use me thus? I know thee not.

---

[1] **dawning:** just before dawn. Oswald probably does not recognise Kent as it is still night

[2] **mire:** mud

[3] **Lipsbury pinfold:** the general sense of this phrase is 'in my clutches'. 'Lipsbury' is usually taken to mean 'between the teeth': Lipsbury=Lips-town. 'Pinfold' is an animal pen.

KENT

Fellow, I know thee.

OSWALD

What dost thou know me for?

KENT

A knave, a rascal, an eater of broken meats,[4] a base, proud,
shallow, beggarly, three-suited,[5] hundred-pound,[6] filthy,
worsted-stocking[7] knave; a lily-livered,[8] action-taking[9]
whoreson, glass-gazing,[10] super-serviceable[11] finical[12] rogue,
one-trunk-inheriting[13] slave; one that wouldst be a bawd in
way of good service,[14] and art nothing but the composition[15]
of a knave, beggar, coward, pandar,[16] and the son and heir of
20 a mongrel bitch; one whom I will beat into clamorous[17]
whining, if thou deniest the least syllable of thy addition.[18]

OSWALD

Why, what a monstrous fellow art thou, thus to rail on one
that is neither known of thee nor knows thee!

KENT

What a brazen-faced varlet[19] art thou, to deny thou knowest
me! Is it two days ago since I tripped up thy heels, and beat
thee before the King? Draw, you rogue: for, though it be
night, yet the moon shines. I'll make a sop o' th' moonshine
of you.[20] *[Drawing his sword]* Draw, you whoreson cullionly
barber-monger,[21] draw!

OSWALD

30 Away! I have nothing to do with thee.

KENT

Draw, you rascal! You come with letters against the King,
and take Vanity the puppet's[22] part against the royalty of her
father. Draw, you rogue, or I'll so carbonado your shanks.[23]
Draw, you rascal! Come your ways!

OSWALD

Help, ho! Murder! Help!

KENT

Strike, you slave! Stand, rogue, stand! You neat[24] slave,
strike! *[Beating him]*

OSWALD

Help, ho! Murder! Murder!

4 **broken meats:** scraps
5 **three-suited:** servants were allowed three suits per year
6 **hundred-pound:** possibly a reference to James I's practice of selling knighthoods for 100 pounds
7 **worsted-stocking:** wearing stockings made from cheap wool rather than silk as a gentleman would
8 **lily-livered:** white-livered i.e. cowardly. It was thought that courage came from the liver, therefore a white or bloodless liver indicated a lack of courage
9 **action-taking:** one who takes legal action rather than fights i.e. a coward
10 **glass-gazing:** vain. 'glass' = mirror
11 **super-serviceable:** overly anxious to serve
12 **finical:** fussy
13 **one-trunk-inheriting:** having few possessions
14 **one that wouldst...service:** one who would perform any base action in service
15 **composition:** compound / mixture / make-up
16 **pandar:** 1 go-between for lovers 2 pimp
17 **clamorous:** noisy
18 **addition:** titles I have given you. Kent is being ironic
19 **brazen-faced varlet:** shameless rascal
20 **sop o' th' moonshine:** sop = a cake soaked in liquid. Kent may mean that he will kill Oswald and leave his body to soak in its own blood in the moonlight. However, the meaning is not certain
21 **cullionly barber-monger:** wretched fop who cares too much for his appearance and goes to the barber's too often
22 **Vanity the puppet:** Lady Vanity was a puppet character from morality plays who represented conceit. Kent is comparing this character to Goneril
23 **carbonado your shanks:** score your legs as if preparing for cooking on a grill
24 **neat:** fancy / foppish

[Enter EDMUND, with his rapier drawn.]

EDMUND
How now! What's the matter? *[Parting them]*

KENT
With you, goodman boy,[25] if you please. Come, I'll flesh ye;[26] come on, young master.

[Enter CORNWALL, REGAN, GLOUCESTER and Servants]

GLOUCESTER
Weapons! Arms! What's the matter here?

CORNWALL
Keep peace, upon your lives!
He dies that strikes again. What is the matter?

REGAN
The messengers from our sister and the King.

CORNWALL
What is your difference?[27] Speak.

OSWALD
I am scarce in breath, my Lord.

KENT
No marvel, you have so bestirred your valour.[28] You cowardly rascal, nature disclaims in thee;[29] a tailor made thee.[30]

CORNWALL
Thou art a strange fellow. A tailor make a man?

KENT
Ay, a tailor, sir. A stone-cutter or painter could not have made him so ill, though he had been but two year o' th' trade.

CORNWALL
Speak yet, how grew your quarrel?

OSWALD
This ancient ruffian, sir, whose life I have spared at suit of[31] his grey beard –

KENT
Thou whoreson zed![32] Thou unnecessary letter! My lord, if you

---

[25] **goodman boy:** impudent youth
[26] **flesh ye:** initiate you. Kent is goading Edmund by suggesting that he is young and inexperienced

[27] **difference:** quarrel

[28] **bestirred your valour:** you have raised your courage
[29] **disclaims in thee:** denies having anything to do with you
[30] **a tailor made thee:** Kent is saying that Oswald's clothes are fine, but Oswald himself is worthless

[31] **at suit of:** at the petition of / out of consideration for
[32] **zed:** superfluous / unnecessary. The letter 'z' was seen as unnecessary at the time as its function could be performed by 's'

will give me leave, I will tread this unbolted[33] villain into
mortar, and daub the wall of a jakes[34] with him.
Spare my grey beard, you wagtail?[35]

CORNWALL

60 Peace, sirrah!
You beastly knave, know you no reverence?

KENT

Yes, sir; but anger hath a privilege.[36]

CORNWALL

Why art thou angry?

KENT

That such a slave as this should wear a sword,
Who wears no honesty. Such smiling rogues as these,
Like rats, oft bite the holy cords a-twain[37]
Which are too intrince[38] t'unloose; smooth every passion
That in the natures of their lords rebel;[39]
Bring oil to fire, snow to their colder moods;

70 Renege, affirm, and turn their halcyon beaks
With every gale and vary of their masters,[40]
Knowing nought, like dogs, but following.
A plague upon your epileptic visage![41]
Smile you my speeches, as I were a fool?
Goose, if I had you upon Sarum Plain,
I'd drive ye cackling home to Camelot.[42]

CORNWALL

What, art thou mad, old fellow?

GLOUCESTER

How fell you out? Say that.

KENT

No contraries hold more antipathy[43]

80 Than I and such a knave.

CORNWALL

Why dost thou call him a knave? What is his offence?

KENT

His countenance likes me not.[44]

CORNWALL

No more, perchance,[45] does mine, nor his, nor hers.

[33] **unbolted:** lumpy, as in poorly mixed mortar

[34] **jakes:** lavatory

[35] **wagtail:** a comparison to a dog that wags its tail for its master

[36] **anger hath a privilege:** anger offers the right to overstep the mark. (See Kent's comments in 1.1)

[37] **holy cords a-twain:** hold cords in two. The 'holy cords' may refer to the bonds of family or marriage

[38] **intrince:** tightly bound

[39] **smooth every...lords rebel:** indulge every passion of their masters that rebels against reason

[40] **turn their halcyon...masters:** It was believed that a dead kingfisher when hung up ('halcyon') would turn its beak with the wind. Kent is saying that servants like Oswald support their masters' changing moods

[41] **epileptic visage:** perhaps a reference to Oswald's twitching face

[42] **Goose...Camelot:** The meaning is unclear. The general sense of these lines is: 'Fool, I'd make you run for your life all the way from Salisbury ('Sarum Plain') to Camelot.' 'Goose' is probably a reference to Oswald's foolish laughter. 'Sarum Plain' (Salisbury) is near Winchester which was sometimes identified with King Arthur's castle 'Camelot'. 'Winchester Goose' was a name for a sexually transmitted disease. Kent's lines may have their roots in these references

[43] **No contraries...antipathy:** No two opposites could be more at odds

[44] **His countenance...not:** His face displeases me

[45] **perchance:** perhaps

KENT
Sir, 'tis my occupation to be plain.[46]
I have seen better faces in my time
Than stands on any shoulder that I see
Before me at this instant.

CORNWALL
                           This is some fellow,
Who, having been praised for bluntness, doth affect
A saucy roughness, and constrains the garb
Quite from his nature.[47] He cannot flatter, he!
An[48] honest mind and plain, he must speak truth!
An they will take it, so; if not, he's plain.[49]
These kind of knaves I know, which in this plainness
Harbour more craft[50] and more corrupter ends
Than twenty silly-ducking observants
That stretch their duties nicely.[51]

KENT
Sir, in good faith, in sincere verity,[52]
Under the allowance of your great aspect,
Whose influence, like the wreath of radiant fire
On flickering Phoebus' front —[53,54]

CORNWALL
                           What mean'st by this?

KENT
To go out of my dialect,[55] which you discommend[56] so much. I
know, sir, I am no flatterer. He that beguiled[57] you in a plain
accent was a plain knave, which for my part I will not be,
though I should win your displeasure to entreat me to 't.[58]

CORNWALL
What was the offence you gave him?

OSWALD
I never gave him any:
It pleased the King his master very late[59]
To strike at me, upon his misconstruction;[60]
When he, compact and flattering his displeasure,[61]
Tripped me behind; being down, insulted, railed,[62]
And put upon him such a deal of man,[63]
That worthied him, got praises of the King
For him attempting who was self-subdued;[64]
And, in the fleshment of this dread exploit,[65]
Drew on me here again.

[46] **'tis my occupation…plain:** it is my habit to be blunt

[47] **constrains…his nature:** forces the blunt manner ('garb') of his speech against its nature, and therefore turns bluntness into a form of deception
[48] **An:** If
[49] **An honest mind…he's plain:** If people tolerate his rude manner, he's satisfied. If not, he says he is just being honest
[50] **Harbour more craft:** hide more cunning
[51] **twenty silly-ducking…nicely:** twenty fawning, bowing attendants that strain to carry out their duties conscientiously
[52] **verity:** honesty
[53] **Phoebus' front:** Apollo's (god of the sun) forehead
[54] **Under the allowance…Phoebus' front:** Kent adopts a mock courtly tone here
[55] **dialect:** manner of speaking
[56] **discommend:** disapprove of
[57] **beguiled:** deceived
[58] **He that beguiled…to 't:** Unclear, possibly: he that deceived you using blunt language was clearly a rogue, which I will not be, even if I could call on your disapproval to beg me to be a plain speaking rogue

[59] **very late:** recently
[60] **misconstruction:** misinterpretation
[61] **compact…his displeasure:** in league with the King and encouraging his ill-temper
[62] **railed:** shouted abuse
[63] **such a deal of man:** such a brave show
[64] **self-subdued:** humbled himself
[65] **fleshment of…exploit:** in the excitement of these terrible actions

KENT

                    None of these rogues and cowards
But Ajax is their fool.[66]

CORNWALL

                    Fetch forth the stocks![67]
You stubborn ancient knave, you reverend braggart,
We'll teach you.

KENT

                    Sir, I am too old to learn:
Call not your stocks for me. I serve the King,
120 On whose employment I was sent to you.
You shall do small respect, show too bold malice
Against the grace and person[68] of my master,
Stocking[69] his messenger.

CORNWALL

                    Fetch forth the stocks!
As I have life and honour. There shall he sit till noon.

REGAN

Till noon! Till night, my Lord, and all night too.

KENT

Why, madam, if I were your father's dog,
You should not use me so.

REGAN

                    Sir, being his knave, I will.

CORNWALL

This is a fellow of the self-same colour[70]
Our sister speaks of. Come, bring away the stocks!

[Stocks brought out]

GLOUCESTER

130 Let me beseech[71] your Grace not to do so.
His fault is much, and the good King his master
Will check[72] him for't. Your purposed low correction[73]
Is such as basest and contemned'st wretches
For pilferings and most common trespasses
Are punished with.[75] The king must take it ill,
That he, so slightly valued in his messenger,
Should have him thus restrained.[76]

[66] **None of these...fool:** None of these rogues and cowards are satisfied until Ajax (or Cornwall) is deceived into being their fool. Ajax is a great Greek warrior. However, he was thought to be stupid. The name 'Ajax' also suggests a lavatory (a jakes), hence Cornwall's anger at the comparison

[67] **stocks:** a punishment whereby the offender's ankles were secured in wooden frame

[68] **grace and person:** dignity of the crown and to Lear himself

[69] **stocking:** placing in the stocks

[70] **self-same colour:** the same character

[71] **beseech:** urge / beg

[72] **check:** reprimand

[73] **low correction:** dishonourable punishment

[74] **basest and contemned'st:** lowly and contemptible

[75] **pilferings...trespasses:** stealing and common crimes

[76] **That he...restrained:** that you have so little respect for him that you should restrain his messenger like this

CORNWALL

       I'll answer that.[77]

REGAN

My sister may receive it much more worse
To have her gentleman abused, assaulted,
For following her affairs. Put in his legs.

[KENT is put in the stocks]

Come, my good Lord, away.

[Exeunt all but GLOUCESTER and KENT]

GLOUCESTER

I am sorry for thee, friend. 'Tis the Duke's pleasure,
Whose disposition, all the world well knows,
Will not be rubbed[78] nor stopped. I'll entreat[79] for thee.

KENT

Pray, do not, sir. I have watched[80] and travelled hard.
Some time I shall sleep out, the rest I'll whistle.
A good man's fortune may grow out at heels.[81]
Give you good morrow!

GLOUCESTER

The Duke's to blame in this: 'twill be ill taken.
[Exit]

KENT

Good King, that must approve the common saw,[82]
Thou out of heaven's benediction com'st
To the warm sun![83]
Approach, thou beacon to this under globe,
That by thy comfortable beams I may
Peruse this letter.[84] Nothing almost sees miracles,
But misery.[85] I know 'tis from Cordelia,
Who hath most fortunately been informed
Of my obscured course;[86] and shall find time
From this enormous state, seeking to give
Losses their remedies.[87] All weary and o'er-watched,
Take vantage,[88] heavy eyes, not to behold
This shameful lodging.
Fortune, good night. Smile once more, turn thy wheel!
[He sleeps]

---

[77] **I'll answer that:** I'll take responsibility for that

[78] **rubbed:** slowed / impeded. In the game of bowls, a 'rub' is anything that impedes the course of the ball
[79] **entreat:** plead / solicit

[80] **watched:** stayed awake
[81] **grow out at heels:** become threadbare (like a worn pair of socks)

[82] **approve the common saw:** confirm the old saying
[83] **Thou...warm sun!:** proverbial: i.e. Things go from bad to worse / Out of the frying pan and into the fire
[84] **Approach...this letter:** come sun to the earth (under globe) so that by your comforting light I can read this letter
[85] **Nothing...misery:** only miserable people see miracles (because their situation is so desperate)
[86] **obscured course:** actions done while in disguise
[87] **and shall...remedies:** this passage is considered to be corrupted by most critics. Possible meaning: (Cordelia) will find an opportunity to rescue us from this calamitous situation ('enormous state') and restore what we have lost
[88] **vantage:** opportunity

Commentary

- **Kent turns on anybody who has been disrespectful to Lear.** He unreservedly insults Oswald, criticising him in the harshest way. Kent sees this as his duty to Lear and tells Cornwall that righteous anger entitles him to speak in such a blunt manner: 'anger hath a privilege'. However, just as it does in Act 1, **Kent's blunt language gets him into trouble**. He does not hesitate to criticise Cornwall, Regan and Edmund:

  > 'Sir, 'tis my occupation to be plain.
  > I have seen better faces in my time
  > Than stands on any shoulder that I see
  > Before me at this instant'

  His plain speaking singles out Cornwall by comparing him to the stupid hero 'Ajax'. Kent is punished for such disrespect by being placed in the stocks. **Like Lear and Gloucester, Kent is a passionate man. However, unlike the other two, Kent's judgement of others is far more astute.**

- **Oswald is shown to be a cowardly, foppish (overly concerned with fashion) character.** Kent's insults plays on these ideas calling him 'a lily-livered, action-taking whoreson, glass-gazing, super-serviceable finical rogue'. This is shown to be true by Oswald's cowardly screams for help and his fawning manner around Cornwall and Regan.

- **The fight between Kent and Oswald parodies the disharmony between their masters: Lear and his daughters,** and reflects the wider conflict in the main plot and sub-plot.

- **The scene is wonderfully comic in parts.** Kent's colourful verbal abuse of Oswald, their fight, and Kent's disrespectful treatment of Cornwall offer the audience some humorous moments. However, these do not undermine the more serious elements of the scene.

- **Cornwall is shown to be a brutal man and disrespectful of Lear.** He punishes Kent by putting him in the stocks; this is disproportionate to Kent's supposed crime and an insult to Lear as Kent is the King's personal messenger. Gloucester points to this last fact: 'The king must take it ill, / That he, so slightly valued in his messenger, / Should have him thus restrained.'

- **Gloucester reveals his compassionate side and his innate sense of justice.** He defends Kent and tries to dissuade Cornwall from using the stocks, pointing to the excessive nature of the punishment: 'Let me beseech your Grace not to do so / ... Your purposed low correction / Is such as basest and contemned'st wretches / For pilferings and most common trespasses / Are punished with.' However, Gloucester proves to be ineffectual and unable to influence Cornwall.

- **Regan shows herself to be a cunning woman.** She looks to increase the severity of Kent's punishment by calling for him to be left in the stocks till night rather than noon. This is a ploy to enrage Lear once he sees his messenger treated so shamefully. Kent's reaction underlines how disrespectful the punishment is to Lear: 'Why, madam, if I were your father's dog, / You should not use me so.'

- **Kent's concern is always for the King.** As Gloucester expresses sympathy for him, Kent stoically accepts the punishment he has received, saying that he will either sleep or whistle through his detention. Kent is far more upset by the fact that his punishment will insult Lear: 'I serve the King / ... You shall do small respect, show too bold malice / Against the grace and person of my master, / Stocking his messenger.'

- **While in the stocks Kent reveals to the audience that Cordelia has written to him.** This scene shows how Cordelia and Kent remain in contact. The audience are now being offered the hope that Cordelia will come to Lear's aid.

Questions

1. (a) Describe how Kent treats Oswald in this scene.
   (b) Do you think Oswald deserves to be treated this way? Why / why not?
2. How do Cornwall and Regan show themselves to be cruel characters in this scene?
3. What is your view of Gloucester from this scene?
4. How does Kent react to the punishment of being placed in the stocks?
5. How do you think Lear will react when he learns that Kent was placed in the stocks?
6. Do you find any aspects of this scene amusing? Explain your answer.

Act 2 — Scene 3

Scene Summary

- In soliloquy, Edgar explains how he has narrowly escaped being apprehended.
- To continue to avoid capture he will now disguise himself as a mad beggar, a 'Poor Tom'.

A Wood near Gloucester's Castle.
Enter EDGAR

EDGAR
I heard myself proclaimed;[1]
And by the happy hollow of a tree
Escaped the hunt. No port[2] is free; no place
That guard and most unusual vigilance
Does not attend my taking.[3] Whiles I may 'scape,
I will preserve myself, and am bethought
To take the basest and most poorest shape
That ever penury,[4] in contempt of man,
Brought near to beast. My face I'll grime with filth,
10 Blanket my loins, elf[5] all my hair in knots,
And with presented nakedness outface[6]
The winds and persecutions of the sky.
The country[7] gives me proof and precedent[8]
Of Bedlam beggars,[9] who, with roaring voices
Strike in their numbed and mortified[10] bare arms
Pins, wooden pricks, nails, sprigs of rosemary;
And with this horrible object,[11] from low farms,
Poor pelting[12] villages, sheep-cotes[13] and mills,
Sometime with lunatic bans,[14] sometime with prayers,
20 Enforce their charity. Poor Turlygod![15] Poor Tom![16]
That's something yet. Edgar I nothing am.[17]
[Exit]

[1] **proclaimed:** proclaimed an outlaw

[2] **port:** 1 seaport 2 gate

[3] **attend my taking:** wait to arrest me

[4] **penury:** extreme poverty

[5] **elf:** tangle / mat
[6] **outface:** confront
[7] **country:** countryside
[8] **proof and precedent:** evidence and examples
[9] **Bedlam beggars:** those released from the Bethlehem hospital for the insane who were given a licence to beg
[10] **mortified:** dead to sensation
[11] **object:** spectacle
[12] **pelting:** paltry / worthless
[13] **sheep-cotes:** shepherds' cottages
[14] **bans:** curses
[15] **Turlygod:** This reference has never been satisfactorily explained. However, as Edgar is feigning madness, no explanation may be necessary
[16] **Poor Tom:** 'Bedlam beggars' referred to themselves as 'Poor Toms'
[17] **That's something...nothing am:** At least as Poor Tom I have some identity. Edgar no longer exists.

Commentary

- This short scene shows how **Gloucester's rash actions and poor judgement have left Edgar as an outlaw**. Edgar is forced to disguise himself as a Bedlam beggar (Poor Tom) to evade capture. Bedlam beggars were reportedly former inmates of the Bethlehem ('Bedlam') lunatic asylum in London. Upon release, these mentally ill individuals were given a licence to beg. They were believed to be possessed by demons and this often kept people away from them.

- **The image of Poor Tom, both mad and homeless, foreshadows Lear's experience in the storm scenes where he is reduced to a similar condition.**

- *King Lear* focuses on the idea of human suffering. In his soliloquy, Edgar (as Poor Tom), highlights how poverty can undermine human dignity as he decides, 'To take the basest and most poorest shape / That ever penury, in contempt of man, / Brought near to beast.' The figure of Poor Tom, sharpens the play's focus on human suffering. It is only through suffering himself that Lear will eventually come to appreciate the suffering of others.

- **Shakespeare's choice of disguise for Edgar goes to the very heart of the play.** The image of a man stripped of all possessions prompts questions about what it means to be human. Poor Tom is an anonymous, 'mad' beggar; what is a man without an identity and reason? Lear has to experience such a state of nothingness to gain insight and wisdom.

- **Disguises and hidden identities are a recurring feature of *King Lear*.** In this scene Edgar disguises himself as Poor Tom. Kent wears a disguise after he is banished. Goneril, Regan and Edmund also disguise who they really are, hiding their true natures from their fathers.

Act 2 — Scene 4

Scene Summary

- Lear comes upon Kent in the stocks and is incredulous at the idea that Regan and Cornwall would treat his messenger like this.
- Lear demands to see Regan and Cornwall. He becomes agitated when his demands are not immediately met.
- Lear complains to Regan about the manner in which he was treated by Goneril. However, Regan sides with her sister, much to Lear's surprise.
- Goneril arrives. Both she and Regan decide to further reduce Lear's train of knights. Lear defiantly says that he will not reside with either daughter and leaves the castle just as a storm breaks.
- Gloucester tries to intervene on Lear's behalf but Goneril, Regan and Cornwall remain indifferent and do nothing to prevent Lear leaving.

Before Gloucester's Castle. KENT in the Stocks.
Enter LEAR, FOOL and Gentleman

LEAR
'Tis strange that they[1] should so depart from home,
And not send back my messenger.[2]

GENTLEMAN
                As I learned,
The night before there was no purpose in them
Of this remove.[3]

KENT
Hail to thee, noble master!

LEAR
Ha!
Mak'st thou this shame thy pastime?[4]

KENT
No, my Lord.

FOOL
Ha, ha! He wears cruel garters.[5] Horses are tied by the heads,
dogs and bears by the neck, monkeys by the loins, and men
10 by the legs. When a man's over-lusty at legs,[6] then he wears
wooden nether-stocks.[7]

---

[1] **they:** Regan and Cornwall
[2] **messenger:** Kent

[3] **no purpose…remove:** they had no intention to move somewhere else

[4] **Mak'st…pastime?:** Are you sitting in the stocks for amusement?

[5] **cruel garters:** the stocks. The Fool is punning on the word 'crewel' which means a twisted yarn used to make hose
[6] **over-lusty at legs:** 1 has a tendency to run away 2 promiscuous
[7] **nether-stocks:** stocks for the lower legs

LEAR
What's he that hath so much thy place[8] mistook
To set thee here?

KENT
          It is both he and she:
Your son and daughter.

LEAR
No.

KENT
Yes.

LEAR
No, I say.

KENT
I say, yea.

LEAR
No, no, they would not.

KENT
Yes, they have.

LEAR
By Jupiter,[9] I swear, no.

KENT
By Juno,[10] I swear, ay.

LEAR
          They durst[11] not do't;
They could not, would not do't. 'Tis worse than murder,
To do upon respect[12] such violent outrage.
Resolve me, with all modest haste,[13] which way
Thou mightst deserve or they impose this usage,
Coming from us.[14]

KENT
          My Lord, when at their home
I did commend your Highness' letters to them,
Ere I was risen from the place that showed
My duty kneeling,[15] came there a reeking post,
Stewed in his haste,[16] half breathless, panting forth
From Goneril his mistress, salutations;

---

8 **place:** position as Lear's servant

9 **Jupiter:** King of the Roman gods

10 **Juno:** Queen of the Roman gods

11 **durst:** dare
12 **upon respect:** 1 upon consideration
   2 upon the respect due (to the King)
13 **Resolve...haste:** Clarify for me as
   quickly as possibly
14 **Coming from us:** seeing as I sent
   you as my messenger. This is the
   last time in the play Lear uses the
   royal plural ('us')

15 **the place...kneeling:** a kneeling
   position that I dutifully occupied
16 **reeking post ...haste:** messenger
   soaked in sweat

Delivered letters, spite of intermission,[17]
Which presently they read; on whose contents
They summoned up their meiny,[18] straight took horse,
Commanded me to follow, and attend
The leisure of their answer; gave me cold looks;
And meeting here the other messenger,
Whose welcome, I perceived, had poisoned mine
40 Being the very fellow that of late
Displayed so saucily[19] against your Highness,
Having more man than wit[20] about me, drew.
He raised the house with loud and coward cries.
Your son and daughter found this trespass worth
The shame which here it suffers.

FOOL
Winter's not gone yet, if the wild-geese fly that way.[21]
        Fathers that wear rags
        Do make their children blind,
        But fathers that bear bags
50   Shall see their children kind.[22]
        Fortune, that arrant whore,
        Ne'er turns the key to the poor.[23]
But, for all this, thou shalt have as many dolours[24] for thy
daughters as thou canst tell in a year.

LEAR
O, how this mother swells up toward my heart!
Hysterica passio,[25] down, thou climbing sorrow!
Thy element's[26] below! Where is this daughter?

KENT
With the Earl, sir, here within.

LEAR
Follow me not; stay here.
[Exit]

GENTLEMAN
60 Made you no more offence but what you speak of?

KENT
None. How chance[27] the King comes with so small a
number?

FOOL
An[28] thou hadst been set i' the stocks for that question, thou
hadst well deserved it.

---

[17] **spite of intermissions:** despite the fact he was interrupting me
[18] **meiny:** servants / retinue

[19] **saucily:** rudely
[20] **more man than wit:** more courage than sense

[21] **Winter's…that way:** i.e. Bad times are ahead. Geese fly south ('that way') when the harsh weather of winter comes
[22] **Fathers that wear…children kind:** Fathers that are poor have children who care little for them, but fathers that hold their purse strings tightly have children that act kindly to them
[23] **Fortune…the poor:** Fortune is like a prostitute who never opens her door to a poor man
[24] **dolours:** 1 pain / grief 2 dollars i.e. money. The Fool is punning here
[25] **this mother…passio:** This is a reference to a disease known as 'The Mother' or 'Hysterica Passio'. The condition was said to arise in the stomach and cause a choking sensation.
[26] **element:** proper place

[27] **How chance:** How has it come about

[28] **An:** If

KENT
Why, Fool?

FOOL
We'll set thee to school to an ant, to teach thee there's no
labouring i' the winter.[29] All that follow their noses are led
by their eyes, but blind men; and there's not a nose among
twenty but can smell him that's stinking.[30] Let go thy hold
when a great wheel runs down a hill, lest it break thy neck
with following it. But the great one that goes upward,[31] let
him draw thee after. When a wise man gives thee better
counsel, give me mine again; I would have none but knaves
follow it, since a fool gives it.
　　　That sir which serves and seeks for gain
　　　And follows but for form,[32]
　　　Will pack[33] when it begins to rain,
　　　And leave thee in the storm.
　　　But I will tarry;[34] the Fool will stay,
　　　And let the wise man fly:
　　　The knave turns fool that runs away;
　　　The Fool no knave, perdy.[35]

KENT
Where learned you this, Fool?

FOOL
Not i' the stocks, fool.

[Re-enter LEAR with GLOUCESTER]

LEAR
Deny to speak with me? They are sick? They are weary?
They have travelled all the night? Mere fetches,[36]
The images of revolt and flying off.[37]
Fetch me a better answer.

GLOUCESTER
　　　　　　　　My dear Lord,
You know the fiery quality of the Duke;
How unremovable[38] and fixed he is
In his own course.

LEAR
Vengeance! Plague! Death! Confusion!
Fiery? What quality? Why, Gloucester, Gloucester,
I'd speak with the Duke of Cornwall and his wife.

[29] **We'll set thee...the winter:** We'll have
you learn from the ant, who will teach
you that it is pointless to work in winter.
The Fool is recalling Aesop's fable in
which the ant worked all summer to
provide for the winter. Lear is now in the
winter of his life and is not provided for
[30] **All that follow...stinking:** All who use
their eyes can walk in a straight line
except the blind; and even they can
smell ruination. The Fool is observing
that Lear's downfall is readily apparent
[31] **great one...upward:** a person whose
fortunes are improving
[32] **form:** appearances
[33] **pack:** leave
[34] **tarry:** wait
[35] **The knave turns...perdy:** The servant
('knave') that deserts his master is a fool;
but the Fool is no villain ('knave'), by
God ('perdy')

[36] **fetches:** excuses / evasions
[37] **flying off:** abandonment

[38] **unremovable:** stubborn / immovable

GLOUCESTER
Well, my good Lord, I have informed them so.

LEAR
Informed them! Dost thou understand me, man?

GLOUCESTER
Ay, my good Lord.

LEAR
The King would speak with Cornwall; the dear father
Would with his daughter speak, commands her service.
100 Are they informed of this? My breath and blood!
Fiery? The fiery Duke? Tell the hot Duke that –
No, but not yet. Maybe he is not well.
Infirmity doth still neglect all office
Whereto our health is bound.[39] We are not ourselves
When Nature, being oppressed, commands the mind
To suffer with the body. I'll forbear,
And am fallen out with my more headier will,
To take the indisposed and sickly fit
For the sound man.[40] *[Looking at KENT]* Death on my state![41]
wherefore
110 Should he sit here? This act persuades me
That this remotion[42] of the Duke and her
Is practice only.[43] Give me my servant forth.
Go tell the Duke and's wife I'd speak with them,
Now, presently! Bid them come forth and hear me,
Or at their chamber-door I'll beat the drum
Till it cry sleep to death.[44]

GLOUCESTER
I would have all well betwixt you.
[Exit]

LEAR
O me, my heart, my rising heart! But down!

FOOL
Cry to it, nuncle, as the cockney did to the eels when she put
120 'em i' the paste alive; she knapped 'em o' the coxcombs with
a stick, and cried 'Down, wantons, down!'[45] 'Twas her
brother that, in pure kindness to his horse, buttered his hay.[46]

[Enter CORNWALL, REGAN, GLOUCESTER and Servants]

[39] **Infirmity...is bound:** Illness causes us to neglect the duties we perform when we are healthy

[40] **am fallen...sound man:** I have taken issue with my initial stronger impulse, and I recognise that Cornwall's actions are the result of sickness

[41] **Death on my state!:** An oath. The word 'state' relates to both the kingdom and Lear's state as an old man

[42] **remotion:** 1 removal i.e. moving from their own castle to Gloucester's 2 remoteness i.e. being aloof

[43] **practice only:** merely a trick

[44] **Till...to death:** until sleep is killed by the noise i.e. until everyone is awoken

[45] **Cry to it...down!:** The Fool draws a parallel between Lear and a cockney woman who placed live eels in a pie to cook. Because she hadn't killed the eels first they tried to wriggle out so she beat them on their heads. Similarly, Lear's attempts to control his heart come too late

[46] **'Twas her brother...hay:** It was her brother who gave buttered hay to his horses to eat. This is an example of folly growing out of attempted kindness. The Fool's metaphors poke fun at Lear's foolish tenderness for his daughters

LEAR
Good morrow[47] to you both.

CORNWALL
         Hail to your Grace!

[KENT is set at liberty]

REGAN
I am glad to see your Highness.

LEAR
Regan, I think you are; I know what reason
I have to think so. If thou shouldst not be glad,
I would divorce me from thy mother's tomb,
Sepulchring an adultress.[48] *[To KENT]* O, are you free?
Some other time for that.

      [Exit KENT]

         Beloved Regan,
Thy sister's naught. O Regan, she hath tied
Sharp-toothed unkindness, like a vulture,[49] here
[Points to his heart]
I can scarce speak to thee – thou'lt not believe
With how depraved a quality[50] – O Regan!

REGAN
I pray you, sir, take patience. I have hope
You less know how to value her desert
Than she to scant her duty.[51]

LEAR
         Say, how is that?

REGAN
I cannot think my sister in the least
Would fail her obligation. If, sir, perchance
She have restrained the riots[52] of your followers,
'Tis on such ground, and to such wholesome end,
As clears her from all blame.

LEAR
         My curses on her!

REGAN
O, sir, you are old.

[47] **morrow:** Lear is being ironic as it is now evening

[48] **If thou shouldst...adultress:** If you weren't glad to see me I would divorce your dead mother and refuse to be buried with a dead adulteress

[49] **vulture:** This is a reference to the legend of Prometheus who stole fire from the gods and was punished by having his liver endlessly pecked at by a vulture
[50] **quality:** manner

[51] **I have hope...her duty:** I hope that it is the case that you are unappreciative of her, rather than her falling short ('scant') in her duty to you

[52] **riots:** unrestrained revelry

Nature in you stands on the very verge
Of her confine.[53] You should be ruled and led
By some discretion,[54] that discerns your state
Better than you yourself. Therefore, I pray you,
That to our sister you do make return.
Say you have wronged her, sir.

LEAR
                      Ask her forgiveness?
Do you but mark how this becomes the house:[55]
150 *[Kneeling]* Dear daughter, I confess that I am old;
Age is unnecessary: on my knees I beg
That you'll vouchsafe me raiment, bed and food![56]

REGAN
Good sir, no more! These are unsightly tricks.
Return you to my sister.

LEAR
                 [Rising] Never, Regan:
She hath abated me of half my train;[57]
Looked black upon me; struck me with her tongue,
Most serpent-like, upon the very heart.
All the stored vengeances of heaven fall
On her ingrateful top![58] Strike her young bones,
160 You taking airs, with lameness![59]

CORNWALL
                   Fie, sir, fie!

LEAR
You nimble lightnings, dart your blinding flames
Into her scornful eyes! Infect her beauty,
You fen-sucked[60] fogs, drawn by the powerful sun,
To fall and blister her![61]

REGAN
O the blest gods! So will you wish on me,
When the rash mood is on.

LEAR
No, Regan, thou shalt never have my curse.
Thy tender-hefted[62] nature shall not give
Thee o'er to harshness. Her eyes are fierce; but thine
170 Do comfort and not burn. 'Tis not in thee
To grudge my pleasures, to cut off my train,
To bandy hasty words, to scant my sizes,[63]

---

[53] **her confine:** i.e. the end of Lear's life

[54] **some discretion:** some discreet person

[55] **becomes the house:** 1 befits the family 2 befits the royal line. Lear is being ironic here

[56] **Dear daughter...food!:** Dear daughter, I admit that I am elderly. Old people are unnecessary. On my knees I beg you to grant ('vouchsafe') me clothing ('raiment'), a bed and food. Lear is being ironic here

[57] **abated...train:** deprived me of half of my entourage

[58] **All the stored...ingrateful top!:** May all of the divine vengeance of heaven fall upon her ungrateful head!

[59] **Strike...lameness!:** Strike her children, you noxious vapours, and make them lame

[60] **fen-sucked:** drawn up from the marsh

[61] **blister her:** cover her face with blisters

[62] **tender-hefted:** 1 tender-hearted 2 set in a delicate frame ('heft')

[63] **scant my sizes:** limit my allowances (food, drink etc.)

And in conclusion to oppose the bolt[64]
Against my coming in. Thou better know'st
The offices[65] of nature, bond of childhood,[66]
Effects of courtesy, dues of gratitude.
Thy half o' the kingdom hast thou not forgot,
Wherein I thee endowed.

REGAN
Good sir, to the purpose.

LEAR
Who put my man i' the stocks?

[Tucket within]

CORNWALL
What trumpet's that?

REGAN
I know't, my sister's. This approves her letter,[67]
That she would soon be here.

[Enter OSWALD]

Is your Lady come?

LEAR
This is a slave, whose easy-borrowed pride[68]
Dwells in the fickle grace[69] of her he follows.
Out, varlet,[70] from my sight!

CORNWALL
What means your Grace?

LEAR
Who stocked my servant? Regan, I have good hope
Thou didst not know on't. Who comes here? O heavens,

[Enter GONERIL]

If you do love old men, if your sweet sway[71]
Allow obedience, if yourselves are old,
Make it your cause! Send down, and take my part!
90 *[To GONERIL]* Art not ashamed to look upon this beard?
O Regan, wilt thou take her by the hand?

[64] **oppose the bolt:** lock the door
[65] **office:** duties
[66] **bond of childhood:** a child's
obligations (to a parent)

[67] **approves her letter:** confirms the
contents of her letter

[68] **easy-borrowed pride:** casual pride.
[69] **fickle grace:** undependable favour
[70] **varlet:** 1 scoundrel 2 servant

[71] **sway:** authority

GONERIL
Why not by the hand, sir? How have I offended?
All's not offence that indiscretion[72] finds
And dotage[73] terms so.

72 **indiscretion:** poor judgement
73 **dotage:** senility

LEAR
O sides, you are too tough!
Will you yet hold?[74] How came my man i' the stocks?

74 **O sides...yet hold?:** Lear wonders
why his chest does not split with the
pain he is experiencing

CORNWALL
I set him there, sir: but his own disorders
Deserved much less advancement.[75]

75 **much less advancement:** less of a
promotion. Cornwall is arguing that
Kent deserves a harsher punishment

LEAR
You! Did you?

REGAN
I pray you, father, being weak, seem so.
If, till the expiration of your month,
200 You will return and sojourn[76] with my sister,
Dismissing half your train, come then to me.
I am now from home, and out of that provision[77]
Which shall be needful for your entertainment.

76 **sojourn:** live with for a while

77 **provision:** necessities

LEAR
Return to her, and fifty men dismissed?
No, rather I abjure[78] all roofs, and choose
To wage[79] against the enmity[80] o' the air,
To be a comrade with the wolf and owl,
Necessity's sharp pinch![81] Return with her?
Why, the hot-blooded[82] France, that dowerless took
210 Our youngest born, I could as well be brought
To knee his throne, and, squire-like,[83] pension beg
To keep base life afoot.[84] Return with her?
Persuade me rather to be slave and sumpter[85]
To this detested groom. *[Pointing at OSWALD]*

78 **abjure:** renounce / swear to avoid
79 **wage:** battle / wage war against
80 **enmity:** hostility
81 **necessity's sharp pinch:** 1 the
hardship of poverty 2 cruel suffering
imposed by Fate
82 **hot-blooded:** passionate
83 **squire-like:** like a servant
84 **base life afoot:** keep a basic
existence continuing
85 **sumpter:** packhorse

GONERIL
At your choice, sir.

LEAR
I prithee, daughter, do not make me mad,
I will not trouble thee, my child. Farewell.
We'll no more meet, no more see one another.
But yet thou art my flesh, my blood, my daughter –
Or rather a disease that's in my flesh
220 Which I must needs call mine. Thou art a boil,

A plague-sore, an embossed carbuncle,[86]
In my corrupted blood.[87] But I'll not chide thee.
Let shame come when it will, I do not call it.
I do not bid the thunder-bearer[88] shoot,
Nor tell tales of thee to high-judging Jove.[89]
Mend[90] when thou canst, be better at thy leisure;
I can be patient; I can stay with Regan,
I and my hundred knights.

REGAN
             Not altogether so.
I looked not for you yet, nor am provided
For your fit welcome. Give ear, sir, to my sister,
For those that mingle reason with your passion[91]
Must be content to think you old, and so –
But she knows what she does.

LEAR
             Is this well spoken?

REGAN
I dare avouch[92] it, sir. What, fifty followers?
Is it not well? What should you need of more?
Yea, or so many, sith[93] that both charge[94] and danger
Speak 'gainst so great a number? How in one house
Should many people, under two commands,
Hold amity?[95] 'Tis hard, almost impossible.

GONERIL
Why might not you, my Lord, receive attendance
From those that she calls servants or from mine?

REGAN
Why not, my Lord? If then they chanced to slack you,
We could control them. If you will come to me –
For now I spy a danger – I entreat[96] you
To bring but five-and-twenty. To no more
Will I give place or notice.

LEAR
I gave you all –

REGAN
             And in good time you gave it.

LEAR
Made you my guardians, my depositaries,[97]

---

86 **embossed carbuncle:** swollen tumour
87 **blood:** lineage / family
88 **thunder-bearer:** Jupiter, King of the gods, and the God of sky and thunder
89 **Jove:** another name for Jupiter
90 **Mend:** Improve

91 **mingle reason...passion:** apply rational thinking to your passionate outburst

92 **avouch:** declare

93 **sith:** since
94 **charge:** cost
95 **Hold amity:** get along / maintain friendly relations

96 **entreat:** plead with

97 **depositaries:** trustees / managers

But kept a reservation[98] to be followed
250 With such a number. What, must I come to you
With five-and-twenty, Regan? Said you so?

REGAN

And speak't again, my Lord. No more with me.

LEAR

Those wicked creatures yet do look well-favoured[99]
When others are more wicked. Not being the worst
Stands in some rank of praise. *[To GONERIL]* I'll go with thee.
Thy fifty yet doth double five-and-twenty,
And thou art twice her love.

GONERIL

                          Hear me, my Lord.
What need you five-and-twenty, ten or five,
To follow[100] in a house where twice so many
260 Have a command to tend you?

REGAN

                          What need one?

LEAR

O, reason not the need![101] Our basest beggars
Are in the poorest thing superfluous.[102]
Allow not nature more than nature needs,
Man's life as cheap as beast's.[103] Thou art a lady;
If only to go warm were gorgeous,
Why, nature needs not what thou gorgeous wear'st,
Which scarcely keeps thee warm.[104] But, for true need –
You heavens, give me that patience, patience I need!
You see me here, you gods, a poor old man,
270 As full of grief as age; wretched in both!
If it be you that stir these daughters' hearts
Against their father, fool me not so much
To bear it tamely;[105] touch me with noble anger,
And let not women's weapons, water-drops,[106]
Stain my man's cheeks! No, you unnatural hags,
I will have such revenges on you both,
That all the world shall – I will do such things –
What they are yet I know not, but they shall be
The terrors of the earth! You think I'll weep –
280 No, I'll not weep.

[Storm and tempest]

[98] **kept a reservation:** retained the right. Lear reserved the right to have 100 knights (see 1.1)

[99] **well-favoured:** good looking

[100] **to follow:** be your followers

[101] **O, reason not the need!:** O, don't try to rationalise my needs!
[102] **Our basest...superfluous:** Our poorest beggars have something superfluous (unnecessary) to their needs
[103] **Allow...beast's:** If you don't allow human nature more than animal nature needs, then man's life is as worthless as a beast's
[104] **If only...keeps thee warm:** If to keep warm was considered gorgeous, why then, human nature wouldn't need your gorgeous clothes, which hardly keep you warm
[105] **bear it tamely:** meekly put up with it
[106] **water-drops:** tears

                 I have full cause of[107] weeping, but this heart
Shall break into a hundred thousand flaws[108]
Or ere I'll weep. O Fool, I shall go mad!
[Exeunt LEAR, GLOUCESTER and FOOL]

CORNWALL
Let us withdraw; 'twill be a storm.

(handwritten note: pathetic fallacy)

REGAN
This house is little; the old man and his people
Cannot be well bestowed.[109]

GONERIL
'Tis his own blame;[110] hath put himself from rest,[111]
And must needs taste his folly.

REGAN
For his particular,[112] I'll receive him gladly,
But not one follower.

GONERIL
                  So am I purposed.
Where is my Lord of Gloucester?

CORNWALL
Followed the old man forth. He is returned.

[Re-enter GLOUCESTER]

GLOUCESTER
The King is in high rage.

CORNWALL
                  Whither is he going?

GLOUCESTER
He calls to horse, but will I know not whither.[113]

CORNWALL
'Tis best to give him way; he leads himself.[114]

GONERIL
My Lord, entreat him by no means to stay.

GLOUCESTER
Alack, the night comes on, and the bleak winds
Do sorely ruffle.[115] For many miles about
There's scarce a bush.

[107] **full cause of:** every reason to
[108] **flaws:** fragments

[109] **bestowed:** accommodated

[110] **blame:** fault
[111] **put himself from rest:** 1 rejected a place to sleep 2 rejected peace of mind / upset himself

[112] **For his particular:** As far as he himself is concerned

[113] **He calls...not whither:** He calls for his horse, but I don't know where he intends to go

[114] **'Tis best...leads himself:** It's best to let him leave; he insists on going his own way

[115] **sorely ruffle:** blow harshly

REGAN

             O, sir, to wilful men
The injuries that they themselves procure[116]
300 Must be their schoolmasters.[117] Shut up your doors.
He is attended with a desperate train,[118]
And what they may incense him to, being apt
To have his ear abused, wisdom bids fear.[119]

CORNWALL

Shut up your doors, my Lord; 'tis a wild night.
My Regan counsels well. Come out o' the storm.
[Exeunt]

[116] **they themselves procure:** they bring on themselves
[117] **be their schoolmasters:** i.e. learn lessons from their mistakes
[118] **desperate train:** band of scoundrels. Regan seems to be under the impression that Lear is accompanied by his knights
[119] **And what...bids fear:** and what they may encourage him to do, seeing how he listens to them and is easily deceived, good sense tells us to fear

Key Quotations

LEAR *O, how this mother swells up toward my heart! / Hysterica passio, down, thou climbing sorrow!*

LEAR *I abjure all roofs, and choose*
To wage against the enmity o' the air,
To be a comrade with the wolf and owl,
Necessity's sharp pinch!

LEAR *You see me here, you gods, a poor old man,*
As full of grief as age; wretched in both!
If it be you that stir these daughters' hearts
Against their father, fool me not so much
To bear it tamely; touch me with noble anger,
And let not women's weapons, water-drops,
Stain my man's cheeks!

LEAR *No, you unnatural hags,*
I will have such revenges on you both,
That all the world shall – I will do such things –
What they are yet I know not, but they shall be
The terrors of the earth! You think I'll weep –
No, I'll not weep.

LEAR *I have full cause of weeping, but this heart / Shall break into a hundred thousand flaws / Or ere I'll weep. O Fool, I shall go mad!*

Commentary

- **This scene is a key moment in Lear's disintegrating relationship with Goneril and Regan.** Having already argued with Goneril, Lear is shocked at the similar manner in which Regan treats him. By the end of this scene, Lear breaks all ties with both daughters and leaves to endure the raging storm outside.

- **Lear is placed under considerable stress in this scene.** The shock at finding Kent in stocks leaves Lear in a state of disbelief that Regan or Cornwall could be so disrespectful: 'They durst not do't; / They could not, would not do't. 'Tis worse than murder, / To do upon respect such violent outrage.' This stress is compounded by the casual and then cruel manner in which Lear is treated. At first Lear tries to ignore the reality of his situation. He struggles to believe that Kent was placed in the stocks by Regan and Cornwall. He then looks to explain Cornwall's delay in coming to speak to him as resulting from illness. Lear then looks to Regan for comfort. However, Goneril's alliance with Regan and the reductions in his train of knights shatters any delusions that Lear entertains.

- **The stress is so great that Lear fears for his sanity.** He senses that he has been pushed to the brink of insanity and cries out to remain sane: 'O, how this mother swells up toward my heart! / Hysterica passio, down, thou climbing sorrow!', 'O, Fool I shall go mad!' The increasing disorder of Lear's mental state is reflected in the chaotic storm that rages outside. The division in his mind is a reflection of the division of his kingdom and the breaking of his natural bond with Cordelia.

- **Lear has to endure a cruel parody of the love-test.** In Act 1, Scene 1, Lear encourages his daughters to compete with each other in flattering him; here they try to outdo each other by eroding the size of Lear's entourage. Lear attempts to choose between them by weighing up which of these unattractive options is the least bad: 'Not being the worst / Stands in some rank of praise. I'll go with thee. / Thy fifty yet doth double five-and-twenty, / And thou art twice her love.' After having his train whittled down to nothing, Lear eventually chooses to leave both daughters. He is still quantifying and measuring love in material terms.

- **Nothingness is a central motif in the play.** In the play's first scene Lear believes that Cordelia's love for him is nothing as she says nothing to gain advantage or quantify her love. Lear's knights are now reduced to nothing. He must himself become nothing (in terms of wealth, power and rationality) if he is to discover who he really is.

- **Goneril and Regan act with extreme cruelty** as together they bully their father. Realising how Lear values his knights as a status symbol, they look to humiliate their father by reducing his train. Lear's pride in himself as a man means he has to fight off the urge to cry as he comes to realise the ingratitude of his daughters: 'let not women's weapons, water-drops, / Stain my man's cheeks!'

- **Despite his wretched situation, Lear still retains his pride.** Lear's need to retain his knights signals his inability to relinquish power and status. His refusal to cry or make peace with Goneril, and his decision to go out into the storm rather than live with his daughters, illustrate this fact.

- **Lear's powerlessness is made clear in this scene.** His threats against his daughters are pathetic and empty as he struggles to find a fitting revenge:

  > 'I will have such revenges on you both,
  > That all the world shall – I will do such things –
  > What they are yet I know not, but they shall be
  > The terrors of the earth! You think I'll weep –
  > No, I'll not weep.'

Commentary (continued)

- **Gloucester again shows that he is a compassionate man** as he appeals to Cornwall, Regan and Goneril to save Lear from the turbulent weather: 'Alack, the night comes on, and the bleak winds / Do sorely ruffle. For many miles about / There's scarce a bush.' However, his pleas fall on deaf ears and he is ignored.

- **Although the Fool is always quick to point out Lear's faults, he is unwavering in his loyalty.**

   The Fool reminds Lear of his foolishness:

   'Fathers that wear rags
   Do make their children blind,
   But fathers that bear bags
   Shall see their children kind.'

   However, the Fool remains steadfast. Even though he sees the difficulty of Lear's situation, he chooses to stay with his master. **It is the Fool's role to help Lear towards self-recognition by highlighting Lear's faults.** In this way the Fool functions as a kind of personification of Lear's conscience.

Questions
---

1. How does Lear react when Kent tells him how he came to be in the stocks?

2. How does the Fool point out Lear's mistakes in this scene?

3. What evidence in this scene shows that Lear is still a proud man?

4. What evidence shows that Lear fears for his mental health?

5. How would you describe the behaviour of Goneril and Regan in this scene? Refer to the text in your answer.

6. (a) In what ways does Lear suffer in this scene?
   (b) What effect do you think this suffering will have on him?

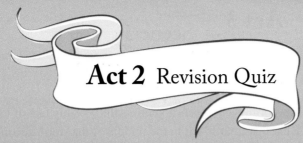

Act 2 Revision Quiz

1. How does Edmund convince Edgar to flee?
   (a) He tells him that Gloucester wants to meet him outside the castle walls
   (b) He tells Edgar that his hiding place is discovered and that Gloucester is angry with him
   (c) He gives Edgar a forged letter
2. True or False: Gloucester promises to make sure that Edmund will inherit his wealth?
3. Why is Kent placed in the stocks?
4. What does Kent read while he is in the stocks?
5. What disguise does Edgar adopt to avoid capture?
6. How does Lear react when he discovers Kent in the stocks?
7. Why does Lear refuse to stay with either Goneril or Regan?
8. Who appeals unsuccessfully to Cornwall, Goneril and Regan to save Lear from the violent weather?
9. What parallels are there between the manner in which Lear and Gloucester are treated by their children?
10. Who says each of the following?

   (a) *I abjure all roofs, and choose*
   To wage against the enmity o' the air,
   To be a comrade with the wolf and owl,
   Necessity's sharp pinch!

   (b) *No, you unnatural hags,*
   I will have such revenges on you both,
   That all the world shall – I will do such things –
   What they are yet I know not, but they shall be
   The terrors of the earth! You think I'll weep –
   No, I'll not weep

   (c) *Fathers that wear rags*
   Do make their children blind,
   But fathers that bear bags
   Shall see their children kind

   (d) *I have full cause of weeping, but this heart*
   Shall break into a hundred thousand flaws
   Or ere I'll weep. O Fool, I shall go mad!

Act 3 Scene 1

Scene Summary

- While out in the raging storm, Kent meets a gentleman (possibly one of Lear's knights).
- The gentleman tells Kent that Lear is out in the middle of the storm accompanied only by the Fool.
- Kent tells the gentleman of the mounting tension between Cornwall and Albany. He also tells him that the King of France has been informed by his spies of Lear's situation.
- Kent explains that French soldiers have landed at Dover. Kent asks the gentleman to go to Dover to bring a message to Cordelia. He gives the gentleman his ring so that Cordelia will know who the message is from.
- Kent leaves to search for Lear.

A Heath. Storm Still.
Enter KENT and a Gentleman, severally.

KENT
Who's there, besides foul weather?

GENTLEMAN
One minded like the weather, most unquietly.[1]

KENT
I know you. Where's the King?

GENTLEMAN
Contending with the fretful elements:[2]
Bids the winds blow the earth into the sea,
Or swell the curled water[3] 'bove the main,[4]
That things might change or cease; tears his white hair,
Which the impetuous blasts, with eyeless rage,[5]
Catch in their fury, and make nothing of;[6]
10 Strives in his little world of man[7] to out-storm[8]
The to-and-fro-conflicting[9] wind and rain.
This night, wherein the cub-drawn[10] bear would couch,[11]
The lion and the belly-pinched[12] wolf
Keep their fur dry, unbonneted[13] he runs,
And bids what will take all.[14]

KENT
                    But who is with him?

GENTLEMAN
None but the Fool, who labours to outjest
His heart-struck injuries.[15]

[1] **minded like...unquietly:** whose mind is unsettled, like the weather

[2] **Contending...elements:** 1 Dealing with the violent weather 2 Competing in fury with the violent weather
[3] **curled water:** waves
[4] **main:** mainland
[5] **eyeless rage:** blind rage
[6] **make nothing of:** care nothing for (Lear's hair)
[7] **little world of man:** microcosm. Lear's body is presented as a reflection of the world around him: violent, unsettled and changeable
[8] **out-storm:** create a greater storm
[9] **to-and-fro-conflicting:** raging
[10] **cub-drawn:** sucked dry by her cubs i.e. very hungry
[11] **couch:** rest
[12] **belly-pinched:** starving
[13] **unbonneted:** hatless
[14] **bids...take all:** says 'Whoever wants the world can have it.' This phrase has a gambling resonance

[15] **who labours...injuries:** who tries to use humour to top Lear's grief

KENT

             Sir, I do know you,
And dare, upon the warrant of my note,[16]
Commend a dear thing to you.[17] There is division,[18]
Although as yet the face of it be covered
With mutual cunning, 'twixt Albany and Cornwall,
Who have – as who have not, that their great stars[19]
Throned and set high? – servants, who seem no less,
Which are to France the spies and speculations[20]
Intelligent of our state. What hath been seen,
Either in snuffs and packings[21] of the Dukes,
Or the hard rein which both of them have borne
Against the old kind King,[22] or something deeper,
Whereof perchance these are but furnishings –[23]
But, true it is, from France there comes a power[24]
Into this scattered[25] kingdom, who already,
Wise in our negligence, have secret feet[26]
In some of our best ports, and are at point[27]
To show their open banner.[28] Now to you:
If on my credit[29] you dare build so far
To make your speed to Dover, you shall find
Some that will thank you, making just report
Of how unnatural and bemadding sorrow[30]
The King hath cause to plain.[31]
I am a gentleman of blood and breeding,[32]
And, from some knowledge and assurance, offer
This office[33] to you.

GENTLEMAN

I will talk further with you.

KENT

              No, do not.
For confirmation that I am much more
Than my out-wall,[34] open this purse, and take
What it contains. If you shall see Cordelia –
As fear not but you shall – show her this ring,
And she will tell you who your fellow[35] is
That yet you do not know. Fie on[36] this storm!
I will go seek the King.

GENTLEMAN

Give me your hand. Have you no more to say?

KENT

Few words, but, to effect, more than all yet:[37]
That, when we have found the King – in which your pain[38]

[16] **warrant of my note:** assurance of my observation of you

[17] **Commend...to you:** trust you with an important matter

[18] **division:** tension / disagreement

[19] **stars:** fortunes

[20] **speculations:** infiltrators / secret agents

[21] **snuffs and packings:** resentments and schemes

[22] **hard rein...kind King:** the mistreatment they have given to the old kind King. The image here is of riding a horse on a tight rein

[23] **furnishings:** decorations / facades

[24] **power:** army

[25] **scattered:** divided

[26] **feet:** foothold

[27] **at point:** ready

[28] **open banner:** display their military banners i.e. reveal themselves

[29] **on my credit:** on my word

[30] **bemadding sorrow:** sorrow that is driving him mad

[31] **plain:** complain

[32] **of blood and breeding:** by noble birth and education

[33] **office:** duty i.e. to go to Dover

[34] **out-wall:** appearance

[35] **fellow:** companion

[36] **Fie on:** i.e. Damn

[37] **to effect...yet:** more important than anything I have said yet

[38] **pain:** efforts

That way, I'll this – he that first lights on[39] him
Holla[40] the other.
[Exeunt severally]

Commentary

- **The conversation between Kent and the gentleman provides the audience with important information:**
  - Tension is mounting between Cornwall and Albany, although this is not out in the open.
  - Lear is out in the middle of the violent storm. Only the Fool is with him.
  - Through his spies, the King of France is aware of Lear's situation.
  - French forces have landed at Dover. Cordelia is also at Dover.
- **The forces of good are starting to militarily unite.** We learn that the King of France is preparing forces to come to Lear's aid. This, along with Kent's communication with Cordelia, offers some hope at this point of the play.
- **The gentleman paints a picture of Lear's wretchedness.** He is described as 'Contending with the fretful elements' shouting at the wind to destroy the earth as he 'tears his white hair'. The image of Lear vulnerably exposed to the harsh weather, yet battling it, is a powerful metaphor for Lear's egocentrism and unwillingness to accept his situation. The image also conjures up the idea of Lear's utter powerlessness. Without power, wealth or status Lear is becoming nothing. This process is paralleled by his growing mental instability.

Act 3 — Scene 2

Scene Summary

- Lear roars at the raging storm, calling on it to bring destruction to the earth and to himself.
- The Fool urges Lear to escape the storm and return to his daughters.
- After searching for Lear Kent finds him.
- Lear says that he is a victim, 'a man / More sinned against than sinning.'
- Kent leads Lear to shelter in a hovel.
- Lear expresses pity for the Fool.

Another Part of the Heath. Storm Still.
Enter LEAR and FOOL

Storm has major symbolic importance in the play (reflects the turmoil)

LEAR
Blow, winds, and crack your cheeks![1] Rage! Blow!
You cataracts and hurricanoes,[2] spout
Till you have drenched our steeples, drowned the cocks![3]
You sulphurous and thought-executing[4] fires,
Vaunt-couriers[5] to oak-cleaving thunderbolts,
Singe my white head! And thou, all-shaking thunder,
Strike flat the thick rotundity o' the world![6]
Crack Nature's moulds,[7] all germens[8] spill at once,
That make ingrateful man!

FOOL
O nuncle, court holy-water[9] in a dry house is better than this
rain-water out o' door. Good nuncle, in, and ask thy daughters'
blessing. Here's a night pities neither wise man nor fool.

LEAR
Rumble thy bellyful! Spit, fire! Spout, rain!
Nor rain, wind, thunder, fire are my daughters.
I tax[10] not you, you elements, with unkindness;
I never gave you kingdom, called you children;
You owe me no subscription;[11] then let fall
Your horrible pleasure. Here I stand, your slave,
A poor, infirm, weak and despised old man.
But yet I call you servile ministers,[12]
That will with two pernicious daughters join
Your high-engendered battles[13] 'gainst a head
So old and white as this. O, ho! 'Tis foul!

1 **crack your cheeks:** On maps, wind is often represented as blowing faces with puffed cheeks
2 **cataracts and hurricanoes:** heavy rain from the air and water spouts from the sea
3 **cocks:** weathercocks
4 **thought-executing:** 1 thought destroying 2 flash as quickly as thoughts arrive 3 destructive like Lear's thoughts
5 **Vaunt-couriers:** heralds
6 **Strike flat...world!:** Strike the round world flat. The world is imagined here as pregnant ('thick rotundity') and Lear calls on the storm to destroy it utterly
7 **Nature's moulds:** the moulds that give shape to all forms in nature
8 **germens:** seeds
9 **court holy-water:** flattery

10 **tax:** accuse / charge

11 **subscription:** loyalty

12 **servile ministers:** slavish agents

13 **high-engendered battles:** armies formed in the heavens

FOOL

He that has a house to put's[14] head in has a good head-
piece.[15]

> The cod-piece[16] that will house
> Before the head has any,
> The head and he shall louse;
> So beggars marry many.[17]
> The man that makes his toe
> What he his heart should make
> Shall of a corn cry woe,
> And turn his sleep to wake.[18]

For there was never yet fair woman but she made mouths in
a glass.[19]

[Enter KENT]

LEAR

No, I will be the pattern of all patience;
I will say nothing.

KENT

Who's there?

FOOL

Marry, here's grace[20] and a cod-piece[21]; that's a wise man
and a fool.[22]

KENT

Alas, sir, are you here? Things that love night
Love not such nights as these. The wrathful skies
Gallow the very wanderers of the dark,[23]
And make them keep their caves. Since I was man,
Such sheets of fire, such bursts of horrid thunder,
Such groans of roaring wind and rain I never
Remember to have heard. Man's nature cannot carry
Th' affliction nor the fear.[24]

LEAR

                 Let the great gods,
That keep this dreadful pudder[25] o'er our heads,
Find out their enemies now. Tremble, thou wretch,
That hast within thee undivulged crimes,
Unwhipped of justice. Hide thee, thou bloody hand;[26]
Thou perjured, and thou simular[27] man of virtue
That art incestuous. Caitiff,[28] to pieces shake,
That under covert and convenient seeming
Hast practised on man's life.[29] Close pent-up guilts,

---

14 **put's:** put his
15 **head-piece:** 1 helmet 2 head/brain

16 **cod-piece:** 1 penis 2 cover worn on the front of the trousers
17 **The cod-piece...marry many:** The man who satisfies his sexual desire before he has a house, will become a beggar with lice. Many beggars marry this way
18 **The man...to wake:** 1 The man that rejects or kicks away ('make his toe') what he should cherish, will experience pain and sleeplessness 2 The man that cherishes something insignificant, like his toe, instead of what he should love, will experience pain and sleeplessness. Both meanings are relevant to Lear's relationship with his daughters
19 **made mouths in glass:** practised faces in the mirror i.e. was vain

20 **grace:** the King
21 **cod-piece:** The Fool's costume may have had a codpiece
22 **that's a...a fool:** The Fool may be suggesting that he is the wise man and Lear is the fool

23 **Gallow...the dark:** Frighten nocturnal animals

24 **cannot carry...the fear:** cannot endure the physical suffering it brings nor the fear

25 **pudder:** turmoil

26 **bloody hand:** murderer
27 **simular:** hypocrite
28 **Caitiff:** Wretch / Villain
29 **That under covert...man's life:** who hides under a deceptive appearance while plotting to take a man's life

Rive your concealing continents[30] and cry
These dreadful summoners grace.[31] I am a man
More sinned against than sinning.[32]

KENT

Alack, bare-headed?
Gracious my Lord, hard by[33] here is a hovel;
Some friendship will it lend you 'gainst the tempest.[34]
Repose you there while I to this hard house —[35]
More harder than the stones whereof 'tis raised;
Which even but now, demanding after you,
Denied me to come in – return and force
Their scanted courtesy.[36]

LEAR

My wits begin to turn.
Come on, my boy. How dost, my boy? Art cold?
I am cold myself. Where is this straw, my fellow?
The art of our necessities is strange
That can make vile things precious.[37] Come, your hovel.
Poor Fool and knave, I have one part in my heart
That's sorry yet for thee.[38]

FOOL

[Singing] *He that has and a little tiny wit,*
     With hey, ho, the wind and the rain,
     Must make content with his fortunes fit,
     For the rain it raineth every day.[39]

LEAR

True, my good boy. Come, bring us to this hovel.
[Exeunt LEAR and KENT]

FOOL

This is a brave night to cool a courtesan.[40] I'll speak a
prophecy ere I go:
     When priests are more in word than matter;[41]
     When brewers mar their malt[42] with water;
     When nobles are their tailors' tutors;[43]
     No heretics burned, but wenches' suitors;[44]
     Then shall the realm of Albion[45]
     Come to great confusion.
     When every case in law is right;
     No squire in debt, nor no poor knight;
     When slanders do not live in tongues;[46]
     Nor cutpurses come not to throngs;[47]
     When usurers tell their gold i' the field;[48]

---

30 **Close pent-up…continents:** Allow buried guilt to burst from the places you have hid it
31 **and cry…summoners grace:** and beg for mercy from those who summon you to divine justice (just like 'summoners' (court officers) bring the accused to an ecclesiastical court)
32 **I am a man…sinning:** More wrong has been done to me than I have done to others
33 **hard by:** nearby
34 **tempest:** violent storm
35 **hard house:** cruel household
36 **force…courtesy:** compel them to offer the courtesy they withhold

37 **The art…precious:** The power of hardship is strange in that it makes valueless things seem precious
38 **I have one part…thee:** There is still a little part of my heart that feels pity for you

39 **He that has…every day:** He that has little sense, must content himself with his fortunes, as every day brings problems

40 **cool a courtesan:** cool the passion of a courtier's mistress
41 **more in word than matter:** i.e. don't practise what they preach
42 **mar their malt:** ruin their beer
43 **when nobles…tutors:** when noblemen teach tailors how to do their job
44 **No heretics…suitors:** The Fool is referring to sexually transmitted disease ('burned') here
45 **Albion:** a Roman name for Britain
46 **When slanders…tongues:** When slanderous statements are not spoken
47 **Nor cutpurses…throngs:** Nor pickpockets come to crowded places
48 **When usurers…field:** When moneylenders count their money publicly

And bawds[49] and whores do churches build;
Then comes the time, who lives to see't,
That going shall be used with feet.[50]
This prophecy Merlin[51] shall make, for I live before his
time.[52]

[Exit]

[49] **bawds:** 1 prostitutes 2 brothel keepers
[50] **going…feet:** people will use their feet for walking i.e. natural order will be restored
[51] **Merlin:** King Arthur's magician
[52] **before his time:** King Lear is set in the 8th century BC; the legend of King Arthur is set in 6th century AD

Key Quotations

LEAR   *Blow, winds, and crack your cheeks! Rage! Blow!*
       You cataracts and hurricanoes, spout
       Till you have drenched our steeples, drowned the cocks!
       You sulphurous and thought-executing fires,
       Vaunt-couriers to oak-cleaving thunderbolts,
       Singe my white head! And thou, all-shaking thunder,
       Strike flat the thick rotundity o' the world!
       Crack Nature's moulds, all germens spill at once,
       That make ingrateful man!

LEAR   *Here I stand, your slave,*
       A poor, infirm, weak and despised old man.
       But yet I call you servile ministers,
       That will with two pernicious daughters join
       Your high-engendered battles 'gainst a head
       So old and white as this. O, ho! 'Tis foul!

LEAR   *I am a man / More sinned against than sinning.*

Commentary

- **This is the first of three scenes set amidst the storm.** An audience during Shakespeare's time would have relied more on language to set the scene than a modern audience more used to special effects. Kent's language portrays the particular ferocity of the storm: 'Since I was man, / Such sheets of fire, such bursts of horrid thunder, / Such groans of roaring wind and rain I never / Remember to have heard'.

- **Lear's egocentrism means he only sees suffering in his own terms.** He identifies the violence of the weather with the cruelty of his two daughters as he imagines Goneril and Regan conspiring with the elements against him:

     '…yet I call you servile ministers,
     That will with two pernicious daughters join
     Your high-engendered battles 'gainst a head
     So old and white as this. O, ho! 'Tis foul!'

His own plight overshadows everything. His despair and pain cause him to cry out for the apocalypse as if *his* problems are the world's problems:
     'And thou, all-shaking thunder,

Strike flat the thick rotundity o' the world!
Crack Nature's moulds, all germens spill at once,
That make ingrateful man!'

- Lear hasn't yet accepted that it was his own poor judgement that brought him to this wretched state. **He still sees himself as a victim:** 'I am a man / More sinned against than sinning'. The weather inspires Lear to imagine the storm unleashing righteous fury on a corrupt world full of criminals and sinners:

'Tremble, thou wretch,
That hast within thee undivulged crimes,
Unwhipped of justice. Hide thee, thou bloody hand;
Thou perjured, and thou simular man of virtue
That art incestuous.'

Lear however does not identify himself as one of these. Instead he still sees himself as a victim rather than the architect of his own downfall.

- However, **there are signs that Lear is starting to grow in wisdom through suffering.** He first takes pity on the Fool and empathises with his suffering: 'Poor Fool and knave, I have one part in my heart / That's sorry yet for thee.' Although for much of the scene Lear focuses on his own plight, there is a growing understanding of the suffering of others. This is really a turning point for Lear. As his own suffering intensifies, Lear becomes a more compassionate figure, recognising the suffering of marginalised figures: the poor and those deemed insane.

- In the first scene of the play, Lear proudly imagines himself as a 'dragon', a powerful figure to be feared. However, in this scene he acknowledges his vulnerability, describing himself as 'A poor, infirm, weak and despised old man.' **Suffering has brought him closer to recognising his own weakness.**

- **The Fool offers a degree of pragmatism next to Lear's dramatic ranting.** He suggests that Lear should beg forgiveness of Goneril and Regan: 'Good nuncle, in, and ask thy daughters' blessing.' However, this is unthinkable for Lear. **The Fool is also a remarkably loyal character.** He tries to diffuse Lear's despair through humour. His concern for Lear is both genuine and admirable as he accompanies his king through these dark moments.

- **The Fool continues to expose Lear to his own folly.** His remarks have a caustic edge as he seeks to remind Lear of the mistakes he has made.

- **Kent too exhibits unwavering loyalty.** He has searched for Lear through a horrendous storm and now accompanies him to some meagre shelter.

Questions

1. Do you agree with Lear's claim that he is 'a man / More sinned against than sinning'? Explain your answer.
2. In the first scene of the play, Lear is both arrogant and proud. Do you think this attitude has changed? Why / why not?
3. What signs are there in this scene that Lear is starting to become a more compassionate figure?
4. Lear is only starting to change and gain wisdom. What in this scene shows that he is still a proud man, unable to accept his role in bringing about his own downfall?

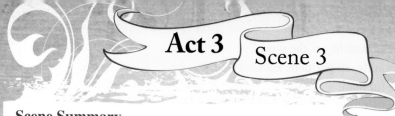

Act 3 Scene 3

Scene Summary

- Gloucester confides in Edmund that he is unhappy with the way Lear has been treated by Goneril, Regan and Cornwall. He also explains that they have taken control of his house and forbidden him to help Lear.
- Gloucester says that he has received a letter informing him of the arrival of French forces. He tells Edmund that he intends to aid Lear even though he may be killed for doing so.
- After Gloucester leaves, Edmund says that he will inform Cornwall of all that Gloucester has told him in the hope that he will win the Duke's favour and be given Gloucester's estate.

A Room in Gloucester's Castle.
Enter GLOUCESTER and EDMUND

GLOUCESTER
Alack, alack, Edmund, I like not this unnatural dealing.[1]
When I desired their leave that I might pity[2] him, they took
from me the use of mine own house, charged me on pain of
their perpetual displeasure, neither to speak of him, entreat
for him, nor any way sustain[3] him.

EDMUND ironic
Most savage and unnatural!

GLOUCESTER
Go to.[4] Say you nothing. There is division between the
Dukes, and a worse matter[5] than that. I have received a letter
this night; 'tis dangerous to be spoken; I have locked the
10 letter in my closet. These injuries the King now bears will be
revenged home.[6] There is part of a power already footed.[7] We
must incline to[8] the King. I will look him, and privily[9] relieve
him. Go you and maintain talk with the Duke, that my charity
be not of him perceived. If he ask for me, I am ill and gone to
bed. If I die for it, as no less is threatened me, the King my
old master must be relieved. There is some strange things
toward,[10] Edmund; pray you, be careful.
[Exit]

EDMUND
This courtesy,[11] forbid thee, shall the Duke
Instantly know, and of that letter too.
20 This seems a fair deserving,[12] and must draw me
That which my father loses – no less than all.[13]
The younger rises when the old doth fall.
[Exit]

---

[1] **dealing:** conduct / behaviour
[2] **pity:** help / take pity on

[3] **sustain:** care for

[4] **Go to:** That's true
[5] **worse matter:** i.e. the threat of a French invasion

[6] **home:** thoroughly
[7] **footed:** landed
[8] **incline to:** side with
[9] **privily:** secretly

[10] **toward:** about to happen

[11] **courtesy:** kindness

[12] **fair deserving:** an action worthy of reward
[13] **and must…than all:** and must get me what my father loses – nothing less than all

Commentary

- **This scene develops the sub-plot.** Blinded to the truth of Edmund's nature, Gloucester confides in Edmund about his intention to help Lear and tells him about the arrival of the French forces. This provides Edmund with an opportunity to betray his father and take all of Gloucester's wealth. This vicious cruelty and lack of compassion is contrasted by Lear's growing empathy for the Fool in the previous scene.

- **There is wonderful dramatic irony* in this scene.** Gloucester expresses his disquiet about the manner in which Lear has been treated by Cornwall and his daughters. However, he is utterly unaware that Edmund intends to treat Gloucester in the same way and will use this conversation as evidence against him.

- **Edmund's dishonesty is readily apparent.** As Gloucester discusses the actions of Cornwall, Goneril and Regan, Edmund's false outrage illustrates his manipulative nature: 'Most savage and unnatural!' No sooner has Gloucester left, than Edmund expresses his intention to betray his father. He justifies his scheme with his self-serving philosophy: 'The younger rises when the old doth fall.'

- **Up to this point of the play Gloucester has been a weak and ineffectual character. However, he now displays new strength as he resolves to help Lear.** Despite the fact that he is risking his life, Gloucester is determined to do the right thing. However, **he lacks the type of bold courage displayed by Kent**. Gloucester is unwilling to publicly support Lear. Instead he seeks to hide his allegiance from Cornwall and asks Edmund to pretend that he has gone to bed so that his support for Lear remains a secret.

*Dramatic irony: When the audience know something that the characters on stage are unaware of.

Questions

1. What does Gloucester tell Edmund in confidence?

2. (a) What does Edmund decide to do with this information?
    (b) What does Edmund hope to gain by this?

3. Do you think Gloucester shows any bravery in this scene? Why / why not?

Act 3 Scene 4

Scene Summary

- Kent brings Lear and the Fool to the hovel for shelter. Lear insists that Kent and the Fool go in ahead of him.
- The Fool rushes out in the belief that there is a spirit in the hovel. Edgar (disguised as Tom o' Bedlam) emerges.
- Lear believes Edgar (Tom) is in a wretched state because he was mistreated by cruel daughters.
- Lear tears off his clothes in an act of solidarity with Edgar (Tom).
- Gloucester arrives and looks to provide Lear with food and shelter.
- Lear treats Edgar (Tom) as if he is a learned scholar.

The Heath. Before a Hovel.
Enter LEAR, KENT and FOOL

KENT
Here is the place, my Lord; good my Lord, enter.
The tyranny of the open night's[1] too rough
For nature[2] to endure.

[Storm still]

LEAR
              Let me alone.

KENT
Good my Lord, enter here.

LEAR
              Wilt break my heart?[3]

KENT
I had rather break mine own. Good my Lord, enter.

LEAR
Thou think'st 'tis much that this contentious[4] storm
Invades us to the skin; so 'tis to thee,
But where the greater malady is fixed,
The lesser is scarce felt.[5] Thou'dst shun a bear;
10 But if thy flight lay toward the raging sea
Thou'dst meet the bear i' the mouth.[6] When the mind's free,[7]
The body's delicate;[8] the tempest in my mind
Doth from my senses take all feeling else[9]

---

1. **open night:** night in the open air
2. **nature:** human nature

3. **Wilt break my heart?:** But will it break my heart? Lear wants to remain outside in the storm as it distracts him from his daughters' behaviour which is breaking his heart

4. **contentious:** tempestuous / wild

5. **But where…scarce felt:** But when a greater pain is rooted in the mind, lesser pain is barely felt
6. **i' the mouth:** head on / face to face
7. **free:** untroubled
8. **delicate:** sensitive
9. **all feeling else:** any other feelings

Save what beats there: filial ingratitude!
Is it not as this mouth should tear this hand
For lifting food to't? But I will punish home.[10]
No, I will weep no more. In such a night
To shut me out! Pour on; I will endure.
In such a night as this! O Regan, Goneril!
Your old kind father, whose frank[11] heart gave all –
O, that way madness lies; let me shun that;
No more of that.

KENT

        Good my Lord, enter here.

LEAR

Prithee, go in thyself; seek thine own ease.
This tempest will not give me leave to ponder
On things would hurt me more. But I'll go in.
[To the FOOL] In boy; go first. You houseless poverty –[12]
Nay, get thee in. I'll pray, and then I'll sleep. *[FOOL goes in]*
Poor naked wretches, whereso'er you are
That bide[13] the pelting of this pitiless storm,
How shall your houseless heads and unfed sides,[14]
Your looped and windowed raggedness,[15] defend you
From seasons such as these? O, I have ta'en
Too little care of this! Take physic, pomp;[16]
Expose thyself to feel what wretches feel,
That thou mayst shake the superflux[17] to them,
And show the heavens more just.[18]

EDGAR

[Within] Fathom and half, fathom and half![19] Poor Tom!

[The FOOL runs out from the hovel]

FOOL

Come not in here, nuncle, here's a spirit.[20]
Help me, help me!

KENT

Give me thy hand. Who's there?

FOOL

A spirit, a spirit! He says his name's poor Tom.

KENT

What art thou that dost grumble there i' the straw?
Come forth.

---

[10] **home:** thoroughly / fully

[11] **frank:** generous

[12] **houseless poverty:** poor homeless person

[13] **bide:** endure
[14] **unfed sides:** hungry bodies
[15] **looped...raggedness:** your torn clothes full of holes

[16] **Take physic, pomp:** Vanity / Pride / Arrogance ('pomp') prepare to be purged
[17] **superflux:** superfluous possessions
[18] **show the heavens more just:** show how the world can be a fairer place

[19] **fathon and half!:** Edgar treats the rain water as if it were the sea

[20] **spirit:** In Shakespeare's time sometimes madness was thought to be the result of possession by evil spirits or the devil

[Enter EDGAR disguised as a madman]

EDGAR
Away! The foul fiend follows me! Through the sharp
hawthorn blows the cold wind. Humh![21] Go to thy cold bed,
and warm thee.

> 21 **Humh!:** Edgar is shivering

LEAR
Didst thou given all to thy two daughters? And art thou
come to this?

EDGAR
Who gives anything to Poor Tom? Whom the foul fiend
50 hath led through fire and through flame, through ford and
whirlpool, e'er bog and quagmire;[22] that hath laid knives
under his pillow, and halters in his pew;[23] set ratsbane[24] by
his porridge;[25] made him proud of heart, to ride on a bay
trotting-horse over four-inched bridges,[26] to course his own
shadow for a traitor.[27] Bless thy five wits![28] Tom's a-cold!
O, do de, do de, do de.[29] Bless thee from whirlwinds, star-
blasting and taking![30] Do Poor Tom some charity, whom the
foul fiend vexes.[31] There could I have him now, and there,
and there again, and there.

> 22 **quagmire:** marsh
> 23 **halters in his pew:** nooses in the church gallery. The devil was said to tempt the desperate to commit suicide
> 24 **ratsbane:** rat poison
> 25 **porridge:** soup
> 26 **four-inched bridges:** 1 Help from the devil would be needed to cross such small bridges on a horse 2 Possibly: small bridges used to train horses to trot. An example of 'pomp'
> 27 **to course…traitor:** to chase his own shadow in the belief that it was a traitor
> 28 **five wits:** common wit, imagination, fantasy, estimation and memory
> 29 **O, do…do de:** possibly chattering teeth
> 30 **star-blasting…taking:** being influenced by an evil star and taken by disease
> 31 **vexes:** torments
> 32 **pass:** predicament

[Storm still]

LEAR
60 What, has his daughters brought him to this pass?[32]
Couldst thou save nothing? Didst thou give 'em all?

FOOL
Nay, he reserved a blanket, else we had been all shamed.

LEAR
Now, all the plagues that in the pendulous air
Hang fated o'er men's faults light on thy daughters![33]

> 33 **Now…daughters!:** Now, all the diseases stored up in the air, waiting to punish men for their faults, let them land on your daughters

KENT
He hath no daughters, sir.

LEAR
Death, traitor! Nothing could have subdued nature[34]
To such a lowness but his unkind daughters.
Is it the fashion, that discarded[35] fathers
Should have thus little mercy on their flesh?[36]
70 Judicious punishment! 'Twas this flesh begot
Those pelican daughters.[37]

> 34 **subdued nature:** diminished his natural powers
> 35 **discarded:** cast aside
> 36 **little mercy…flesh:** A reference to the thorns Edgar has stuck in his flesh
> 37 **pelican daughters:** It was said that young pelicans fed on the blood and flesh of their parents

EDGAR

    Pillicock sat on Pillicock Hill[38]
    Alow, alow, loo, loo!

FOOL

This cold night will turn us all to fools and madmen.[39]

EDGAR

Take heed o' the foul fiend; obey thy parents; keep thy word justly; swear not; commit not with man's sworn spouse;[40] set not thy sweet heart on proud array.[41] Tom's a-cold.

LEAR

What hast thou been?

EDGAR

A serving-man, proud in heart and mind, that curled my hair,[42] wore gloves in my cap,[43] served the lust of my mistress' heart, and did the act of darkness[44] with her, swore as many oaths as I spake words, and broke them in the sweet face of heaven; one that slept in the contriving of lust,[45] and waked to do it. Wine loved I deeply, dice[46] dearly, and in woman out-paramoured the Turk.[47] False of heart, light of ear,[48] bloody of hand; hog in sloth,[49] fox in stealth, wolf in greediness, dog in madness,[50] lion in prey. Let not the creaking of shoes nor the rustling of silks betray thy poor heart to woman. Keep thy foot out of brothels, thy hand out of plackets,[51] thy pen from lenders'[52] books, and defy the foul fiend. Still through the hawthorn blows the cold wind, says suum, mun, nonny.[53] Dolphin[54] my boy, boy, cessez! Let him trot by.

[Storm still]

LEAR

Thou wert better in thy grave[55] than to answer with thy uncovered body this extremity of the skies. Is man no more than this? Consider him well. Thou ow'st the worm[56] no silk, the beast no hide, the sheep no wool, the cat[57] no perfume. Ha! Here's three on's are sophisticated![58] Thou art the thing itself! Unaccommodated[59] man is no more but such a poor bare, forked[60] animal as thou art. Off, off, you lendings![61] Come unbutton here.
[Tearing off his clothes]

FOOL

Prithee, nuncle, be contented; 'tis a naughty[62] night to swim

---

38 **Pillicock Hill:** 1 'Pillicock': slang for penis. 'Pillicock Hill' is therefore a reference to female genitalia 2 'Pillicock' was also a term of endearment like 'darling'

39 **This cold night…madmen:** The Fool now speaks with common sense as his former role as jester and the speaker of cryptic rhymes is taken by Edgar

40 **commit…spouse:** do not commit adultery with another man's wife

41 **proud array:** expensive clothes

42 **curled my hair:** i.e. a courtier

43 **wore gloves…cap:** i.e. was rewarded for doing favours for my mistress

44 **act of darkness:** sex

45 **slept…lust:** dreamt lustful plans

46 **dice:** gambling

47 **out-paramoured the Turk:** had more lovers than the Turkish Sultan (who was famed for his harem)

48 **light of ear:** impressionable / easily fooled

49 **hog in sloth:** lazy like a pig

50 **dog in madness:** mad like a rabid dog

51 **plackets:** openings in the fronts of women's petticoats (underskirts)

52 **lenders:** money-lenders

53 **suum, mun, nonny:** Possibly: Edgar is mimicking the sound of the wind

54 **Dolphin:** Possibly means 'Dauphin' (the Prince of France) whose crest was a dolphin. Some critics offer that 'Dauphin' suggests the Prince of Darkness as the French were hated by the English

55 **Thou wert…grave:** You would be better off dead

56 **worm:** silkworm

57 **cat:** civet-cat. A type of mammal that is used to produce musk for perfume

58 **Here's three…sophisticated!:** Here are three of us who are no longer natural / simple

59 **Unaccommodated:** Lacking the comforts of civilization: clothes etc.

60 **forked:** two-legged

61 **lendings:** clothes, which have been lent to us by animals

62 **naughty:** nasty

in. Now a little fire in a wild field were like an old lecher's heart;[63] a small spark, all the rest on's body cold. Look, here comes a walking fire!

[Enter GLOUCESTER, with a torch]

EDGAR
This is the foul fiend Flibbertigibbet.[64] He begins at curfew, and walks till the first cock.[65] He gives the web and the pin,[66] squinies[67] the eye, and makes the harelip; mildews the white[68] wheat, and hurts the poor creature of earth.
110 *[Chants] Swithold footed thrice the old;*
         He met the night-mare, and her nine-fold;
         Bid her alight,
         And her troth plight,
         And, aroint thee, witch, aroint thee![69]

KENT
How fares your Grace?

LEAR
What's he?

KENT
[To GLOUCESTER] Who's there? What is't you seek?

GLOUCESTER
What are you there? Your names?

EDGAR
Poor Tom, that eats the swimming frog, the toad, the
120 todpole, the wall-newt[70] and the water; that in the fury of his heart, when the foul fiend rages, eats cow-dung for sallets,[71] swallows the old rat and the ditch-dog,[72] drinks the green mantle[73] of the standing pool, who is whipped from tithing to tithing,[74] and stock-punished and imprisoned, who hath had three suits[75] to his back, six shirts to his body,
         Horse to ride, and weapon to wear
         But mice and rats, and such small deer,[76]
         Have been Tom's food for seven long year.
Beware my follower.[77]
130 Peace, Smulkin![78] Peace, thou fiend!

GLOUCESTER
What, hath your Grace no better company?

63 **Now a little fire…heart:** The Fool sees Gloucester approaching with a torch in the night

64 **Flibbertigibbet:** The name of a devil. Shakespeare took this name from a publication by Harsnett who criticised the belief in witches and possessions
65 **He begins…first cock:** He starts at dusk and finishes at dawn
66 **web and the pin:** cataracts of the eye
67 **squinies:** squints
68 **white:** ready for harvest
69 **Swithold…aroint thee!:** A chant to ward off demons. It describes how St Withold overcame a demon and her nine offspring by commanding her to leave the chest of her victim and promise to do no further harm

70 **the todpole…wall-newt:** the tadpole and the lizard on the wall
71 **sallets:** salad
72 **ditch-dog:** dead dog lying in a ditch
73 **green mantle:** pond scum
74 **tithing:** parish. Each household in a parish had to pay a tithe (a tenth of their income) to the Church
75 **three suits:** the clothes allowance for a serving man
76 **deer:** game
77 **follower:** spirit
78 **Smulkin:** A devil (from Harsnett. See above)

EDGAR
The Prince of Darkness is a gentleman. Modo he's called
and Mahu.[79]

[79] **Modo; Mahu:** Devils (from Harsnett)

GLOUCESTER
Our flesh and blood is grown so vile, my Lord,
That it doth hate what gets it.[80]

[80] **Our flesh...gets it:** Our children have
become so dreadful, my Lord, that they
hate their own parents

EDGAR
Poor Tom's a-cold.

GLOUCESTER
Go in with me. My duty cannot suffer[81]
T'obey in all your daughters' hard commands;
Though their injunction[82] be to bar my doors
And let this tyrannous night take hold upon you,
Yet have I ventured to come seek you out
And bring you where both fire and food is ready.

[81] **suffer:** bear
[82] **injunction:** order

LEAR
First let me talk with this philosopher.[83]
[To EDGAR] What is the cause of thunder?

[83] **philosopher:** 1 natural scientist
2 magician

KENT
Good my Lord, take his offer; go into th' house.

LEAR
I'll talk a word with this same learned Theban.[84]
[To EDGAR] What is your study?[85]

[84] **Theban:** scholar from the city of Thebes
in Ancient Egypt
[85] **study:** academic area of interest

EDGAR
How to prevent[86] the fiend, and to kill vermin.

[86] **prevent:** frustrate

LEAR
Let me ask you one word in private.

KENT
Importune[87] him once more to go, my Lord.
His wits begin t' unsettle.

[87] **Importune:** Urge

GLOUCESTER
Canst thou blame him?

[Storm still]

His daughters seek his death. Aha, that good Kent!
He said it would be thus, poor banished man!

Thou say'st the King grows mad. I'll tell thee, friend,
I am almost mad myself. I had a son,
Now outlawed from my blood;[88] he sought my life,
But lately,[89] very late, I loved him, friend,
No father his son dearer. Truth to tell thee,
160 The grief hath crazed my wits. What a night's this!
I do beseech your Grace –

88 **outlawed from my blood**: banished
    as a criminal and disowned as a son
89 **lately**: recently

LEAR
                          O, cry you mercy,[90] sir.
[To EDGAR] Noble philosopher, your company.

90 **cry you mercy**: beg your pardon

EDGAR
Tom's a-cold.

GLOUCESTER
In, fellow, there, into th' hovel. Keep thee warm.

LEAR
Come, let's in all.

KENT
                    This way, my Lord.

LEAR
                                    With him.
I will keep still with[91] my philosopher.

91 **keep still with**: stay with

92 **soothe**: placate / humour

KENT
Good my Lord, soothe[92] him; let him take the fellow.

GLOUCESTER
Take him you on.

KENT
Sirrah, come on. Go along with us.

93 **Athenian**: Philosopher from Athens
    in Ancient Greece
94 ***Child Rowland…British man***:
    Rowland was the heroic nephew of
    Charlemagne (European Emperor).
    This reference is mixed with the
    famous tale of Jack the Giant Killer.
    Shakespeare writes 'British man'
    rather than 'English man', possibly as
    a tribute to James I whose coronation
    united the realm. The whole rhyme
    may be a suggestion that Edgar will
    act heroically and slay the 'giant'
    Edmund, thus helping to reunite
    Lear's kingdom

LEAR
170 Come, good Athenian.[93]

GLOUCESTER
No words, no words! Hush.

EDGAR
          Child Rowland to the dark tower came,
          His word was still, 'Fie, foh, and fum,
          I smell the blood of a British man.'[94]

[Exeunt]

--- **Key Quotations** ---

LEAR   *The body's delicate; the tempest in my mind*
           Doth from my senses take all feeling else
           Save what beats there: filial ingratitude!

LEAR   *Poor naked wretches, whereso'er you are*
           That bide the pelting of this pitiless storm,
           How shall your houseless heads and unfed sides,
           Your looped and windowed raggedness, defend you
           From seasons such as these? O, I have ta'en
           Too little care of this! Take physic, pomp;
           Expose thyself to feel what wretches feel,
           That thou mayst shake the superflux to them,
           And show the heavens more just.

LEAR   *Is it the fashion, that discarded fathers*
           Should have thus little mercy on their flesh?
           Judicious punishment! 'Twas this flesh begot
           Those pelican daughters

LEAR   *Unaccommodated man is no more but such a poor bare, forked animal as thou art.*

--- **Commentary** ---

- **Lear's anguish is so great that he welcomes the storm as a distraction from his mental suffering:** 'the tempest in my mind / Doth from my senses take all feeling else / Save what beats there: filial ingratitude!' The physical discomfort which exposure to the raging storm brings is overshadowed by his 'greater malady': his mental turmoil.
- **As Lear suffers, his compassion for others grows.** He expresses pity for the Fool and all destitute people. Lear tells the Fool to go before him into the hovel: 'In boy; go first. You houseless poverty – / Nay, get thee in'. He then expresses huge pity for those who live in poverty:

  > 'Poor naked wretches, whereso'er you are
  > That bide the pelting of this pitiless storm,
  > How shall your houseless heads and unfed sides,
  > Your looped and windowed raggedness, defend you
  > From seasons such as these? O, I have ta'en
  > Too little care of this! Take physic, pomp;
  > Expose thyself to feel what wretches feel,
  > That thou mayst shake the superflux to them,
  > And show the heavens more just.'

- As he becomes nothing himself, Lear is ashamed of the way he ignored the plight of the poor in the past ('O, I have ta'en / Too little care of this!) and the vanity or pride that accompanies wealth: 'Take physic, pomp; / Expose thyself to feel what wretches feel'. **This awareness of social justice and acknowledgement that he neglected his responsibilities as King, mark an important step in Lear's growth towards wisdom.**

─────── **Commentary** (continued) ───────

- However, Lear's personal growth is a gradual and unsteady process. He still has not achieved full self-awareness. His compassion for Poor Tom is expressed in terms that relate purely to himself. Recognising Poor Tom's suffering, Lear immediately sees an echo of his own situation and assumes that Poor Tom was mistreated by his daughters: 'What, has his daughters brought him to this pass? / Couldst thou save nothing? Didst thou give 'em all?' Despite his steps towards wisdom Lear is still a flawed individual with much to learn about himself and the world.

- Lear still sees himself largely as a victim, rather than the orchestrator of his own wretched situation:

  'To shut me out! Pour on; I will endure.
  In such a night as this! O Regan, Goneril!
  Your old kind father, whose frank heart gave all –
  O, that way madness lies; let me shun that;
  No more of that.'

  It interesting to note that Lear's first thought here is to pity himself and blame his daughters. However, he turns away from this idea ('No more of that') either because he cannot bear to entertain this idea or because he is starting to reject the idea of himself as a helpless victim.

- Although, his understanding is not complete, Lear has a growing sense of his role in bringing about his own downfall. Upon seeing the suffering of Poor Tom, Lear exclaims:

  'Is it the fashion, that discarded fathers
  Should have thus little mercy on their flesh?
  Judicious punishment! 'Twas this flesh begot
  Those pelican daughters.'

  Pelicans were thought to feed on the flesh of their parents; Lear imagines Goneril and Regan feeding on him, but he sees this as a 'judicious punishment' as it was he who created ('begot') them.

- Paradoxically, it is only as Lear grows in madness that he starts to attain wisdom. Lear is clearly confused as he treats the supposedly mad Poor Tom as a learned scholar; the greatest in the kingdom now admires the least. Seeing Tom half-naked, Lear gets a vision of humanity stripped down to its bare essence: 'Thou art the thing itself! Unaccommodated man is no more but such a poor bare, forked animal as thou art.' In an act of solidarity with Tom's poverty, Lear tears off his own clothes. Lear has now rejected the trappings of wealth and pomp that were so important to him before. As he loses touch with reality, his insight into human suffering and the emptiness of human pride increases.

- In the first scene of the play Lear acted as if he had god-like status, now he sees humanity as equal in status to a beast: 'man is no more but…[a] forked animal'. Lear is clearly eroding the arrogant pride he displayed earlier but he is yet to understand the dignity of being human.

─────── **Questions** ───────

1. In this scene, why does Lear say he wants to be exposed to the violence of the storm?
2. How does the appearance of Poor Tom affect Lear?
3. Why do you think Lear tears off his clothes in this scene?
4. What suggestions are there in this scene that Lear is starting to be become a more compassionate character?
5. In your opinion, is Lear now less proud and arrogant than he was in the first scene of the play? Explain your answer.
6. Do you agree that in this scene Lear still sees himself as a victim? Explain your answer.

Act 3 — Scene 5

Scene Summary

- Edmund talks with Cornwall after alerting him to the fact that Gloucester is trying to help Lear. Edmund has just shown Cornwall the letter that proves Gloucester is in touch with the French forces.
- Edmund pretends to be upset that he informed on his father and tells Cornwall that he feels torn between loyalty to his father and his duty to Cornwall.
- Cornwall rewards Edmund by making him Earl of Gloucester.
- Edmund swears allegiance to Cornwall. In return, Cornwall offers to act like a father to Edmund from this point on.

Gloucester's Castle.
Enter CORNWALL and EDMUND

CORNWALL
I will have my revenge[1] ere I depart his house.

EDMUND
How, my Lord, I may be censured, that nature thus gives
way to loyalty, something fears me to think of.[2]

CORNWALL
I now perceive, it was not altogether your brother's evil
disposition made him seek his death, but a provoking merit,
set a-work by a reprovable badness in himself.[3]

EDMUND
How malicious is my fortune that I must repent to be just![4]
This is the letter he spoke of, which approves[5] him an
intelligent party[6] to the advantages of France. O heavens!
That this treason were not, or not I the detector!

CORNWALL
Go with me to the Duchess.

EDMUND
If the matter of this paper be certain,[7] you have mighty
business in hand.

CORNWALL
True or false, it hath made thee Earl of Gloucester. Seek out
where thy father is, that he may be ready for our
apprehension.[8]

---

1. **my revenge:** i.e. his revenge on Gloucester

2. **How, my Lord...think of:** How, my Lord, I will be thought of, if I place my loyalty to you over my duty to my father, frightens me somewhat

3. **I now perceive...in himself:** I now see that it was not just your brother's evil nature that made him look to murder Gloucester, but he was encouraged by a sense of his own worth ('provoking merit') and enticed by Gloucester's reprehensible bad nature

4. **just:** i.e. righteous to reveal his father's disloyalty

5. **approves:** proves

6. **intelligent party:** spy

7. **certain:** true

8. **apprehension:** arrest

EDMUND

[Aside] If I find him comforting the King, it will stuff his
suspicion more fully. *[Aloud]* I will persever[9] in my course of
loyalty, though the conflict be sore between that and my
20 blood.[10]

9 **persever:** continue / persist

10 **my blood:** 1 my family 2 my
feelings for my father

CORNWALL

I will lay trust upon thee, and thou shalt find a dearer father
in my love.
[Exeunt]

Commentary

- **Edmund's ruthless, self-serving nature is illustrated in this scene** as he betrays his father.
  Without scruples, Edmund tells Cornwall about Gloucester's efforts to help Lear and about
  the letter which proves Gloucester has been in contact with the French forces. Edmund is
  motivated by the pursuit of power, and his treachery is rewarded when Cornwall awards him
  the title Earl of Gloucester. Having previously framed his brother, Edmund now betrays his
  father as he ruthlessly pursues social status.

- **Edmund's manipulative and devious nature is evident in his conversation with
  Cornwall.** To avoid suspicion and to increase Cornwall's regard for him, Edmund pretends
  to be conflicted in exposing Gloucester: 'O heavens! That this treason were not, or not I the
  detector!'

Questions

1. Do you agree that Edmund is very crafty in the manner in which he deals with Cornwall in
   this scene?
2. What is your impression of Cornwall from this scene?
3. Comment on the use of dramatic irony* in this scene.

*Dramatic irony: When the audience know something that the characters on stage are unaware of.

Scene Summary
- Gloucester brings Lear and the others to find shelter in a farmhouse on his estate.
- Lear conducts a mock-trial of Goneril and Regan. The Fool and Edgar (as Poor Tom) act as assistant judges to Lear.
- Gloucester tells of a plot to assassinate Lear. He urges Kent to bring Lear to safety in Dover. Kent reluctantly agrees but worries that Lear needs rest to soothe his frayed nerves.
- The scene ends with Edgar in soliloquy. He acknowledges that Lear's suffering is greater than his own. Edgar decides that he will reveal his true identity when his name has been cleared.

A chamber in a farmhouse adjoining Gloucester's Castle.
Enter GLOUCESTER, LEAR, KENT, FOOL and EDGAR

GLOUCESTER
Here is better than the open air; take it thankfully. I will piece out the comfort[1] with what addition I can. I will not be long from you.

KENT
All the power of his wits have given way to his impatience.[2] The gods reward your kindness!

[Exit GLOUCESTER]

EDGAR
Frateretto calls me; and tells me Nero is an angler in the lake of darkness.[3] Pray, innocent, and beware the foul fiend.

FOOL
Prithee, nuncle, tell me whether a madman be a gentleman or a yeoman?[4]

LEAR
A king, a king!

FOOL
No, he's a yeoman that has a gentleman to his son; for he's a mad yeoman that sees his son a gentleman before him.[5]

LEAR
To have a thousand[6] with red burning spits
Come hissing in upon 'em!

---

1 **piece out the comfort:** make it more comfortable

2 **impatience:** 1 passion / lack of self-control 2 inabiltiy to endure

3 **Frateretto...darkness:** More of Tom's ramblings. Frateretto: a dancing devil (name taken from Harsnett). Nero: Roman Emperor who apparently played fiddle as Rome burned. Angler: 1 fisherman 2 fiddler

4 **yeoman:** A free man who owned his own farm but did not have a coat of arms

5 **No...before him:** The Fool is saying that only a mad yeoman would allow his son to become a gentleman before him as the yeoman would then be his son's inferior. This parallels Lear's situation

6 **thousand:** i.e. thousand devils

EDGAR
The foul fiend bites my back.[7]

FOOL
He's mad that trusts in the tameness of a wolf, a horse's
health,[8] a boy's love, or a whore's oath.

LEAR
It shall be done; I will arraign[9] them straight.
[To EDGAR] Come, sit thou here, most learned justicer;[10]
20 *[To the FOOL]* Thou, sapient[11] sir, sit here. Now, you she
foxes!

EDGAR
Look, where he[12] stands and glares! Want'st thou eyes[13] at
trial, madam?
        [Sings] Come o'er the bourn, Bessy, to me —[14]

FOOL
[Sings] Her boat hath a leak,
        And she must not speak
        Why she dares not come over to thee.[15]

EDGAR
The foul fiend haunts Poor Tom in the voice of a
nightingale.[16] Hoppedance[17] cries in Tom's belly for two
white[18] herring. Croak not,[19] black angel; I have no food for
30 thee.

KENT
How do you, sir? Stand you not so amazed.
Will you lie down and rest upon the cushions?

LEAR
I'll see their trial first. Bring in their evidence.
[To EDGAR] Thou robed man of justice, take thy place;
[To the FOOL] And thou, his yoke-fellow of equity,[20]
Bench by his side. *[To KENT]* You are o' the commission;[21]
Sit you too.

EDGAR
Let us deal justly.
        Sleepest or wakest thou, jolly shepherd?
40   *Thy sheep be in the corn;*
        And for one blast of thy minikin mouth,
        Thy sheep shall take no harm.[22]
Purr! The cat is grey.[23]

[7] **The foul...back:** Edgar imagines the devil as a biting louse

[8] **horse's health:** horses were thought to have poor health

[9] **arraign:** bring to court. Lear now holds a mock trial for his daughters. This episode is not included in all versions of the play
[10] **justicer:** judge
[11] **sapient:** wise

[12] **he:** i.e. an imaginary devil
[13] **eyes:** spectators. Possibly Poor Tom is asking the imaginary daughter of Lear if she would like the devil as an audience
[14] **Come o'er...to me:** A line from an old song in which a lover invites his sweetheart across a river ('bourn') to meet him
[15] **Her boat...to thee:** The Fool's response is invented and carries possible obscene meanings

[16] **nightingale:** Possibly, Edgar is referring to the Fool's singing
[17] **Hoppedance:** The name of a devil
[18] **white:** unsmoked
[19] **Croak not:** Don't grumble

[20] **yoke-fellow of equity:** 1 judicial partner 2 Possibly, a reference to the Courts of Chancery which settled disputes according to natural justice
[21] **o' the commission:** appointed a Justice of the Peace
[22] **Sleepest...no harm:** A fragment of a song in which a shepherd's sheep are in danger if they eat too much corn but one whistle from his delicate ('minikin') mouth and they will return from the cornfield
[23] **Purr!...grey:** Devils were thought to take the form of witches' cats. 'Purr' is the name of a devil in Harsnett (see p.98)

LEAR

Arraign[24] her first; 'tis Goneril. I here take my oath before
this honourable assembly: she kicked the poor King her
father.

FOOL

Come hither, mistress. Is your name Goneril?

LEAR

She cannot deny it.

FOOL

Cry you mercy, I took you for a joint-stool.[25]

LEAR

And here's another,[26] whose warped[27] looks proclaim
What store[28] her heart is made on. Stop her there!
Arms, arms, sword, fire![29] Corruption in the place!
False justicer, why hast thou let her 'scape?

EDGAR

Bless thy five wits![30]

KENT

O pity! Sir, where is the patience now
That thou so oft have boasted to retain?

EDGAR

[Aside] My tears begin to take his part so much
They mar my counterfeiting.[31]

LEAR

               The little dogs and all,
Tray, Blanch, and Sweetheart,[32] see, they bark at me.

EDGAR

Tom will throw his head[33] at them. Avaunt, you curs![34]
     Be thy mouth or black or white,
     Tooth that poisons if it bite;
     Mastiff, grey-hound, mongrel grim,
     Hound or spaniel, brach[35] or lym,[36]
     Or bobtail tike or trundle-tail,[37]
     Tom will make them weep and wail:
     For, with throwing thus my head,
     Dogs leap the hatch,[38] and all are fled.
Do de, de, de.[39] Cessez![40] Come, march to wakes[41] and fairs
and market towns. Poor Tom, thy horn is dry.[42]

---

[24] **Arraign:** Bring before the court

[25] **Cry you mercy...joint-stool:** i.e. Pardon me, I didn't notice you

[26] **another:** i.e. Regan
[27] **warped:** distorted
[28] **store:** abundance. Lear is being ironic here
[29] **fire:** In Lear's imagination the courtroom has become hell

[30] **five wits:** common wit, imagination, fantasy, estimation and memory

[31] **mar my counterfeiting:** ruin my performance (as Poor Tom)
[32] **Tray...Sweetheart:** The names of pet dogs. Some commentators see these names as suggesting the names of Lear's daughters: Tray – Goneril in that she be'tray'ed her father; Blanch – Regan in that she made Lear pale with fear; Sweetheart – Cordelia in that she is Lear's darling
[33] **throw his head:** Unexplained, possibly means 'shout at'
[34] **Avaunt...curs!:** Get out here, you dogs!
[35] **brach:** bitch hound
[36] **lym:** i.e. liemer, a type of bloodhound
[37] **bobtail...tail:** a terrier with a docked tail or one with a long tail
[38] **hatch:** bottom part of a split door
[39] **Do...de:** Tom's teeth are probably chattering
[40] **Cessez!:** Stop!
[41] **wakes:** parish festivals
[42] **thy horn is dry:** 1 A beggar's cry for drink 2 Edgar may mean that he can no longer play the part of Poor Tom

LEAR

Then let them anatomize[43] Regan; see what breeds about her
heart. Is there any cause in nature that makes these hard
hearts? *[To EDGAR]* You, sir, I entertain[44] for one of my
hundred, only I do not like the fashion of your garments. You
will say they are Persian attire,[45] but let them be changed.

KENT

Now, good my Lord, lie here and rest awhile.

LEAR

Make no noise, make no noise; draw the curtains: so, so, so.
We'll go to supper i' the morning. So, so, so. *[Sleeps]*

FOOL

And I'll go to bed at noon.[46]

[Re-enter GLOUCESTER]

GLOUCESTER

80 Come hither, friend; where is the King my master?

KENT

Here, sir; but trouble him not; his wits are gone.

GLOUCESTER

Good friend, I prithee, take him in thy arms.
I have o'erheard a plot of death upon[47] him.
There is a litter[48] ready; lay him in't,
And drive towards Dover, friend, where thou shalt meet
Both welcome and protection. Take up thy master:
If thou shouldst dally[49] half an hour, his life,
With thine, and all that offer to defend him,
Stand in assured loss. Take up, take up,
90 And follow me, that will to some provision
Give thee quick conduct.[50]

KENT

          Oppressed nature sleeps:
This rest might yet have balmed thy broken sinews,[51]
Which, if convenience will not allow,[52]
Stand in hard cure.[53] *[To the Fool]* Come, help to bear thy
master;
Thou must not stay behind.

GLOUCESTER

          Come, come, away!
[Exeunt all but EDGAR, with the FOOL supporting LEAR]

---

[43] **anatomize:** dissect

[44] **entertain:** take into service

[45] **Persian attire:** Persians were thought to wear luxurious clothes; Edgar is dressed in rags

[46] **I'll go to…noon:** Proverbial i.e. I'll act the fool too

[47] **upon:** made against
[48] **litter:** a frame made of sticks used to carry a sick person

[49] **dally:** wait / delay

[50] **will to some provision…quick conduct:** will bring you quickly to some supplies for your journey

[51] **This rest…sinews:** Rest may have brought relief to your frayed nerves
[52] **if convenience…allow:** if it isn't convenient
[53] **Stand in hard cure:** are unlikely to be cured

EDGAR

When we our betters see bearing our woes,
We scarcely think our miseries our foes.[54]
Who alone suffers, suffers most i' the mind,
Leaving free things and happy shows behind.[55]
But then the mind much sufferance doth o'erskip,
When grief hath mates, and bearing fellowship.[56]
How light and portable[57] my pain seems now,
When that which makes me bend makes the King bow,
He childed as I fathered![58] Tom, away!
Mark the high noises;[59] and thyself bewray[60]
When false opinion,[61] whose wrong thought defiles[62] thee,
In thy just proof, repeals and reconciles thee.[63]
What will hap more tonight, safe 'scape the King![64]
Lurk, lurk![65]
[Exit]

[54] **When we our betters...our foes:** When we see our superiors bearing our own troubles, we find it easier to endure our own sufferings

[55] **Leaving...shows behind:** leaving carefree thoughts and happy displays behind

[56] **But then...fellowship:** But then the mind can avoid much suffering, even when grief multiples if the ability to endure it does also

[57] **portable:** bearable

[58] **He childed...fathered!:** i.e. He has unkind children just like I have an unkind father

[59] **Mark...noises:** i.e. Listen to the rumours about the feuding Dukes

[60] **thyself bewray:** reveal yourself (by disposing of the disguise of Poor Tom)

[61] **false opinion:** i.e. Gloucester's incorrect opinion of Edgar

[62] **defiles:** tarnishes (your reputation)

[63] **In thy...reconciles thee:** proof of your innocence will undo your banishment and reconcile you to your father

[64] **What will hap...King!:** Whatever happens tonight, may the King escape!

[65] **Lurk, lurk!:** Stay hidden!

Key Quotations

KENT   *All the power of his wits have given way to his impatience.*

EDGAR   *When we our betters see bearing our woes,*
        We scarcely think our miseries our foes.
        Who alone suffers, suffers most i' the mind,
        Leaving free things and happy shows behind.
        But then the mind much sufferance doth o'erskip,
        When grief hath mates, and bearing fellowship.
        How light and portable my pain seems now,
        When that which makes me bend makes the King bow

Commentary

- **The mock-trial dramatically illustrates that Lear still blames Goneril and Regan for his intense suffering.** During the mock-trial he imagines arraigning Goneril and Regan, and then calls for Regan's heart to be dissected to find the source of her cruel nature: 'let them anatomize Regan; see what breeds about her heart. Is there any cause in nature that makes these hard hearts?'

- **The mock-trial points to the absurdity of human justice.** The mad nature of the trial combined with its inability to successfully apportion blame offers a jaundiced view of human justice.

- **The depth of Kent's and Gloucester's love for Lear is clear from this scene.** They both act to protect Lear: Gloucester brings him to the farmhouse and then moves to protect Lear from a potential assassination attempt. Kent urges Lear to rest and only reluctantly agrees to bring Lear to Dover so worried is he about Lear's fraught nerves.

- **Edgar shows his deeply empathetic and compassionate nature.** He is moved to tears by the pitiful sight of Lear acting out the mock-trial: 'My tears begin to take his part so much / They mar my counterfeiting.'

- **Edgar's loyalty to Lear is readily apparent.** When faced with the suffering of Lear, Edgar dismisses his own pain: 'How light and portable my pain seems now, / When that which makes me bend makes the King bow'. Edgar puts concern for Lear ahead of concern for himself.

- **This is the last scene in which the Fool appears.** He is neither heard from nor discussed again in the play. Some critics suggest that this is because the same actor would play the parts of both the Fool and Cordelia. Both roles are also symbolically linked in that they hold a mirror up to Lear, directing his journey towards self-awareness. The Fool's disappearance is also important thematically. **As Lear grows in compassion and learns to recognise his own flaws, there is no more need for the Fool.** In earlier scenes the Fool acted as Lear's conscience; Lear now has to see his own faults and mistakes himself.

Questions
---

1. Gloucester, Kent and Edgar all show their love for King Lear. Find examples of this in the scene.
2. Think about the Fool's role in the earlier scenes of the play, how has his function on stage changed?
3. In his soliloquy, Edgar acts as a foil (a contrast) that deepens our understanding of Lear. Explain how this is true.
4. Some versions of *King Lear* contain neither the mock-trial nor Edgar's soliloquy. Make the case for retaining both of these in a production of the play.

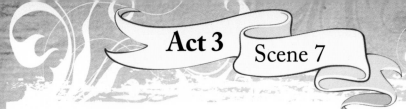

Scene Summary

- Cornwall sends Goneril to alert Albany to the news that French forces have arrived at Dover.
- Oswald tells Cornwall that Lear is making his way to Dover.
- Gloucester is bound and brought before Cornwall and Regan.
- Cornwall and Regan question Gloucester and call him a traitor.
- Regan plucks his beard. Cornwall gouges out one of his eyes and stamps on it.
- Regan calls for the other eye to be gouged.
- A servant intervenes. Cornwall attacks him but is seriously wounded. Regan stabs the servant from behind, killing him.
- Cornwall gouges out Gloucester's other eye.
- Gloucester cries out for Edmund. Regan mocks Gloucester and reveals that Edmund was the one that betrayed him. Gloucester now sees that Edgar was innocent.
- Gloucester is cast out of the castle.
- Alone on stage, two servants criticise Regan and Cornwall for their cruelty. They decide to help Gloucester and bring him to Poor Tom to be led.

Gloucester's Castle.
Enter CORNWALL, REGAN, GONERIL, EDMUND and
Servants

CORNWALL
[To GONERIL] Post speedily[1] to my lord your husband.
Show him this letter:[2] the army of France is landed. *[To*
Servants] Seek out the villain Gloucester.

[Exeunt some of the Servants]

REGAN
Hang him instantly!

GONERIL
Pluck out his eyes!

CORNWALL
Leave him to my displeasure. Edmund, keep you our sister[3]
company; the revenges we are bound[4] to take upon your
traitorous father are not fit for your beholding.[5] Advise the
Duke, where you are going, to a most festinate preparation;[6]
we are bound to the like.[7] Our posts[8] shall be swift and
intelligent[9] betwixt us. Farewell, dear sister; farewell, my
Lord of Gloucester.[10]

[Enter OSWALD]

---

1 **Post speedily:** ride quickly
2 **letter:** i.e. the letter Edmund gave to Cornwall

3 **sister:** sister-in-law
4 **bound:** duty-bound / obliged
5 **for your beholding:** for you to see
6 **festinate preparation:** quick preparation (for war)
7 **we are...the like:** likewise, we also plan to prepare for war
8 **posts:** messengers / couriers
9 **intelligent:** informative
10 **Lord of Gloucester:** i.e. Edmund. Cornwall refers to Edmund by his new title. However, Oswald below still refers to Edmund's father by the same title

How now! Where's the King?

OSWALD
My Lord of Gloucester hath conveyed him hence.
Some five–or six–and thirty of his knights,
Hot questrists[11] after him, met him at gate,
Who, with some other of the Lord's[12] dependants,
Are gone with him towards Dover, where they boast
To have well-armed friends.

CORNWALL
                    Get horses for your mistress.[13]

GONERIL
20 Farewell, sweet Lord, and sister.

CORNWALL
Edmund, farewell.

[Exeunt GONERIL, EDMUND and OSWALD]

             Go seek the traitor Gloucester,
Pinion him[14] like a thief, bring him before us.

[Exeunt other Servants]

Though well we may not pass upon his life[15]
Without the form of justice,[16] yet our power
Shall do a courtesy to our wrath,[17] which men
May blame, but not control. Who's there? The traitor?

[Enter GLOUCESTER, brought in by two or three Servants]

REGAN
Ingrateful fox,[18] 'tis he.

CORNWALL
Bind fast his corky[19] arms.

GLOUCESTER
              What means your Graces?
Good my friends, consider; you are my guests.
30 Do me no foul play, friends.

CORNWALL
             Bind him, I say.[20]

[Servants bind him]

---

[11] **Hot questrists:** excited seekers

[12] **Lord:** i.e. Gloucester

[13] **mistress:** i.e. Goneril

[14] **Pinion him:** bind him / tie him up

[15] **pass upon his life:** sentence him to death
[16] **form of justice:** a trial
[17] **our power...our wrath:** my rightful power will give way to my anger

[18] **Ingrateful fox:** Ungrateful, sneaky individual

[19] **corky:** withered

[20] **Bind...I say:** The fact that Cornwall has to ask twice suggests that servants may be reluctant to follow his order

REGAN
Hard, hard!²¹ O filthy traitor!

²¹ **Hard, hard!:** Bind him tightly!

GLOUCESTER
Unmerciful lady as you are, I'm none.

CORNWALL
To this chair bind him. Villain, thou shalt find –

[REGAN plucks his beard]²²

²² **plucks his beard:** This would have been an outrageously disrespectful thing to do

GLOUCESTER
By the kind gods, 'tis most ignobly²³ done
To pluck me by the beard.

²³ **ignobly:** dishonourably / disrespectfully

REGAN
So white, and such a traitor!

GLOUCESTER
                  Naughty²⁴ Lady,
These hairs, which thou dost ravish²⁵ from my chin,
Will quicken,²⁶ and accuse thee. I am your host;
With robbers' hands my hospitable favours
You should not ruffle thus.²⁷ What will you do?

²⁴ **Naughty:** Wicked
²⁵ **ravish:** pluck. The word suggests rape and thus stresses Gloucester's sense of violation
²⁶ **quicken:** come to life
²⁷ **You should...thus:** You should not treat me like this

CORNWALL
Come, sir, what letters had you late²⁸ from France?

²⁸ **late:** recently

REGAN
Be simple answered,²⁹ for we know the truth.

²⁹ **Be simple answered:** Answer clearly

CORNWALL
And what confederacy³⁰ have you with the traitors
Late footed³¹ in the kingdom?

³⁰ **confederacy:** conspiracy
³¹ **Late footed:** recently landed

REGAN
               To whose hands
You have sent the lunatic King? Speak!

GLOUCESTER
I have a letter guessingly set down,³²
Which came from one that's of a neutral heart,
And not from one opposed.³³

³² **guessingly set down:** written without particular information
³³ **opposed:** i.e. opposed to Cornwall

CORNWALL
             Cunning.

REGAN

And false.

CORNWALL
Where hast thou sent the King?

GLOUCESTER

To Dover.

REGAN
50 Wherefore to Dover? Wast thou not charged at peril —[34]

[34] **at peril:** at the risk of execution

CORNWALL
Wherefore to Dover? Let him first answer that.

GLOUCESTER
I am tied to the stake, and I must stand the course.[35]

[35] **I am tied...the course:** The image here is of bear-baiting. Gloucester imagines himself as a bear tied to a stake who is attacked by dogs

REGAN
Wherefore to Dover, sir?

GLOUCESTER

Because I would not see
Thy cruel nails pluck out his poor old eyes;
Nor thy fierce sister in his anointed flesh[36]
Stick boarish[37] fangs. The sea, with such a storm
As his bare head in hell-black night endured,
Would have buoyed[38] up, and quenched the stelled fires.[39]
Yet, poor old heart, he holp the heavens to rain.[40]
60 If wolves had at thy gate howled that stern time,
Thou should'st have said, 'Good porter, turn the key,
All cruels else subscribed';[41] but I shall see
The winged vengeance[42] overtake such children.

[36] **anointed flesh:** During the coronation ceremony, kings were anointed with holy oil
[37] **boarish:** like a wild boar
[38] **buoyed:** risen
[39] **quenched the stelled fires:** put out the light of the stars
[40] **he holp the heavens to rain:** he helped the heavens to rain with his own tears
[41] **turn the key...subscribed:** Possibly: 1 'open the door and let the wolves in, and whatever other cruel beings sought entry' 2 'open the door and let the wolves in.' All other cruel creatures display compassion in such circumstances. The interpretation of these lines depends on whether the inverted commas close after *key* or *subscribed*

CORNWALL
See't shalt thou never. Fellows, hold the chair;
Upon these eyes of thine I'll set my foot.

GLOUCESTER
He that will think to live till he be old,[43]
Give me some help! – O cruel! O you gods!

[42] **winged vengeance:** the gods' vengeance
[43] **He that will...old:** i.e. He that values his life

REGAN
One side will mock another – the other too!

CORNWALL
If you see vengeance –

FIRST SERVANT

> Hold your hand, my Lord!
I have served you ever since I was a child,
But better service have I never done you
Than now to bid you hold.[44]

44 **bid you hold:** urge you to stop

REGAN

> How now, you dog!

FIRST SERVANT

If you did wear a beard upon your chin,
I'd shake it on this quarrel.[45] What do you mean?[46]

45 **If you did...quarrel:** If you were a man, I'd pull your beard
46 **What do you mean?:** Possibly this line is a response to Cornwall drawing his sword. Some editors attribute this line to Regan, others to Cornwall
47 **villain:** 1 servant 2 wicked person

CORNWALL

My villain![47]
[They draw and fight]

FIRST SERVANT

Nay, then, come on, and take the chance of anger.[48]
[He wounds CORNWALL]

48 **take the chance of anger:** run the risk of fighting me when I am enraged

REGAN

[To another Servant] Give me thy sword. A peasant stand up thus![49]
[Takes a sword, and runs at him behind]

49 **A peasant...thus!:** I can't believe that a peasant would make a challenge like this!

FIRST SERVANT

O, I am slain! My Lord, you have one eye left
To see some mischief on him.[50] O!
[Dies]

50 **see some mischief on him:** see that he comes to harm

CORNWALL

Lest it see more, prevent it. Out, vile jelly!
Where is thy lustre[51] now?

51 **lustre:** 1 brightness 2 beauty

GLOUCESTER

All dark and comfortless. Where's my son Edmund?
Edmund, enkindle all the sparks of nature
To quit this horrid act.[52]

52 **enkindle...horrid act:** arouse all of your love for your father and take revenge for this terrible action

REGAN

> Out, treacherous villain!
Thou call'st on him that hates thee. It was he
That made the overture[53] of thy treasons to us,
Who is too good to pity thee.

53 **made the overture:** disclosed

GLOUCESTER
O my follies! Then Edgar was abused.[54]
Kind gods, forgive me that, and prosper him!

REGAN
90 *[To a Servant]* Go thrust him out at gates, and let him smell
His way to Dover.

[Exit Servant with GLOUCESTER]

How is't, my Lord? How look you?[55]

CORNWALL
I have received a hurt: follow me, Lady.
[To Servants] Turn out that eyeless villain. Throw this slave
Upon the dunghill. Regan, I bleed apace.[56]
Untimely[57] comes this hurt. Give me your arm.
[Exit CORNWALL, led by REGAN]

SECOND SERVANT
I'll never care what wickedness I do
If this man come to good.[58]

THIRD SERVANT
If she live long,
And in the end meet the old course of death,
100 Women will all turn monsters.[59]

SECOND SERVANT
Let's follow the old Earl, and get the Bedlam[60]
To lead him where he would. His roguish madness
Allows itself to anything.[61]

THIRD SERVANT
Go thou: I'll fetch some flax and whites of eggs[62]
To apply to his bleeding face. Now, heaven help him!

[Exeunt severally]

---

[54] **abused:** wronged

[55] **How look you?:** 1 How are you feeling? 2 What does your expression mean?

[56] **apace:** quickly
[57] **Untimely:** At a bad time

[58] **If this…good:** if Cornwall survives this wound

[59] **If she live…monsters:** If Regan lives long, and dies in old age, all women will turn into monsters (because they will escape punishment for their crimes)
[60] **Bedlam:** i.e. Edgar as Poor Tom
[61] **His roguish…anything:** Poor Tom's homelessness and madness allows him to get away with all sorts of things
[62] **flax and whites of eggs:** bandages soaked in egg whites. This was a treatment for an eye injury

---
Key Quotations

GLOUCESTER   *Because I would not see*
               Thy cruel nails pluck out his poor old eyes;
               Nor thy fierce sister in his anointed flesh
               Stick boarish fangs.

CORNWALL   *Out, vile jelly! / Where is thy lustre now?*

GLOUCESTER   *O my follies! Then Edgar was abused. / Kind gods, forgive me that,*
               and prosper him!

REGAN   *Go thrust him out at gates, and let him smell / His way to Dover.*

Commentary

- **The sub-plot parallels the play's main plot in this hugely dramatic scene.** Lear has experienced much suffering up to this point; Gloucester's suffering in this scene is an echo of this. However, **whereas Lear's suffering is psychological, Gloucester's is largely physical.** Lear's error was one of judgement, it is therefore appropriate that he experiences mental anguish. Gloucester's 'sin' in fathering Edmund outside of marriage is a physical one, it is therefore fitting that he suffers physically. The horror of being blinded and the violence Gloucester experiences is deeply disquieting for the audience. We appreciate Gloucester's physical pain as Cornwall stamps on his gouged eyeball. The shock and horror of this act is compounded by Cornwall's callous language: 'Out, vile jelly!'

- **Blindness is an important motif (recurring idea) in *King Lear*.** This motif is central to this scene. It is only when Gloucester is physically blinded does he learn to see the true natures of his sons and achieve insight. After his second eye is gouged, Gloucester calls out for Edmund. Regan cruelly mocks him for his gullibility; it is then that Gloucester appreciates Edgar's innocence and his own poor judgement: 'O my follies! Then Edgar was abused./ Kind gods, forgive me that, and prosper him!' **By the end of this scene Gloucester is physically blinded, but, in a moral sense, he now sees much clearer.**

- **Shakespeare offers a disturbing vision of human cruelty.** Regan, Goneril and Cornwall all participate in the torture of Gloucester. Goneril cries, 'Pluck out his eyes!' Cornwall does so, adding to the violence by stamping on the eyeball. It is Regan who then says, 'One side will mock another – the other too!' Cornwall obliges, celebrating the act with the bitter comment, 'Out, vile jelly! / Where is thy lustre now?' **In this way we can see how a 'mob mentality' develops as the characters physically torture Gloucester, embracing all that is cruel and vicious in human nature.** Regan looks to amplify Gloucester's pain by mocking him for trusting Edmund. The torture is finished only when Gloucester is thrown out of his own castle upon Regan's instruction that he must, 'smell / His way to Dover.'

- **Shakespeare adds to the vision of human evil through the use of animal imagery.** Gloucester imagines himself as a bear tied to a stake and set upon by dogs: 'I am tied to the stake, and I must stand the course.' When asked why he sent Lear to Dover, Gloucester uses bestial imagery to depict Goneril and Regan:

      'Because I would not see
      Thy cruel nails pluck out his poor old eyes;

> Nor thy fierce sister in his anointed flesh
> Stick boarish fangs.'

- However, **Shakespeare balances this spectacle of human evil with the brave, self-sacrificing actions of the servants**. The First Servant's intervention is reminiscent of Gloucester's attempts to help Lear, and also of Kent's intervention on Cordelia's behalf in the play's first scene. By fighting Cornwall, the First Servant illustrates his duty to Gloucester and helps to highlight how corrupt Cornwall, Regan and Goneril have become. The other two servants also show humanity's potential for compassion as they leave to soothe Gloucester's eyes and help him find his way.

Questions
---

1. Explain how Goneril, Regan and Cornwall all contribute to the mistreatment and torture of Gloucester.
2. Why do you think Shakespeare makes use of animal imagery in this scene?
3. Although physically blinded by the end of the scene, how is Gloucester better able to see in a moral sense?
4. (a) In what way is Gloucester's situation an echo of Lear's?
   (b) In what way is it different?
5. What do you think is the significance of the servants' actions in this scene?
6. Imagine you are Edmund. You have just been sent out of the room before Gloucester is brought in. Using modern English, write a soliloquy in which you discuss your thoughts and feelings about your situation and Gloucester's.

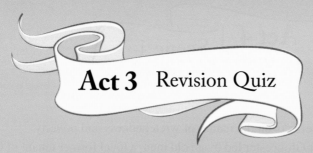

Act 3 Revision Quiz

1. In Act 3, Scene 1, Kent explains that soldiers have landed at Dover. Where have these forces come from?
2. Kent sends a gentleman to bring a message to the forces at Dover. What token does Kent give him to prove his identity to Cordelia?
3. How does Edmund betray his father to Cornwall?
4. How does Lear treat Poor Tom (Edgar) when he first meets him in Act 3, Scene 4?
5. How does Cornwall reward Edmund for betraying Gloucester?
6. Gloucester brings Lear to find shelter. Where does he bring him to?
   (a) A hovel
   (b) An abandoned castle
   (c) A farmhouse
   (d) A cabin in the woods

7. How is Gloucester tortured by Cornwall and Regan?

8. At the end of this act Cornwall is fatally wounded. Who wounds him?

9. Who says each of the following?
   (a) *Blow, winds, and crack your cheeks! Rage! Blow!*
       You cataracts and hurricanoes, spout
       Till you have drenched our steeples, drowned the cocks!

   (b) *Here I stand, your slave,*
       A poor, infirm, weak and despised old man

   (c) *O my follies! Then Edgar was abused.*
       Kind gods, forgive me that, and prosper him!

   (d) *Because I would not see*
       Thy cruel nails pluck out his poor old eyes;
       Nor thy fierce sister in his anointed flesh
       Stick boarish fangs

10. Rewrite these quotations. In each case, write the speaker's name and fill in the blanks.
    (a) *I am a man*
        More sinned against than _____
    (b) *Out, vile _____!*
        Where is thy lustre now?
    (c) *Go thrust him out at gates, and let him _____*
        His way to Dover

Act 4 — Scene 1

Scene Summary

- Edgar in soliloquy reflects on the nature of wretchedness and poverty.
- Edgar sees his father Gloucester led by an old man, a loyal former tenant of Gloucester's. Edgar is moved by the sight of his father in such a state of wretchedness.
- Gloucester sends the old man to get clothes for Edgar who is disguised as Poor Tom.
- Gloucester gives Edgar his money purse. He then asks Edgar to lead him to Dover where he intends to kill himself by jumping from a cliff.
- Edgar (as Poor Tom) agrees to lead him.

The Heath.
Enter EDGAR

EDGAR
Yet better thus, and known to be contemned¹
Than still contemned and flattered.² To be worst,
The lowest and most dejected thing of fortune,
Stands still in esperance,³ lives not in fear.
The lamentable change is from the best,
The worst returns to laughter.⁴ Welcome then,
Thou unsubstantial air that I embrace!
The wretch that thou hast blown unto the worst
Owes nothing to thy blasts.⁵

[Enter GLOUCESTER, led by an OLD MAN]

                     But who comes here?
10 My father, poorly led?⁶ World, world, O world!
But that thy strange mutations make us hate thee,
Life would not yield to age.⁷

OLD MAN
                O, my good Lord!
I have been your tenant, and your father's tenant,
These fourscore years.

GLOUCESTER
Away, get thee away; good friend, be gone.
Thy comforts⁸ can do me no good at all;
Thee they may hurt.

OLD MAN
            Alack, sir, you cannot see your way.

¹ **contemned:** despised
² **Yet better…flattered:** It is better to be like this (a beggar), knowingly despised, than to be flattered and secretly despised
³ **Stands…esperance:** is always hoping for something better
⁴ **The lamentable…laughter:** Change brings sadness to those in a fortunate position; the most wretched person's circumstance can only improve
⁵ **The wretch…blasts:** The wretched person who has suffered misfortune, owes nothing to the wind
⁶ **poorly led:** 1 led by a poor man 2 led in a fashion inappropriate to a man of his social status
⁷ **But that thy…to age:** If it was not for the odd changes of the world that make us hate life, we would never accept growing old
⁸ **comforts:** efforts to bring me comfort

GLOUCESTER
I have no way, and therefore want no eyes:
I stumbled when I saw. Full oft 'tis seen
Our means secure us, and our mere defects
Prove our commodities.[9] O dear son Edgar,
The food of thy abused father's wrath![10]
Might I but live to see thee in my touch,
I'd say I had eyes again!

OLD MAN
                              How now! Who's there?

EDGAR
[Aside] O gods! Who is't can say 'I am at the worst'?
I am worse than e'er I was.

OLD MAN
                              'Tis poor mad Tom.

EDGAR
[Aside] And worse I may be yet; the worst is not
So long as we can say 'This is the worst.'[11]

OLD MAN
Fellow, where goest?

GLOUCESTER
                              Is it a beggar-man?

OLD MAN
Madman and beggar too.

GLOUCESTER
He has some reason,[12] else he could not beg.
I' the last night's storm I such a fellow saw,
Which made me think a man a worm. My son
Came then into my mind; and yet my mind
Was then scarce friends with him. I have heard more since.
As flies to wanton boys, are we to the gods.
They kill us for their sport.[13]

EDGAR
            [Aside] How should this be?
Bad is the trade that must play fool to sorrow,
Angering itself and others.[14] *[Aloud]* Bless thee, master!

GLOUCESTER
Is that the naked fellow?

9 **Full oft...commodities:** Too often it is seen that our wealth gives us a false sense of security, and our problems turn out to be beneficial

10 **The food...wrath:** Edgar was the 'food' that fed Gloucester's anger when he was misled ('abused') by Edmund

11 **And worse...worst:** I may be worse off yet; we haven't reached the worst if we can say 'This is as bad as it gets' (because this suggests that the situation can improve). Edgar is rejecting his earlier optimistic view expressed at the start of this scene

12 **reason:** sense / intelligence

13 **As flies...their sport:** Just like flies are to reckless boys, so are we to the gods. They kill us for their own amusement

14 **Bad is the trade...others:** It's a bad business that I must play the fool as Poor Tom in spite of my father's sorrow, thus causing distress to myself and others

OLD MAN

Ay, my Lord.

GLOUCESTER

Then, prithee, get thee away. If, for my sake,
Thou wilt o'ertake us hence a mile or twain[15]
I' the way toward Dover, do it for ancient love,[16]
And bring some covering for this naked soul,
Who I'll entreat[17] to lead me.

Reflects Lear's kindness

[15] **twain:** two
[16] **ancient love:** longstanding loyalty
[17] **entreat:** ask

OLD MAN

Alack, sir, he is mad.

GLOUCESTER

'Tis the times' plague,[18] when madmen lead the blind.
Do as I bid thee, or rather do thy pleasure;
Above the rest,[19] be gone.

[18] **times' plague:** a problem of the times we live in
[19] **Above the rest:** above all

OLD MAN

I'll bring him the best 'parel[20] that I have,
50 Come on't what will.[21]
[Exit]

[20] **'parel:** apparel / clothes
[21] **Come...will:** whatever happens

GLOUCESTER

Sirrah, naked fellow.

EDGAR

Poor Tom's a-cold. *[Aside]* I cannot daub[22] it further.

[22] **daub:** pretend (to be Poor Tom)

GLOUCESTER

Come hither, fellow.

EDGAR

[Aside] And yet I must. *[To GLOUCESTER]* Bless thy
sweet eyes, they bleed.

GLOUCESTER

Know'st thou the way to Dover?

EDGAR

Both stile and gate, horseway[23] and footpath. Poor Tom hath
been scared out of his good wits. Bless thee, goodman's son,
from the foul fiend! Five fiends[24] have been in Poor Tom at
once; of lust, as Obidicut; Hobbididence, prince of darkness;
60 Mahu, of stealing; Modo, of murder; Flibbertigibbet, of
mopping and mowing,[25] who since possesses chambermaids
and waiting-women. So, bless thee, master!

[23] **horseway:** bridle-path
[24] **Five fiends:** Five evil spirits. The names are taken from Harsnett (see p.98)

[25] **mopping and mowing:** making faces and grimacing

GLOUCESTER
Here, take this purse, thou whom the heavens' plagues
Have humbled to all strokes.[26] That I am wretched
Makes thee the happier.[27] Heavens, deal so still![28]
Let the superfluous and lust-dieted man[29]
That slaves your ordinance,[30] that will not see
Because he doth not feel, feel your power quickly;
So distribution should undo excess,[31]
And each man have enough. Dost thou know Dover?

EDGAR
Ay, master.

GLOUCESTER
There is a cliff, whose high and bending head[32]
Looks fearfully in the confined deep:[33]
Bring me but to the very brim of it,
And I'll repair the misery thou dost bear
With something rich about me.[34] From that place
I shall no leading need.

EDGAR
                Give me thy arm:
Poor Tom shall lead thee.
[Exeunt]

[26] **humbled to all strokes:** made you bear all kinds of afflictions
[27] **That I...happier:** The fact that I am wretched, should make you happier (because you are getting my money)
[28] **Heavens...still!:** May heaven always act this way (to help distribute wealth more fairly)
[29] **Let the superfluous...man:** Allow the man who has more than is necessary and who satisfies every whim
[30] **That slaves your ordinance:** 1 who treats your instruction (that we should be generous) as if it was his own to break 2 who treats the rules laid down by heaven as if they were his own to break if he chooses
[31] **So distribution...excess:** this would allow wealth to be fairly distributed and prevent anybody becoming excessively rich
[32] **bending head:** summit leaning over its base
[33] **confined deep:** waters held (between Dover and France)
[34] **about me:** about my person

Key Quotations

EDGAR	*The lamentable change is from the best, / The worst returns to laughter.*
EDGAR	*World, world, O world! / But that thy strange mutations make us hate thee, / Life would not yield to age.*
GLOUCESTER	*I have no way, and therefore want no eyes: / I stumbled when I saw. Full oft 'tis seen / Our means secure us, and our mere defects / Prove our commodities. O dear son Edgar, / The food of thy abused father's wrath! / Might I but live to see thee in my touch, / I'd say I had eyes again!*
GLOUCESTER	*As flies to wanton boys, are we to the gods. / They kill us for their sport.*
GLOUCESTER	*Heavens, deal so still! / Let the superfluous and lust-dieted man / That slaves your ordinance, that will not see / Because he doth not feel, feel your power quickly; / So distribution should undo excess, / And each man have enough.*

──────────────── **Commentary** ────────────────

- **Gloucester is a man of compassion.** We see this as he urges the old man to leave, in case his enemies hurt him: 'Away, get thee away; good friend, be gone. / Thy comforts can do me no good at all; / Thee they may hurt.' Similarly, Gloucester asks the old man to find clothes for Poor Tom, extending his compassion to those in need.

- After experiencing considerable trauma in the previous scene, **Gloucester now grows in wisdom and insight. Suffering has brought him a new understanding of poverty and deprivation.** Gloucester's message of social justice echoes Lear's in Act 3. Suffering has brought both men to the same conclusion. Gloucester argues for a radical redistribution of wealth to alleviate suffering and undermine the excesses of the rich: 'distribution should undo excess, / And each man have enough.' **Like Lear, Gloucester is coming to a position of greater compassion and philosophical insight.**

- **Gloucester is starting to recognise the gross error of judgement he made with regards to his sons.** He becomes aware of his moral blindness and blames himself for rejecting Edgar: 'I have no way, and therefore want no eyes: / I stumbled when I saw.' Gloucester cries out for Edgar as he feels the pain of rejecting the son that loved him dearly: 'O dear son Edgar, / . . . Might I but live to see thee in my touch, / I'd say I had eyes again!' It is this personal pain that allows Gloucester to grow in understanding.

- **This recognition leaves Gloucester in a state of despair.** Faced with his own mistakes and the physical traumas he has suffered, Gloucester now collapses spiritually and embraces death. His solution is take his own life by leaping from a cliff at Dover.

- It is interesting to note that, despite his personal growth, **Gloucester still sees himself as a victim of both the gods and of Edmund. He has not fully accepted that he has brought about his own downfall.** Gloucester depicts himself as a pawn of the Gods: 'As flies to wanton boys, are we to the gods. / They kill us for their sport', doomed to suffer and powerless to change his fate. However, it was Gloucester's own lust that resulted in Edmund; Shakespeare's audience would have seen Gloucester as being punished for this 'sin'.

- **This scene reflects on the meaning of deprivation and human suffering.** In soliloquy Edgar begins the scene by arguing that those who are wretched can always look forward to the possibility of their situation improving. This is summed up by Edgar's assertion that 'The worst returns to laughter.' Edgar's view reflects his lack of self-pity, his optimism and unshakeable faith in divine justice. However, when he sees the pitiful sight of his blinded father led by an old man, Edgar glimpses an even greater level of suffering. He appreciates that there is nothing hopeful about his father's wretched state and that suffering encourages us to accept old age: 'World, world, O world! / But that thy strange mutations make us hate thee, / Life would not yield to age.' Edgar thought he had arrived at 'the worst' but now he understands that humanity has an even greater capacity to endure suffering.

──────────────── **Questions** ────────────────

1. (a) What view of human suffering does Edgar offer in his soliloquy at the opening of the scene?
   (b) How does Edgar's view change?
2. What signs are there that Gloucester has become a more compassionate man?
3. How has Gloucester's suffering changed his view of wealth and the way it is distributed throughout society?
4. Do you think Gloucester feels regret for the way he treated Edgar earlier in the play? Refer directly to the text to explain your answer.
5. What evidence is there to show that Gloucester has reached a state of utter despair in this scene?

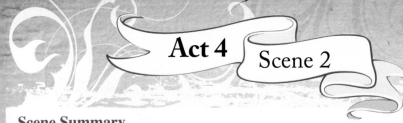

Scene Summary

- Upon returning from Albany's castle, Oswald tells Goneril that Albany has sided with Lear and Gloucester.
- Goneril and Edmund display affection for each other. Their language is loaded with sexual suggestion. Goneril makes it clear that she desires Edmund as a lover and as someone to rule the kingdom with.
- Albany and Goneril exchange harsh insults. Albany is deeply critical of her treatment of Lear and Gloucester.
- A messenger announces Cornwall's death.
- Goneril sees Regan as a competitor for Edmund's affections.

Before Albany's palace
Enter GONERIL and EDMUND

GONERIL
Welcome, my Lord. I marvel our mild husband
Not met us on the way.[1]

[Enter OSWALD]

              Now, where's your master?

OSWALD
Madam, within; but never man so changed.
I told him of the army that was landed;
He smiled at it. I told him you were coming;
His answer was 'The worse.' Of Gloucester's treachery,
And of the loyal service of his son,
When I informed him, then he called me sot,[2]
And told me I had turned the wrong side out.[3]
What most he should dislike seems pleasant to him,
What like, offensive.[4]

GONERIL
    [To EDMUND] Then shall you go no further.
It is the cowish[5] terror of his spirit,
That dares not undertake.[6] He'll not feel wrongs
Which tie him to an answer.[7] Our wishes on the way
May prove effects.[8] Back, Edmund, to my brother;[9]
Hasten his musters and conduct his powers.[10]
I must change arms at home, and give the distaff
Into my husband's hands.[11] This trusty servant

[1] **I marvel...the way:** It's amazing we didn't meet my meek husband on the way

[2] **sot:** idiot

[3] **turned...side out:** got things the wrong way round

[4] **What most...offensive:** What he should most dislike he finds pleasant, whereas the things he should like only offend him

[5] **cowish:** cowardly

[6] **undertake:** assume responsibility

[7] **He'll not feel...an answer:** He ignores offences which would require him to respond

[8] **Our wishes...effects:** What we were hoping for as we travelled here, may indeed come true

[9] **brother:** brother-in-law i.e. Cornwall

[10] **Hasten...his powers:** Urge him to quickly call up his armies and direct his forces

[11] **I must change...hands:** I will take the sword from my husband and give him the distaff (staff for spinning). Goneril sees Albany as womanish and feels she must assume a traditional manly role

125

Shall pass between us. Ere long you are like to hear,
20 If you dare venture in your own behalf,
A mistress's command.[12] Wear this. *[Giving a favour]*[13]
                       Spare speech;
Decline your head.[14] This kiss,[15] if it durst speak,
Would stretch thy spirits up into the air.
Conceive,[16] and fare thee well –

EDMUND
Yours in the ranks of death.[17]

GONERIL
                  – my most dear Gloucester!

[Exit EDMUND]

O, the difference of man and man![18]
To thee a woman's services are due;
My fool usurps my bed.[19]

OSWALD
30 Madam, here comes my Lord.
[Exit]

[Enter ALBANY]

GONERIL
I have been worth the whistling.[20]

ALBANY
                  O Goneril!
You are not worth the dust which the rude[21] wind
Blows in your face. I fear your disposition;
That nature, which contemns its origin,
Cannot be bordered certain in itself.[22]
She that herself will sliver and disbranch
From her material sap, perforce must wither
And come to deadly use.[23]

GONERIL
No more; the text[24] is foolish.

ALBANY
40 Wisdom and goodness to the vile seem vile;
Filths savour but themselves.[25] What have you done?
Tigers, not daughters, what have you performed?
A father, and a gracious aged man
Whose reverence even the head-lugged bear[26] would lick,

---

[12] **mistress's command:** 1 as a powerful female ruler 2 as a lover to Edmund

[13] **favour:** 1 love token 2 symbol of favour

[14] **Decline your head:** bend your head (to accept a kiss)

[15] **kiss:** After she kisses him, Goneril stops using the formal 'you' showing the intimacy between them

[16] **Conceive:** Goneril's language is peppered with sexual suggestions: 'Conceive', 'spirits', 'woman's services', 'bed'

[17] **Yours...death:** 1 I am yours until I die 2 I am yours to enjoy sexually (the language suggests orgasm)

[18] **O, the difference...man!:** Oh, the difference between one man and another i.e. between Edmund and Albany

[19] **To thee...my bed:** You deserve all that a woman may do for you. A fool (i.e. Albany) has taken over my bed

[20] **I have been...whistling:** I am worth waiting for. This recalls the proverb, 'It is a poor dog that is not worth the whistling'. She is reproaching Albany for not coming to meet her

[21] **rude:** rough

[22] **I fear...in itself:** I fear your nature; someone who abandons their parent cannot be trusted to keep within moral bounds

[23] **She that herself...deadly use:** She who cuts herself off from her essential roots, will wither and come to a bad end. The image here is of a branch severing itself from the tree

[24] **text:** subject on which Albany is speaking

[25] **Filths...themselves:** vile individuals only enjoy their own stink

[26] **head-lugged bear:** a bear pulled by the head and therefore enraged

Most barbarous, most degenerate, have you madded.[27]
Could my good brother suffer you to do it?
A man, a prince, by him so benefitted![28]
If that the heavens do not their visible spirits[29]
Send quickly down to tame these vilde offences,[30]
It will come,
Humanity must perforce prey on itself,
Like monsters of the deep.[31]

GONERIL

               Milk-livered[32] man!
That bear'st a cheek for blows,[33] a head for wrongs,
Who hast not in thy brows an eye discerning
Thine honour from thy suffering;[34] that not know'st
Fools do those villains pity who are punished
Ere they have done their mischief.[35] Where's thy drum?[36]
France spreads his banners in our noiseless[37] land;
With plumed helm thy slayer begins threat;
Whiles thou, a moral fool, sits still, and cries
'Alack, why does he so?'

ALBANY

               See thyself, devil!
Proper deformity seems not in the fiend
So horrid as in woman.[38]

GONERIL

              O vain fool!

ALBANY
Thou changed and self-covered thing,[39] for shame,
Be-monster not thy feature.[40] Were't my fitness[41]
To let these hands obey my blood,[42]
They are apt enough to dislocate and tear
Thy flesh and bones. Howe'er thou art a fiend,
A woman's shape doth shield thee.

GONERIL
Marry, your manhood, mew –[43]

[Enter a Messenger]

ALBANY
What news?

MESSENGER
O, my good lord, the Duke of Cornwall's dead,
Slain by his servant, going to put out
The other eye of Gloucester.

27 **Most barbarous...madded:** You are wild and totally immoral; you have driven your father insane

28 **Could my good...benefitted!:** How could my brother-in-law (Cornwall) allow you to do it? How could he seeing that he is a man, a prince and someone who benefitted so much from Lear!

29 **visible spirits:** 1 avenging angels 2 thunderbolts

30 **vilde offences:** vile offenders. 'vilde' also suggests 'wild'

31 **Humanity...the deep:** humanity will inevitably devour itself just like big fish in the sea eat the smaller ones

32 **Milk-livered:** Cowardly. Cowardice was associated with a lack of blood in the liver, 'milk' suggests effeminacy

33 **That bear'st...blows:** that only has a cheek so as to be hit

34 **Who hast not...suffering:** who doesn't have an eye in his head to tell the difference between what can be honourably tolerated and what should cause resentment

35 **that not know'st...mischief:** who doesn't realise that fools pity villains (such as Lear and Gloucester) that need to be punished before they commit crimes

36 **drum:** i.e. call to war

37 **noiseless:** undefended because there are no drums calling the army to battle

38 **Proper deformity...woman:** The ugly appearance of the devil does not seem as horrid as it does in a woman (because it is 'proper' to the devil)

39 **Thou changed...thing:** You have changed and hidden your womanly self under the appearance of a fiend

40 **Be-monster...feature:** Don't let monstrousness be your defining feature

41 **Were't...fitness:** If it was appropriate behaviour for me

42 **blood:** passion

43 **mew:** Goneril mocks Albany's masculinity by imitating a kitten

ALBANY

Gloucester's eyes!

MESSENGER

A servant that he bred,[44] thrilled with remorse,[45]
Opposed against the act, bending[46] his sword
To his great master, who, thereat enraged,
Flew on him, and amongst them felled him dead;
But not without that harmful stroke which since
80 Hath plucked him after.[47]

ALBANY

This shows you are above,
You justicers,[48] that these our nether crimes[49]
So speedily can venge![50] But, O poor Gloucester!
Lost he his other eye?

MESSENGER

Both, both, my Lord.
[To GONERIL] This letter, madam, craves a speedy answer;
'Tis from your sister. *[Presents a letter]*

GONERIL

[Aside] One way I like this well;[51]
But being widow, and my Gloucester with her,
May all the building in my fancy pluck
Upon my hateful life.[52] Another way,
The news is not so tart.[53] *[Aloud]* I'll read, and answer.
[Exit]

ALBANY

90 Where was his son when they did take his eyes?

MESSENGER

Come with my Lady hither.

ALBANY

He is not here.

MESSENGER

No, my good Lord; I met him back again.[54]

ALBANY

Knows he the wickedness?

MESSENGER

Ay, my good Lord; 'twas he informed against him

---

[44] **bred:** trained
[45] **thrilled with remorse:** moved to act by pity (for Gloucester)
[46] **bending:** turning
[47] **plucked him after:** i.e. killed him later

[48] **justicers:** judges
[49] **nether crimes:** crimes committed down here on earth
[50] **venge:** avenge

[51] **One way…well:** In one way I like this
[52] **But being widow…life:** But if she is a widow and my Lord Gloucester (Edmund) is with her, it might pull all the plans I have built down upon me, leaving me with a hateful life
[53] **tart:** sour. The news is somewhat welcome to Goneril as it offers her the possibility of ruling over the entire kingdom

[54] **back again:** returning

And quit[55] the house on purpose, that their punishment
Might have the freer course.[56]

ALBANY

                  Gloucester, I live
To thank thee for the love thou show'dst the King,
And to revenge thine eyes. Come hither, friend,
Tell me what more thou know'st.
[Exeunt]

[55] **quit:** left
[56] **have the freer course:** be unrestrained

Key Quotations

ALBANY   *O Goneril!*
                    You are not worth the dust which the rude wind
                    Blows in your face. I fear your disposition;
                    That nature, which contemns its origin,
                    Cannot be bordered certain in itself.
                    She that herself will sliver and disbranch
                    From her material sap, perforce must wither
                    And come to deadly use.

ALBANY   *Wisdom and goodness to the vile seem vile; / Filths savour but themselves.*
                    What have you done? / Tigers, not daughters, what have you performed?

ALBANY   *Humanity must perforce prey on itself, / Like monsters of the deep.*

Commentary

- **One of the most striking aspects of this scene is the dramatic change in Albany.** Earlier in the play Albany is presented as ineffectual and weak, a man dominated by his wife. Oswald now describes him as radically different ('but never man so changed') and unequivocal in his opposition to Cornwall's call to unite in battle.
- **The change in Albany's character is further reflected in his heated argument with Goneril.** Albany criticises his wife in the harshest terms, effectively severing his relationship with her: 'O Goneril! / You are not worth the dust which the rude wind / Blows in your face.' Rather than the 'Milk-livered man' Goneril describes him as, Albany shows himself to be intensely passionate as he threatens to tear Goneril limb from limb:

      'Were't my fitness
      To let these hands obey my blood,
      They are apt enough to dislocate and tear
      Thy flesh and bones.'

  The scene finishes with Albany promising to help Lear and avenge Gloucester's blinding. Albany now understands his wife as both cruel and evil; it is this that helps to explain the radical change in his personality as he sides with the forces of good.
- **Goneril is a strong yet vicious character.** Once she learns of Albany's opposition to war she becomes assertive and instructs Edmund to return to Cornwall with a message to prepare for battle. Her argument with Albany reflects her twisted, bitter personality as she

matches the intensity of Albany's outrage with disdain for her husband:

> 'Milk-livered man!
> That bear'st a cheek for blows, a head for wrongs,
> Who hast not in thy brows an eye discerning
> Thine honour from thy suffering'.

However, there is nothing admirable about Goneril's strength. An audience in Shakespeare's time would have seen her behaviour as unnatural for a woman and a sign of her twisted nature.

- **Goneril remains a self-serving and conniving character.** Goneril opportunistically sees Cornwall's death in a positive light as it offers her the potential to wrest power from her sister. She always looks to do what is best for herself and acts without regard for others. Once she learns of Albany's opposition to the idea of war she immediately begins to attach herself to Edmund. The audience must appreciate Goneril's conduct as deeply unnatural. She has abandoned her marriage vows and neglected her aged father. It is this that prompts Albany to describe her as a 'devil', 'fiend' and 'tiger'.

- **This scene establishes a plotline in which Edmund has the opportunity to further consolidate his power through romance or marriage.** Cornwall's death and Goneril's strained relationship with Albany mean that Goneril and Regan are now competitors for Edmund's attention. Edmund now has the potential to be king. The idea that a 'bastard' would inherit the kingdom would have been appalling to an audience of Shakespeare's time.

Questions

1. How does Goneril treat Edmund in this scene?
2. Goneril describes her husband as a 'Milk-livered man'. In what ways is this shown to be untrue of his behaviour in this scene?
3. Goneril has mixed feelings about the news of Cornwall's death. Explain her reaction.

Act 4 — Scene 3

Scene Summary

- At the French camp, Kent talks with a gentleman.
- Kent learns that the King of France has returned to his own kingdom on a matter of great urgency.
- Kent asks the gentleman about Cordelia's reaction to the communication he sent her. The gentleman describes how she was moved by the news of Lear's suffering but admirably retained her composure.
- The audience also learn that Lear is reluctant to meet Cordelia as he is ashamed of the way in which he treated Cordelia.
- Kent says that he will remain in disguise for a while longer.

The French camp near Dover
Enter KENT and a Gentleman

KENT
Why the King of France is so suddenly gone back, know you the reason?

GENTLEMAN
Something he left imperfect in the state, which since his coming forth is thought of, which imports to the kingdom so much fear and danger,[1] that his personal return was most required and necessary.

KENT
Who hath he left behind him General?

GENTLEMAN
The Marshal of France, Monsieur la Far.

KENT
Did your letters pierce the Queen to any demonstration of grief?[2]

GENTLEMAN
Ay, sir. She took them, read them in my presence,
And now and then an ample tear trilled[3] down
Her delicate cheek. It seemed she was a queen
Over her passion, who, most rebel-like,

---

[1] **Something…danger:** He left some unfinished business in his country, which poses a dangerous threat to the kingdom

[2] **Did your letters…grief?:** Did your letters move the Queen to cry? Kent sent Cordelia a verbal message with his ring as proof. He did not send a written letter. However, an audience are unlikely to notice this inconsistency

[3] **trilled:** trickled

131

Sought to be king o'er her.[4]

KENT

O, then it moved her.

GENTLEMAN

Not to a rage, patience[5] and sorrow strove
Who should express her goodliest.[6] You have seen
Sunshine and rain at once, her smiles and tears
Were like a better way.[7] Those happy smilets,[8]
20 That played on her ripe lip, seemed not to know
What guests were in her eyes, which parted thence,
As pearls from diamonds dropped. In brief,
Sorrow would be a rarity most beloved,
If all could so become it.[9]

KENT

Made she no verbal question?[10]

GENTLEMAN

Faith, once or twice she heaved[11] the name of 'father'
Pantingly forth, as if it pressed[12] her heart;
Cried 'Sisters! Sisters! Shame of ladies! Sisters!
Kent! Father! Sisters! What, i' the storm, i' the night?
Let pity not be believed!' There she shook
30 The holy water from her heavenly eyes,
And clamour moistened;[13] then away she started,
To deal with grief alone.

KENT

It is the stars,
The stars above us, govern our conditions,[14]
Else one self mate and make could not beget
Such different issues.[15] You spoke not with her since?

GENTLEMAN

No.

KENT

Was this before the King returned?

GENTLEMAN

No, since.

KENT

Well, sir, the poor distressed Lear's i' the town,
Who sometime, in his better tune,[16] remembers
40 What we are come about, and by no means

---

[4] **It seemed...o'er her:** It seems that she controlled her emotions ('passion'), even though they tried to overwhelm her

[5] **patience:** self-control

[6] **express her goodliest:** best express her. The Gentleman explains that self-control and sorrow fought to define her facial expression

[7] **Were like a better way:** were similar, only better

[8] **smilets:** little smiles

[9] **Sorrow...become it:** Sadness would be a rare state most cherished if it made everyone look so well

[10] **Made...question?:** Did she not ask anything?

[11] **heaved:** struggled with the word

[12] **pressed:** weighed upon

[13] **clamour moistened:** her cries subdued by tears

[14] **conditions:** natures / qualities

[15] **Else one self...issues:** or else the same couple ('mate and make') could not have had such different children (i.e. Cordelia is so different to her sisters yet they have the same parents)

[16] **better tune:** better frame of mind

Will yield to see his daughter.

GENTLEMAN

Why, good sir?

KENT

A sovereign shame so elbows him.[17] His own unkindness,
That stripped her from his benediction,[18] turned her
To foreign casualties,[19] gave her dear rights
To his dog-hearted daughters, these things sting
His mind so venomously, that burning shame
Detains[20] him from Cordelia.

GENTLEMAN

Alack, poor gentleman!

KENT

Of Albany's and Cornwall's powers[21] you heard not?

GENTLEMAN

'Tis so, they are afoot.[22]

KENT

Well, sir, I'll bring you to our master Lear,
And leave you to attend him. Some dear cause
Will in concealment wrap me up awhile.[23]
When I am known aright[24] you shall not grieve
Lending me this acquaintance.[25] I pray you,
Go along with me.
[Exeunt]

[17] **A sovereign...him:** Shame overpowers him and holds him back
[18] **benediction:** blessing
[19] **foreign casualties:** take her chances abroad
[20] **Detains:** holds him back
[21] **powers:** armies
[22] **afoot:** marching
[23] **Some dear cause...awhile:** An important reason means I will have to remain disguised a while. Kent never explains what this 'dear cause' is
[24] **known aright:** known for who I truly am
[25] **Lending me this acquaintance:** being my friend

Key Quotations

GENTLEMAN *And now and then an ample tear trilled down*
Her delicate cheek. It seemed she was a queen
Over her passion, who, most rebel-like,
Sought to be king o'er her.

GENTLEMAN *There she shook*
The holy water from her heavenly eyes,
And clamour moistened; then away she started,
To deal with grief alone

KENT *It is the stars,*
The stars above us, govern our conditions,
Else one self mate and make could not beget
Such different issues.

Commentary

- **Shakespeare underlines the quality of Cordelia's character in this scene.** Kent asks the gentleman how she reacted to the news he sent of Lear's situation. **The gentleman remarks on the depth of feeling she showed for her father but also the admirable way in which she controlled her passion:**

  > 'And now and then an ample tear trilled down
  > Her delicate cheek. It seemed she was a queen
  > Over her passion, who, most rebel-like,
  > Sought to be king o'er her.'

  The gentleman explains that Cordelia acted with great composure and dignity before leaving to privately 'deal with grief alone.' **Cordelia's control over her passion is in marked contrast to Lear's behaviour in the first scene of the play,** where he was led by pride, anger and arrogance. Through contrast, Cordelia's obvious humanity and natural love for her father emphasises the unnatural conduct of her sisters. She is motivated by love; they are driven by lust and greed.

- **The gentleman describes Cordelia in terms that emphasise her regal nature** ('she was a queen / Over her passion') **and her saintly goodness:** 'she shook / The holy water from her heavenly eyes'. Cordelia's beauty is stressed in this exchange: 'Sorrow would be a rarity most beloved, / If all could so become it.' Shakespeare is keen to underscore the idea of Cordelia as a Christ-like figure opposing the forces of evil and destruction.

- **Lear is coming to recognise his own flaws and mistakes.** Kent explains that amidst his madness, Lear has moments of clarity in which he expresses deep shame for his mistreatment of Cordelia. So great is this that he cannot bring himself to even face her:

  > 'A sovereign shame so elbows him. His own unkindness,
  > That stripped her from his benediction, turned her
  > To foreign casualties, gave her dear rights
  > To his dog-hearted daughters, these things sting
  > His mind so venomously, that burning shame
  > Detains him from Cordelia.'

  This expression of guilt, although painful, is another positive step in Lear's personal growth as he comes to attain wisdom.

- **Through Kent the idea of fate is explored.** Kent discusses the influence of the stars upon human lives. He looks to the heavens to account for the difference between Cordelia and her sisters in light of the fact that they had the same parents:

  > 'It is the stars,
  > The stars above us, govern our conditions,
  > Else one self mate and make could not beget
  > Such different issues.'

  However, in much the same way as Gloucester looks to the gods to make sense of his suffering (Act 4, Sc 1), Kent looks to the stars to explain evil. Kent does not see that the origins of evil lie within the hearts of people. *King Lear* shows that we all have the capacity for evil if we make poor moral choices. Human beings must look within themselves for an answer to the problem of evil.

Questions

1. What impression of Cordelia is given by the Gentleman's description of her? Quote from the text in your answer.
2. (a) Why does Lear refuse to meet with Cordelia?
   (b) What does this suggest about his development as a character?
3. How does Kent explain the differences between Cordelia and her sisters? Quote from the text in your answer.

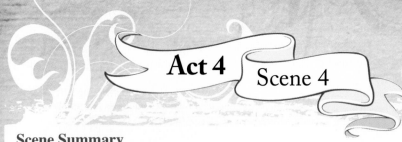

Act 4 — Scene 4

Scene Summary

- Cordelia describes Lear's mad behaviour: he has been seen singing in the fields wearing a crown of weeds and flowers. She sends soldiers out to look for him.
- The Doctor tells Cordelia that Lear needs rest to help restore his sanity.
- Cordelia says that she hopes a herbal remedy can be found for him.
- A messenger warns of the approaching British forces. Cordelia says that her army is prepared for the battle.
- Cordelia explains that she is motivated to go to war by love rather than ambition.

The Same. A Tent.
Enter, with drum and colours,[1] CORDELIA, DOCTOR and Soldiers

CORDELIA
Alack, 'tis he.[2] Why, he was met even now
As mad as the vexed sea,[3] singing aloud,
Crowned with rank fumiter[4] and furrow-weeds,[5]
With hardokes, hemlock, nettles, cuckoo-flowers,
Darnel[6] and all the idle weeds that grow
In our sustaining[7] corn. A century[8] send forth;
Search every acre in the high-grown field,
And bring him to our eye.

[Exit an Officer]

              What can man's wisdom
In the restoring his bereaved sense?[9]
He that helps him take all my outward worth.[10]

DOCTOR
There is means, madam.
Our foster-nurse of nature is repose,[11]
The which he lacks; that to provoke in him,
Are many simples operative,[12] whose power
Will close the eye of anguish.

CORDELIA
            All blest secrets,

---

1 **colours:** military banners

2 **Alack, 'tis he:** Alas, it is him (Lear). i.e. Lear is as mad as he has been described

3 **vexed sea:** stormy sea

4 **rank fumiter:** abundant fumitory weed, also known as 'smoke of the earth'

5 **furrow-weeds:** weeds that grow in the furrows of a ploughed field

6 **hardokes...Darnel:** types of weeds and wild flowers

7 **sustaining:** life-sustaining

8 **century:** 100 soldiers

9 **What can...sense?:** What can human knowledge do to restore his sanity?

10 **outward worth:** material possessions

11 **Our foster-nurse...repose:** Our natures are restored by rest

12 **simples operatives:** effective medicinal herbs

All you unpublished virtues[13] of the earth,
Spring with my tears! Be aidant and remediate[14]
In the good man's distress! Seek, seek for him,
Lest his ungoverned rage[15] dissolve the life
20 That wants the means to lead it.[16]

[Enter a Messenger]

MESSENGER
             News, madam:
The British powers are marching hitherward.[17]

CORDELIA
'Tis known before.[18] Our preparation[19] stands
In expectation of them. O dear father,
It is thy business that I go about;[20]
Therefore great France[21]
My mourning and importuned[22] tears hath pitied.
No blown ambition doth our arms incite,[23]
But love, dear love, and our aged father's right.
Soon may I hear and see him!
[Exeunt]

[13] **unpublished virtues:** unknown medicinal herbs
[14] **aidant and remediate:** helpful and remedial
[15] **ungoverned rage:** uncontrolled madness
[16] **dissolve the life...lead it:** destroy the life that lacks the sanity it requires to govern it
[17] **hitherward:** towards here
[18] **before:** already
[19] **preparation:** waiting soldiers
[20] **O dear father...about:** A reference to Christ's words: 'I must go about my father's business' (Luke 2.49)
[21] **France:** i.e. the King of France, Cordelia's husband
[22] **importuned:** importunate / urgent
[23] **No blown ambition...incite:** It is not inflated ambition that prompts us to go to battle

---
Key Quotations

CORDELIA   *He that helps him take all my outward worth.*

CORDELIA   *No blown ambition doth our arms incite, / But love, dear love, and our aged father's right.*

Commentary

- **The depth of Cordelia's love for her father is made clear.** Cordelia explains that she would give up all of her wealth and material possessions to help her father: 'He that helps him take all my outward worth.' She passionately pleads for any medicinal cure to help Lear:

  > 'All blest secrets,
  > All you unpublished virtues of the earth,
  > Spring with my tears! Be aidant and remediate
  > In the good man's distress!'

  The contrast with her sisters' treatment of Lear is stark.

- **Cordelia pointedly explains that her motivation for going to war is neither pride nor ambition but rather love:** 'No blown ambition doth our arms incite, / But love, dear love, and our aged father's right.' As a dutiful daughter, Cordelia's concern is for her father rather than politics. This is in marked contrast to the ambitions of Edmund and the greed of Goneril and Regan. Cordelia again proves herself to be a pure and noble character, whose virtues show up the flaws of the other characters.

- **Shakespeare makes use of nature imagery in this scene.** It represents both Lear's untempered madness but also Cordelia's restorative powers. Cordelia says that Lear is 'mad as the vexed sea' and describes him crowned with flowers and weeds, singing amongst the 'sustaining corn'. The association with weeds represents the uncontrolled nature of Lear's mind. Cordelia is associated with natural, herbal remedies to help restore Lear's sanity. The imagery suggests that she has the potential to soothe Lear's pain but also in a wider context heal the divisions within the fractured kingdom.

Questions

1. Explain how Cordelia displays the following qualities in this scene:
    (a) compassion
    (b) forgiveness
    (c) leadership
    (d) love
2. Explain the function of the nature imagery in this scene.

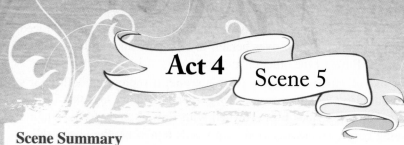

Act 4 Scene 5

Scene Summary

- Regan learns that Goneril has sent a letter to Edmund.
- She understands that Goneril is her rival for Edmund.
- Regan unscrupulously asks Oswald to allow her to open the letter but Oswald declines.
- Through Oswald, Regan sends a message to Goneril. Regan says that she is a more suitable partner for Edmund and that Goneril should stop making advances towards him.
- Regan declares that she will promote anybody that kills Gloucester.

Gloucester's Castle.
Enter REGAN and OSWALD

REGAN
But are my brother's powers set forth?[1]

OSWALD
                      Ay, madam.

REGAN
Himself in person there?

OSWALD
               Madam, with much ado:[2]
Your sister is the better soldier.

REGAN
Lord Edmund spake[3] not with your Lord at home?

OSWALD
No, madam.

REGAN
What might import my sister's letter to him?[4]

OSWALD
I know not, Lady.

REGAN
Faith, he is posted[5] hence on serious matter.
It was great ignorance,[6] Gloucester's eyes being out,

[1] **But are...forth?:** But have my brother-in-law's armies set off?

[2] **with much ado:** with a lot of fuss

[3] **spake:** spoke

[4] **What might import...him?:**
1. What did my sister write to him?
2. What might the fact that my sister wrote to him mean?

[5] **posted:** ridden quickly away
[6] **ignorance:** mistake (politically speaking)

To let him live. Where[7] he arrives he moves
All hearts against us. Edmund, I think, is gone,
In pity of his misery,[8] to dispatch
His nighted life[9] – moreover, to descry[10]
The strength o' the enemy.

OSWALD

I must needs after him, madam, with my letter.

REGAN

Our troops set forth tomorrow: stay with us;
The ways are dangerous.

OSWALD

                       I may not, madam:
My Lady charged my duty[11] in this business.

REGAN

Why should she write to Edmund? Might not you
Transport her purposes by word? Belike –[12]
Some things, I know not what – I'll love thee much;
Let me unseal the letter.

OSWALD

                Madam, I had rather –

REGAN

I know your lady does not love her husband –
I am sure of that – and at her late being here
She gave strange oeillades[13] and most speaking looks
To noble Edmund. I know you are of her bosom.[14]

OSWALD

I, madam?

REGAN

I speak in understanding; y'are, I know't.
Therefore I do advise you, take this note.[15]
My Lord is dead; Edmund and I have talked,
And more convenient[16] is he for my hand
Than for your Lady's. You may gather more.[17]
If you do find him, pray you give him this;[18]
And when your mistress hears thus much[19] from you,
I pray desire her call her wisdom to her.[20]
So, fare you well.
If you do chance to hear of that blind traitor,
Preferment falls on him that cuts him off.[21]

---

7 **Where:** Wherever
8 **In pity of his misery:** Regan is being ironic here
9 **to dispatch...life:** to end his (Gloucester's) life, darkened by blindness
10 **descry:** discover

11 **charged my duty:** insisted upon my total obedience

12 **Belike:** Perhaps

13 **oeillades:** amorous glances / passionate looks
14 **of her bosom:** in her confidence

15 **take this note:** take note of what I'm telling you
16 **convenient:** suitable

17 **gather more:** deduce more
18 **this:** Regan gives Oswald a token or letter to pass on to Edmund
19 **thus much:** an account of what I have said
20 **desire...to her:** urge her to be sensible

21 **Preferment...him off:** I will promote whoever kills him (Gloucester)

OSWALD

Would[22] I could meet him, Madam! I should show

40 What party I do follow.

REGAN

              Fare thee well.

[Exeunt]

[22] **Would:** I wish

Commentary

- **The rivalry between Goneril and Regan for Edmund intensifies in this scene.** Both sisters have proved disloyal to their father; they now show that same disloyalty to one another.

- **Whereas the previous scene is characterised by expressions of love and tenderness, this scene focuses on hatred.** Cordelia's capacity for love and forgiveness is counter-balanced by Regan's hatred and callous nature. Cordelia forgets the injustice of being disowned by her father, whereas Regan is consumed by the thought that she should have killed Gloucester while she had the chance: 'It was great ignorance, Gloucester's eyes being out, / To let him live.'

- **Regan's judgement is clouded by jealous passion and lust.** She feels threatened by Goneril and jealous of her sister's relationship with Edmund: 'She gave strange oeillades and most speaking looks / To noble Edmund.' She fails to act calmly and instead deepens her rift with Goneril by warning her sister off Edmund:

  'Edmund and I have talked,

  And more convenient is he for my hand

  Than for your Lady's…

  I pray desire her call her wisdom to her.'

  Regan is being led by her jealousy and lust; passion has clouded her judgement.

Questions

1. What message does Regan send to Goneril through Oswald?
2. Do you think it was a good idea for Regan to send this message? Why / why not?
3. Explain how Regan is led by each of the following emotions in this scene:
   (a) Jealousy
   (b) Hatred
4. Contrast the actions of Regan in this scene with Cordelia's in the previous scene.
5. What do you think is the main function of this short scene?

Act 4 — Scene 6

Scene Summary

- Edgar (in disguise) leads Gloucester and convinces him that they are at the edge of a cliff.
- Gloucester jumps from what he believes is the top of the cliff.
- Edgar pretends to be somebody who was standing on the beach. He tells Gloucester that he saw him land safely.
- Gloucester decides to endure his suffering until he dies naturally.
- Lear arrives wearing flowers and weeds. He acknowledges how flatterers fed his inflated ego.
- Lear criticises human justice and talks of how money protects sinners and criminals.
- Lear runs away from the group sent by Cordelia to find him.
- Edgar learns that Goneril and Regan's army is fast approaching.
- Edgar offers to lead Gloucester to safety. On the way they meet Oswald. Oswald plans to kill Gloucester. Edgar fights and kills Oswald.
- Edgar reads the letter from Goneril to Edmund which Oswald was carrying. The letter asks Edmund to kill Albany. Edgar decides to deliver the letter to Albany.

Fields near Dover.
Enter GLOUCESTER, and EDGAR dressed like a peasant[1]

GLOUCESTER
When shall I come to the top of that same hill?[2]

EDGAR
You do climb up it now. Look how we labour.[3]

GLOUCESTER
Methinks the ground is even.

EDGAR
                  Horrible steep.
Hark,[4] do you hear the sea?

GLOUCESTER
             No, truly.

[1] **peasant:** Edgar is wearing the clothes the Old Man gave him in 4.1. He no longer speaks like Poor Tom

[2] **same hill:** the hill they were talking about in 4.1

[3] **labour:** struggle

[4] **Hark:** Listen

141

EDGAR
Why, then, your other senses grow imperfect
By your eyes' anguish.[5]

5 **By your...anguish:** by the suffering of your eyes

GLOUCESTER
                    So may it be, indeed.
Methinks thy voice is altered and thou speak'st
In better phrase and matter[6] than thou didst.

6 **better phrase and matter:** improved expression and more sensible subject matter

EDGAR
You're much deceived. In nothing am I changed
10 But in my garments.

GLOUCESTER
                    Methinks you're better spoken.

EDGAR
Come on, sir, here's the place. Stand still. How fearful
And dizzy 'tis, to cast one's eyes so low!
The crows and choughs[7] that wing the midway air
Show scarce so gross as beetles.[8] Halfway down
Hangs one that gathers samphire,[9] dreadful trade!
Methinks he seems no bigger than his head.
The fishermen that walk upon the beach
Appear like mice, and yon tall anchoring bark,[10]
Diminished to her cock, her cock a buoy[11]
20 Almost too small for sight. The murmuring surge[12]
That on the unnumbered idle pebbles[13] chafes,
Cannot be heard so high.[14] I'll look no more,
Lest my brain turn, and the deficient sight
Topple down headlong.[15]

7 **choughs:** jackdaws
8 **Show scarce...beetles:** That barely look as large ('gross') as beetles
9 **samphire:** a type of edible plant

10 **bark:** ship
11 **Diminished...buoy:** reduced to the size of her rowing-boat ('cock'), and her rowing boat is the size of a buoy
12 **surge:** tide
13 **unnumbered...pebbles:** countless, barren pebbles
14 **so high:** i.e. as high as we are up here
15 **Lest my brain...headlong:** in case I become dizzy, cannot see properly and topple over the edge headfirst

GLOUCESTER
                    Set me where you stand.

EDGAR
Give me your hand; you are now within a foot
Of th' extreme verge.[16] For all beneath the moon
Would I not leap upright.[17]

16 **extreme verge:** very edge
17 **upright:** straight up (in case I didn't land exactly on the same spot and then fell)

GLOUCESTER
                    Let go my hand.
Here, friend, is another purse, in it a jewel
Well worth a poor man's taking. Fairies[18] and gods

18 **Fairies:** Superstition held that fairies made wealth multiply

Prosper it with thee! Go thou farther off;
Bid me farewell, and let me hear thee going.

EDGAR
Now fare you well, good sir.

GLOUCESTER
                          With all my heart.

EDGAR
[Aside] Why I do trifle thus with his despair
Is done to cure it.[19]

> [19] **Why I do trifle...cure it:** The only reason I play with his despair is so I can cure him of it

GLOUCESTER
[Kneeling] O you mighty gods!
This world I do renounce and in your sights
Shake patiently my great affliction off.
If I could bear it longer and not fall
To quarrel with your great opposeless[20] wills,
My snuff and loathed part of nature should
Burn itself out.[21] If Edgar live, O, bless him!
Now, fellow, fare thee well.

> [20] **opposeless:** irresistible
> [21] **My snuff...itself out:** The smouldering end and hated part of my life will soon burn itself out. The image here is of a smouldering candle

EDGAR
                          Gone, sir. Farewell.

[GLOUCESTER throws himself forward]

And yet I know not how conceit may rob
The treasury of life, when life itself
Yields to the theft.[22] Had he been where he thought,
By this had thought been past. *[Aloud]* Alive or dead?
Ho, you sir! Friend! Hear you, sir? Speak![23]
[Aside] Thus might he pass[24] indeed, yet he revives.
[Aloud] What are you, sir?

> [22] **I know...theft:** I'm not sure how imagination ('conceit') may rob him of his life, when he wants to die
> [23] **Alive...Speak!:** Edgar is putting on yet another voice
> [24] **pass:** pass away / die

GLOUCESTER
                          Away, and let me die.

EDGAR
Hadst thou been aught but gossamer,[25] feathers, air,
So many fathom down precipitating,[26]
Thou'dst shivered[27] like an egg; but thou dost breathe,
Hast heavy substance, bleed'st not, speak'st, art sound.

> [25] **aught but gossamer:** anything other than cobwebs
> [26] **precipitating:** falling headlong
> [27] **shivered:** smashed

Ten masts at each make not the altitude[28]
Which thou hast perpendicularly fell.
Thy life's a miracle. Speak yet again.

GLOUCESTER
But have I fallen, or no?

EDGAR
From the dread summit of this chalky bourn.[29]
Look up a-height; the shrill-gorged lark[30] so far
60 Cannot be seen or heard. Do but look up.

GLOUCESTER
Alack, I have no eyes.
Is wretchedness deprived that benefit
To end itself by death? 'Twas yet some comfort
When misery could beguile the tyrant's rage,[31]
And frustrate his proud will.

EDGAR
                    Give me your arm.
Up, so. How is't? Feel you your legs? You stand.

GLOUCESTER
Too well, too well.

EDGAR
                    This is above all strangeness.
Upon the crown o' the cliff, what thing was that
Which parted[32] from you?

GLOUCESTER
                    A poor unfortunate beggar.

EDGAR
70 As I stood here below methought his eyes
Were two full moons. He had a thousand noses,
Horns whelked[33] and waved like the enridged[34] sea:
It was some fiend. Therefore, thou happy father,[35]
Think that the clearest[36] gods, who make them honours
Of men's impossibilities,[37] have preserved thee.

GLOUCESTER
I do remember now. Henceforth I'll bear

28 **Ten masts…altitude:** Ten ship-masts, laid on top of one another, would not have reached that height

29 **bourn:** boundary of England, made by the cliff
30 **shrill-gorged lark:** shrill sounding lark (lark is a type of bird)

31 **beguile…rage:** i.e. commit suicide

32 **parted:** departed

33 **whelked:** twisted (like the shell of whelk)
34 **enridged:** furrowed
35 **happy father:** lucky, old man
36 **clearest:** righteous
37 **make…impossibilities:** are honoured for performing feats that are impossible for people to do

Affliction till it do cry out itself
'Enough, enough' and die.[38] That thing you speak of,
I took it for a man. Often 'twould say
'The fiend, the fiend': he led me to that place.

EDGAR
Bear free and patient thoughts.[39] But who comes here?

[Enter LEAR, fantastically dressed with wild flowers]

The safer sense will ne'er accommodate
His master thus.[40]

LEAR
No, they cannot touch me for coining;[41] I am the King
himself.

EDGAR
O thou side-piercing[42] sight!

LEAR
Nature's above art in that respect.[43] There's your press-
money.[44] That fellow handles his bow like a crow-keeper:[45]
draw me a clothier's yard.[46] Look, look, a mouse! Peace,
peace; this piece of toasted cheese will do't. There's my
gauntlet;[47] I'll prove it on a giant. Bring up the brown bills.[48]
O, well flown, bird, i' the clout,[49] i' the clout! Hewgh! Give
the word.[50]

EDGAR
Sweet marjoram.[51]

LEAR
Pass.

GLOUCESTER
I know that voice.

LEAR
Ha! Goneril, with a white beard! They flattered me like a
dog and told me I had white hairs in my beard ere the black
ones were there.[52] To say 'ay' and 'no' to everything that I
said 'ay' and 'no' to was no good divinity.[53] When the rain
came to wet me once and the wind to make me chatter; when
the thunder would not peace at my bidding, there I found

[38] **Henceforth...and die:** From now on, I'll bear pain until it cries out itself, 'Enough, enough' and lets me die naturally

[39] **free...thoughts:** untroubled thoughts with the capacity to bear suffering

[40] **The safer sense...thus:** Nobody in his right mind would dress like this

[41] **touch me for coining:** arrest me for minting coins. A king had the right to mint coins

[42] **side-piercing:** heart-rending

[43] **Nature's...respect:** Possibly: 1 Nature is better at providing heart-rending sights than art 2 A king's natural right to mint coins ('Nature') is superior to a forger's 'art'
[44] **press-money:** money given to army recruits when they were 'impressed' (conscripted)
[45] **crow-keeper:** scarecrow
[46] **draw...yard:** draw the bow back fully. A 'clothier's yard' was an arrow, so called because it was the length of a yard of cloth (36 inches)
[47] **gauntlet:** challenge, often offered by throwing a glove down
[48] **brown bills:** soldiers armed with pikes, their weapons were painted brown to protect against rust
[49] **clout:** centre of the target
[50] **word:** password
[51] **Sweet marjoram:** A herb used to treat diseases of the brain

[52] **had white hairs...were there:** had the wisdom of old age, before I was old enough to grow a beard
[53] **To say...divinity:** Saying 'yes' and 'no' to everything I said 'yes' and 'no' to was not good theology ('divinity'). The reference to 'divinity' suggests Lear was treated like a god

'em, there I smelt 'em out.[54] Go to, they are not men o' their words: they told me I was everything; 'tis a lie, I am not ague-proof.[55]

GLOUCESTER
The trick[56] of that voice I do well remember:
Is't not the King?

LEAR
                    Ay, every inch a king.
When I do stare, see how the subject quakes.
I pardon that man's life. What was thy cause?[57] Adultery?
110 Thou shalt not die – die for adultery? No!
The wren goes to't, and the small gilded fly
Does lecher[58] in my sight.
Let copulation thrive; for Gloucester's bastard son
Was kinder to his father than my daughters
Got 'tween the lawful sheets.[59]
To't, luxury,[60] pell-mell,[61] for I lack soldiers.
Behold yond simpering dame,
Whose face between her forks presages snow,[62]
That minces virtue,[63] and does shake the head[64]
120 To hear of pleasure's name –[65]
The fitchew,[66] nor the soiled[67] horse, goes to't
With a more riotous appetite.
Down from the waist they are Centaurs,[68]
Though women all above;
But to the girdle[69] do the gods inherit,
Beneath is all the fiend's; there's hell, there's darkness, there's the sulphurous pit – burning, scalding, stench, consumption![70] Fie, fie, fie! Pah, pah! Give me an ounce of civet,[71] good apothecary,[72] to sweeten my imagination:
130 there's money for thee.

GLOUCESTER
O, let me kiss that hand!

LEAR
Let me wipe it first; it smells of mortality.[73]

GLOUCESTER
O ruined piece of nature! This great world[74]
Shall so wear out to nought. Dost thou know me?

---

[54] **there I found...'em out:** that's when I saw who they truly are, when I exposed them
[55] **ague-proof:** immune to sickness or shivering

[56] **trick:** character

[57] **cause:** criminal case

[58] **lecher:** fornicate

[59] **Got 'tween...sheets:** conceived in the marriage bed
[60] **luxury:** lust
[61] **pell-mell:** 1 to rush into promiscuity 2 rushing into battle
[62] **Whose face...snow:** whose face predicts ('presages') cold chastity ('snow') between her legs ('forks')
[63] **minces virtue:** 1 affects virtue by her mincing walk 2 offers a show of dainty virtue
[64] **shake the head:** shakes her head in embarrassment or disapproval
[65] **pleasure's name:** mention of sex
[66] **fitchew:** polecat, slang for prostitute
[67] **soiled:** frisky, after being fed too much fresh grass
[68] **Centaurs:** Mythical creatures that were human above the waste, and horse below
[69] **girdle:** waist
[70] **consumption:** destruction
[71] **civet:** perfume
[72] **apothecary:** chemist / druggist

[73] **mortality:** 1 death 2 the condition of being human

[74] **great world:** universe

LEAR
I remember thine eyes well enough. Dost thou squiny[75] at me? No, do thy worst, blind Cupid![76] I'll not love. Read thou this challenge; mark but the penning of it.[77]

GLOUCESTER
Were all the letters suns, I could not see one.

EDGAR
[*Aside*] I would not take this from report;[78] it is,
50 And my heart breaks at it.

LEAR
Read.

GLOUCESTER
What, with the case[79] of eyes?

LEAR
O, ho, are you there with me?[80] No eyes in your head, nor no money in your purse? Your eyes are in a heavy case, your purse in a light, yet you see how this world goes.

GLOUCESTER
I see it feelingly.[81]

LEAR
What, art mad? A man may see how this world goes with no eyes. Look with thine ears. See how yond justice rails[82] upon yond simple thief. Hark, in thine ear: change places and,
60 handy-dandy,[83] which is the justice, which is the thief? Thou hast seen a farmer's dog bark at a beggar?

GLOUCESTER
Ay, sir.

LEAR
And the creature[84] run from the cur? There thou mightst behold the great image of authority: a dog's obeyed in office.[85]
Thou rascal beadle,[86] hold thy bloody hand!
Why dost thou lash that whore? Strip thine own back;
Thou hotly lusts to use her in that kind
For which thou whipp'st her.[87] The usurer hangs the
60 cozener.[88]

---

75 **squiny:** squint
76 **blind Cupid:** the god of love who was represented as blind
77 **mark...of it:** just note the way it was written

78 **I would...from report:** I wouldn't believe this if I heard it

79 **case:** 1 socket 2 condition of

80 **are you...me?:** is that your excuse?

81 **feelingly:** 1 by touch 2 passionately

82 **justice rails:** judge reprimands
83 **handy-dandy:** take your choice, a game in which a child chooses a hand to find a hidden object

84 **creature:** person
85 **a dog's...office:** even a dog is obeyed if it is given authority
86 **beadle:** parish constable: an officer appointed to keep order in an area
87 **Thou hotly...her:** You desire her for the same thing for which you are whipping her
88 **The usurer...cozener:** The money-lender hangs the petty thief

Through tattered clothes small vices do appear;
Robes and furred gowns hide all. Plate sin with gold,
And the strong lance of justice hurtless breaks;[89]
Arm it in rags, a pigmy's straw does pierce it.
None does offend, none, I say, none; I'll able 'em:[90]
Take that of me,[91] my friend, who have the power   *Justice*
To seal the accuser's lips. Get thee glass eyes,[92]
And like a scurvy politician,[93] seem
To see the things thou dost not. Now, now, now, now![94]
170 Pull off my boots: harder, harder – so.

EDGAR
[*Aside*] O, matter and impertinency[95] mixed! Reason in
madness! *Paradox*

LEAR
If thou wilt weep my fortunes, take my eyes.
I know thee well enough, thy name is Gloucester.
Thou must be patient. We came crying hither: *Justice*
Thou know'st the first time that we smell the air,
We wawl[96] and cry. I will preach to thee: mark.

GLOUCESTER
Alack, alack the day!

LEAR
When we are born, we cry that we are come
180 To this great stage of fools.[97] This a good block:[98]
It were a delicate stratagem[99] to shoe
A troop of horse with felt. I'll put it in proof[100]
And when I have stolen upon these son-in-laws,
Then, kill, kill, kill, kill, kill, kill!

[*Enter a Gentleman, with Attendants*]

GENTLEMAN
O, here he is: lay hand upon him. [*To LEAR*] Sir,
Your most dear daughter –

LEAR
No rescue? What, a prisoner? I am even
The natural fool of Fortune.[101] Use me well;
You shall have ransom. Let me have surgeons;
190 I am cut to the brains.

---

89 **Plate sin...breaks:** If sin is armoured in gold plate, the strong lance of justice breaks harmlessly on it. Lear argues that wealth defends sinners against justice

90 **None does offend...able 'em:** Nobody is a sinner if all do sin; therefore I'll vouch for all criminals

91 **Take that of me:** Learn that lesson from me

92 **glass eyes:** spectacles

93 **scurvy politician:** contemptible deceiver

94 **Now...now!:** Possibly: 1 Lear is consoling Gloucester 2 Lear is sitting down to remove his boots

95 **matter and impertinency:** sense and nonsense

96 **wawl:** wail

97 **stage of fools:** i.e. the world

98 **block:** Possibly: 1 hat 2 mounting-block for horses 3 a tree stump

99 **delicate stratagem:** ingenious plan

100 **put it in proof:** put it to the test

101 **natural...Fortune:** born to be Fortune's fool

GENTLEMAN

You shall have anything.

LEAR

No seconds?[102] All myself?
Why, this would make a man a man of salt,[103]
To use his eyes for garden water-pots.
Ay, and laying autumn's dust.[104]

GENTLEMAN

Good sir –

LEAR

I will die[105] bravely,[106] like a smug bridegroom.
What! I will be jovial.[107] Come, come;
I am a king, my masters, know you that?

GENTLEMAN

You are a royal one, and we obey you.

LEAR

Then there's life in't.[108] Come and you get it, you shall get
it by running. Sa, sa, sa, sa.[109]
[Exit running, followed by Attendants]

GENTLEMAN

A sight most pitiful in the meanest[110] wretch,
Past speaking of in a king! Thou hast one daughter
Who redeems nature from the general[111] curse
Which twain[112] have brought her to.

EDGAR

Hail, gentle sir.

GENTLEMAN

Sir, speed you. What's your will?

EDGAR

Do you hear aught, sir, of a battle toward?[113]

GENTLEMAN

Most sure and vulgar.[114] Everyone hears that
Which can distinguish sound.[115]

---

[102]**seconds**: supporters
[103]**salt**: tears

[104]**To use...dust**: to use his eyes to water the garden and keep down the dust of autumn

[105]**die**: 1 die (as in the end of life) 2 reach sexual climax
[106]**bravely**: 1 courageously 2 in fine clothes
[107]**jovial**: merry

[108]**there's life in't**: all is not lost
[109]**Sa, sa, sa, sa**: A hunting cry used to urge the hounds on. Lear is challenging the attendants to catch him

[110]**meanest**: lowliest / poorest
[111]**general**: universal
[112]**twain**: two others i.e.1 Goneril and Regan (who cursed Lear with this situation or caused Lear to curse nature) 2 Adam and Eve (who brought humanity the 'general curse')

[113]**toward**: pending

[114]**vulgar**: generally known
[115]**sound**: 1 the noise of battle drums 2 audible rumours

EDGAR

But, by your favour,
How near's the other army?[116]

GENTLEMAN
210 Near and on speedy foot;[117] the main descry
Stands on the hourly thought.[118]

EDGAR
I thank you, sir: that's all.

GENTLEMAN
Though that the Queen on special cause[119] is here,
Her army is moved on.

EDGAR

I thank you, sir.

[Exit Gentleman]

GLOUCESTER
You ever-gentle gods, take my breath from me.
Let not my worser spirit[120] tempt me again
To die before you please!

EDGAR

Well pray you, father.

GLOUCESTER
Now, good sir, what are you?

EDGAR
A most poor man, made tame to Fortune's blows;[121]
220 Who, by the art of known and feeling sorrows,
Am pregnant to[122] good pity. Give me your hand,
I'll lead you to some biding.[123]

GLOUCESTER

Hearty[124] thanks:
The bounty[125] and the benison[126] of heaven
To boot, and boot![127]

[Enter OSWALD] — Episode 3

[116] **other army:** i.e. Goneril and Regan's army

[117] **speedy foot:** quickly approaching
[118] **the main...thought:** sight of the main part of the army is thought to arrive any hour now

[119] **on special cause:** for a particular reason i.e. to care for Lear

[120] **worser spirit:** evil angel

[121] **made tame...blows:** weakened by misfortune

[122] **Am pregnant to:** is full of
[123] **biding:** resting place

[124] **Hearty:** Heartfelt
[125] **bounty:** generosity
[126] **benison:** blessing
[127] **To boot:** to reward you, as well as my thanks

OSWALD

          A proclaimed prize! Most happy![128]
That eyeless head of thine was first framed flesh[129]
To raise my fortunes. Thou old unhappy[130] traitor,
Briefly thyself remember;[131] the sword is out
That must destroy thee.

GLOUCESTER

          Now let thy friendly hand
Put strength enough to't.

[EDGAR interposes]

OSWALD

          Wherefore, bold peasant,
Darest thou support a published[132] traitor? Hence,
Lest that the infection of his fortune take
Like hold on thee. Let go his arm.

EDGAR

Ch'ill not let go, zir, without vurther 'casion.[133]

OSWALD

Let go, slave, or thou diest!

EDGAR

Good gentleman, go your gait,[134] and let poor volk[135] pass.
An 'chud ha' bin zwaggered out of my life, 'twould not ha'
bin zo long as 'tis by a vortnight.[136] Nay, come not near th'
old man; keep out, che vor ye,[137] or I'se try whether your
costard or my ballow be the harder.[138] Ch'ill be plain with
you.

OSWALD

Out, dunghill!

EDGAR

Ch'ill pick your teeth, zir. Come, no matter vor your foins.[139]
[They fight and EDGAR knocks him down]

OSWALD

Slave, thou hast slain me. Villain, take my purse.
If ever thou wilt thrive, bury my body,
And give the letters[140] which thou find'st about me
To Edmund Earl of Gloucester. Seek him out

[128] happy: lucky / fortunate
[129] framed flesh: born
[130] unhappy: unfortunate
[131] thyself remember: remember your sins (so you can prepare for death)
[132] published: declared
[133] Ch'ill...'casion: I'll not let go, sir, without further occasion (reason). Edgar now adopts a rural accent so as to hide his identity from Oswald
[134] go your gait: be on your way
[135] volk: folk / people
[136] An 'chud...vortnight: And if I could be scared out of my skin by swaggering like yours, I would not have lived so long as a fortnight
[137] che vor ye: I warrant you
[138] or I'se...harder: or I shall try and see which is harder, your head ('costard' = a type of apple) or my cudgel ('ballow')
[139] Ch'ill...foins: I'm more than a match for you. Come on, your sword thrusts don't matter
[140] letters: 'letters' in Shakespeare often means the singular. In this case the reference is to Goneril's letter to Edmund.

Upon[141] the English party. O, untimely death, death!

[He dies]

EDGAR

I know thee well; a serviceable villain,[142]

As duteous to the vices of thy mistress

As badness would desire.

GLOUCESTER

What, is he dead?

EDGAR

250 Sit you down, father; rest you –

Let's see these pockets: the letters that he speaks of

May be my friends. He's dead; I am only sorry

He had no other deathsman.[143] Let us see.

Leave,[144] gentle wax;[145] and manners, blame us not.

To know our enemies' minds, we rip their hearts,

Their papers,[146] is more lawful.

[Reads] 'Let our reciprocal vows[147] be remembered. You

have many opportunities to cut him off.[148] If your will want

not,[149] time and place will be fruitfully[150] offered. There is

260 *nothing done[151] if he return the conqueror;[152] then am I the*

prisoner, and his bed my goal, from the loathed warmth

whereof deliver me, and supply the place for your labour.[153]

Your wife, (so I would say) –

Affectionate servant,[154] Goneril.'

O undistinguished space of woman's will![155]

A plot upon her virtuous husband's life

And the exchange[156] my brother! Here, in the sands

Thee I'll rake up,[157] the post unsanctified[158]

Of murderous lechers; and in the mature time[159]

270 With this ungracious[160] paper strike the sight

Of the death-practised[161] Duke. For him 'tis well

That of thy death and business I can tell.

GLOUCESTER

The King is mad: how stiff is my vile sense,[162]

That I stand up, and have ingenious[163] feeling

Of my huge sorrows! Better I were distract;[164]

So should my thoughts be severed from my griefs,

And woes by wrong imaginations[165] lose

The knowledge of themselves.

[Drum afar off]

---

[141] **Upon:** amongst

[142] **serviceable villain:** a scoundrel who will perform any sort of evil duty

[143] **deathsman:** executioner

[144] **Leave:** By your leave

[145] **wax:** Edgar is breaking the wax seal on the letter

[146] **Their papers:** i.e. to rip open their letters

[147] **reciprocal vows:** exchanged promises

[148] **cut him off:** kill him i.e. Albany

[149] **If your will want not:** If you don't lack ('want') the will (or the lust for me)

[150] **fruitfully:** plentifully. The word also suggests sexual fulfilment

[151] **There is nothing done:** Nothing will have been achieved

[152] **conqueror:** victor

[153] **for your labour:** 1 as reward for your hard work 2 to reward your sexual desire

[154] **servant:** lover

[155] **undistinguished…will:** limitless lust of woman

[156] **the exchange:** the replacement

[157] **Here…rake up:** Here in the sand I'll bury ('rake up') you (Oswald)

[158] **post unsanctified:** unholy messenger

[159] **mature time:** when the time is ripe

[160] **ungracious:** wicked

[161] **death-practised:** plotted against

[162] **stiff is my vile sense:** stubborn are my powers of sensation

[163] **ingenious:** conscious

[164] **distract:** mad

[165] **wrong imaginations:** delusions

EDGAR

Give me your hand:

Far off, methinks, I hear the beaten drum.[166]

Come, father, I'll bestow[167] you with a friend.

[Exeunt]

[166]drum: battle drum
[167]bestow: leave

Key Quotations

EDGAR   *Why I do trifle thus with his despair / Is done to cure it.*

GLOUCESTER   *O you mighty gods! / This world I do renounce and in your sights / Shake patiently my great affliction off.*

GLOUCESTER   *Henceforth I'll bear / Affliction till it do cry out itself / 'Enough, enough' and die.*

LEAR   *They flattered me like a dog and told me I had white hairs in my beard ere the black ones were there. To say 'ay' and 'no' to everything that I said 'ay' and 'no' to was no good divinity.*

LEAR   *Go to, they are not men o' their words: they told me I was everything; 'tis a lie, I am not ague-proof.*

LEAR   *Through tattered clothes small vices do appear; / Robes and furred gowns hide all.*

LEAR   *When we are born, we cry that we are come / To this great stage of fools.*

LEAR   *I am even / The natural fool of Fortune.*

GLOUCESTER   *You ever-gentle gods, take my breath from me. / Let not my worser spirit tempt me again / To die before you please!*

Commentary

- **The sub-plot and the main plot converge in this moving scene as Shakespeare brings together the mad Lear and the blinded Gloucester.** Both men's suffering bring them to despair but both grow in wisdom.
- **This scene explores the ideas of deception, appearance and reality.** Edgar tricks his father in order to save him. By fooling his father into believing that he has thrown himself from a cliff, Edgar hopes to restore Gloucester's will to live. Edgar describes the dizzying height, a man collecting samphire and how the 'fishermen that walk upon the beach / Appear like mice'. After Gloucester 'jumps', Edgar adds to the illusion by adopting the persona of a witness on the beach. Unlike Edmund who deceived Gloucester to enrich himself, Edgar's deception is motivated by love and deep concern for his father: 'Why I do trifle thus with his despair / Is done to cure it.'
- **Edgar's role is to lead Gloucester to full self-realisation.** Much like Lear is helped to wisdom by the Fool and Cordelia, Gloucester overcomes his despair and finds renewed faith in the gods through Edgar.

- **Gloucester learns to accept his fate and comes to understand that suffering is part of the human condition.** At the start of the scene Gloucester is unwilling to accept his great suffering and in a state of despair is resolved to take his own life. His cry to the gods is an expression of defiance as he looks to control his own destiny: 'O you mighty gods! / This world I do renounce and in your sights / Shake patiently my great affliction off.' However, after he believes the gods have spared him and then witnesses Lear's fraying psychological state, Gloucester's tone is more humble as he comes to accept that he cannot steer his own fate: 'You ever-gentle gods, take my breath from me. / Let not my worser spirit tempt me again / To die before you please!' Gloucester comes to accept that suffering is part of being human, something he must endure: 'I'll bear / Affliction till it do cry out itself / 'Enough, enough' and die.'

- **Lear's continuing personal growth is evidenced in this scene.** In a marked change of attitude from the first scene of the play, **Lear now recognises the emptiness of flattery** and how it feeds the ego: 'They flattered me like a dog and told me I had white hairs in my beard ere the black ones were there… they told me I was everything; 'tis a lie, I am not ague-proof.' However, it is interesting to note that Lear is not taking personal responsibility for courting flattery; he still sees himself as a victim.

- **Lear's suffering has allowed him to see the immorality of excessive wealth and its corrupting influence.** Lear notes how wealth may disguise immorality and corruption, whereas the vices of the poor are visible to all: 'Through tattered clothes small vices do appear; / Robes and furred gowns hide all.' This continues Lear's growing disillusionment with pomp and privilege and his new found empathy with the poor. The clothing imagery shows that Lear identifies with the common humanity, once he is 'stripped' of power (see Act 3, Scene 4).

- **Interestingly, for Lear, insight arrives in the midst of madness.** As his mental distress grows, so does his wisdom. Edgar notes this paradox: 'O, matter and impertinency mixed! Reason in madness!'

- As Gloucester is brought to the edge of utter despair, **Lear's suffering has brought him to the brink of madness.** Towards the end of the scene, his behaviour becomes erratic as he runs merrily from Cordelia's men: 'I will die bravely, like a smug bridegroom. / What! I will be jovial.' However, these 'mad' moments punctuate moments of philosophical insight. Lear describes the experience of being human as one of misery and foolishness: 'When we are born, we cry that we are come / To this great stage of fools.' If Lear is to complete his personal journey to a state of wisdom he must be brought back from the brink of madness, in the same way that Gloucester is brought back from despair.

- **Goneril's ruthlessness is evident in her letter to Edmund.** Her unscrupulous plot to kill her husband causes Edgar's moral outrage and shock: 'O undistinguished space of woman's will! / A plot upon her virtuous husband's life / And the exchange my brother!'

--------------------------------- **Questions** ---------------------------------

1. (a) How does Edgar deceive Gloucester in this scene?
  (b) What is his motivation for doing so?
2. Comment on the transformation of Gloucester's attitude in this scene.
3. In what ways does this scene show that Lear's insight has grown?
4. What do you understand by Edgar's comment that Lear exhibits 'reason in madness'?
5. Would you agree that Lear still exhibits some of the behaviour he displayed in the first scene of the play?

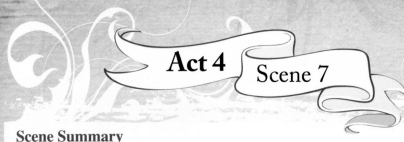

Act 4 — Scene 7

Scene Summary

- Cordelia thanks Kent for his loyalty.
- Kent says that he wishes to remain disguised for the time being.
- Lear is carried on stage dressed in his royal robes. He is asleep.
- Lear wakes. He thinks he is dead and that Cordelia is an angel.
- Lear then recognises Cordelia and begs her forgiveness. Cordelia says he has no need to ask for it.
- Kent and a gentleman discuss the pending battle. The gentleman says that Edmund now leads Cornwall's army.

A Tent in the French Camp.
Enter CORDELIA, KENT, DOCTOR and Gentleman

CORDELIA
O thou good Kent, how shall I live and work,
To match thy goodness? My life will be too short,
And every measure fail me.[1]

KENT
To be acknowledged, madam, is o'erpaid.
All my reports go with the modest truth,[2]
Nor more, nor clipped,[3] but so.

CORDELIA
                    Be better suited:[4]
These weeds[5] are memories of those worser hours.
I prithee,[6] put them off.

KENT
                    Pardon me, dear madam,
Yet to be known shortens my made intent.[7]
My boon[8] I make it that you know me not
Till time and I think meet.

---

[1] **every measure fail me:** every measure of goodness will see me coming up short

[2] **All my reports...truth:** All that I have told you has been the simple truth

[3] **Nor more, nor clipped:** neither exaggerated nor with omissions

[4] **suited:** dressed. Kent is still wearing the clothes of his disguise

[5] **weeds:** clothes

[6] **I prithee:** I pray thee

[7] **to be known...intent:** to have my identity revealed, ruins my plan. It is never made clear what Kent's plan is

[8] **boon:** request / favour

CORDELIA
Then be't so, my good Lord. *[To the DOCTOR]* How does
the King?

DOCTOR
Madam, sleeps still.

CORDELIA
O you kind gods,
Cure this great breach in his abused nature![9]
Th' untuned[10] and jarring senses, O, wind up[11]
Of this child-changed[12] father!

DOCTOR
                                                     So please your Majesty
That we may wake the King? He hath slept long.

CORDELIA
20 Be governed by your knowledge,[13] and proceed
I'the sway of your own will.[14] Is he arrayed?[15]

                [Enter LEAR in a chair, carried by servants]

GENTLEMAN
Ay, madam. In the heaviness of his sleep[16]
We put fresh garments on him.

DOCTOR
Be by,[17] good madam, when we do awake him;
I doubt not of his temperance.[18]

CORDELIA
                                    Very well.

DOCTOR
Please you, draw near. Louder the music there.

CORDELIA
O my dear father! Restoration hang
Thy medicine on my lips,[19] and let this kiss
Repair those violent harms that my two sisters
30 Have in thy reverence[20] made!

KENT
                                    Kind and dear princess!

9   **great breach...nature:** great
    wound to his mistreated self
10 **untuned:** discordant / lacking
    harmony
11 **wind up:** tune (by winding the
    strings)
12 **child-changed:** 1 changed by his
    children 2 become childlike

13 **Be governed...knowledge:** Let
    your medical knowledge guide
    you
14 **I'the...will:** as you see fit
15 **arrayed:** dressed in his royal
    robes

16 **heaviness of his sleep:** while he
    was sleeping deeply

17 **Be by:** remain nearby
18 **temperance:** sanity / self-control

19 **Restoration...lips:** Let restorative
    medicine hang on my lips

20 **thy reverence:** your revered self

CORDELIA
Had you not been their father, these white flakes[21]
Did challenge[22] pity of them. Was this a face
To be opposed against the warring winds?
To stand against the deep dread-bolted thunder,[23]
In the most terrible and nimble stroke
Of quick, cross-lightning?[24] To watch,[25] poor perdu,[26]
With this thin helm?[27] Mine enemy's dog,
Though he had bit me, should have stood that night
Against my fire; and wast thou fain,[28] poor father,
To hovel thee with swine, and rogues forlorn[29]
In short and musty straw?[30] Alack, alack!
'Tis wonder that thy life and wits at once
Had not concluded all. He wakes; speak to him.

DOCTOR
Madam, do you;[31] 'tis fittest.

CORDELIA
How does my royal Lord? How fares your Majesty?

LEAR
You do me wrong to take me out o' the grave.
Thou art a soul in bliss;[32] but I am bound
Upon a wheel of fire,[33] that mine own tears
Do scald like molten lead.

CORDELIA
Sir, do you know me?

LEAR
You are a spirit, I know. Where did you die?

CORDELIA
Still, still, far wide![34]

DOCTOR
He's scarce awake; let him alone awhile.

LEAR
Where have I been? Where am I? Fair daylight?
I am mightily abused.[35] I should e'en die with pity
To see another thus. I know not what to say.
I will not swear these are my hands: let's see –

---

21 **flakes:** hair
22 **challenge:** claim

23 **dread-bolted thunder:** thunder that sends dreaded lightning bolts
24 **cross-lightning:** forked lightning
25 **To watch:** To be on guard
26 **poor perdu:** 1 doomed sentry 2 lost soul
27 **thin helm:** covering i.e. his head
28 **wast thou fain:** were you glad
29 **rogues forlorn:** outcast vagrants
30 **short and musty straw:** thinly spread, old straw

31 **do you:** you should

32 **bliss:** ecstatic heavenly joy
33 **wheel of fire:** one of the punishments thought to await the damned according to medieval thought

34 **wide:** Lear's mind is wandering

35 **abused:** 1 mistreated 2 deluded

I feel this pinprick. Would I were assured
Of my condition!³⁶

³⁶ **Would...condition!:** If only I
could be certain about my state
of being

CORDELIA
          O, look upon me, sir,
60 And hold your hands in benediction³⁷ o'er me!
No, sir, you must not kneel.

³⁷ **benediction:** blessing

LEAR
          Pray, do not mock me.
I am a very foolish, fond old man,
Fourscore and upward,³⁸ not an hour more nor less;
And to deal plainly,³⁹
I fear I am not in my perfect mind.
Methinks I should know you, and know this man,
Yet I am doubtful, for I am mainly ignorant
What place this is and all the skill⁴⁰ I have
Remembers not these garments; nor I know not
70 Where I did lodge⁴¹ last night. Do not laugh at me,
For, as I am a man, I think this Lady
To be my child Cordelia.

³⁸ **Fourscore and upward:** over
eighty years of age
³⁹ **deal plainly:** be honest

⁴⁰ **skill:** knowledge

⁴¹ **lodge:** stay

CORDELIA
          And so I am, I am.

LEAR
Be your tears wet? Yes, faith. I pray, weep not.
If you have poison for me, I will drink it.
I know you do not love me; for your sisters
Have, as I do remember, done me wrong.
You have some cause,⁴² they have not.

⁴² **cause:** reason

CORDELIA
          No cause, no cause.

LEAR
Am I in France?

KENT
          In your own kingdom, sir.

LEAR
Do not abuse⁴³ me.

⁴³ **abuse:** 1 trick 2 mistreat

DOCTOR
Be comforted, good madam, the great rage,[44]
You see, is killed in him, and yet it is danger
To make him even o'er[45] the time he has lost.
Desire him to go in. Trouble him no more
Till further settling.[46]

CORDELIA
                    Will't please your Highness walk?

LEAR
You must bear with me. Pray you now, forget and forgive; I
am old and foolish.
[Exeunt all but KENT and GENTLEMAN]

GENTLEMAN
Holds it true, sir, that the Duke of Cornwall was so slain?

KENT
Most certain, sir.

GENTLEMAN
Who is conductor[47] of his people?

KENT
As 'tis said, the bastard son of Gloucester.

GENTLEMAN
They say Edgar, his banished son, is with the Earl of Kent
in Germany.

KENT
Report is changeable.[48] 'Tis time to look about. The powers
of the kingdom approach apace.[49]

GENTLEMAN
The arbitrement[50] is like to be bloody. Fare you well, sir.
[Exit]

KENT
My point and period will be throughly wrought,
Or well or ill, as this day's battle's fought.[51]
[Exit]

44 **rage**: madness

45 **even o'er**: smooth out i.e. fill in the gaps

46 **Till further settling**: until he settles down more

47 **conductor**: leader

48 **Report is changeable**: reports vary
49 **The powers…apace**: the kingdom's armies approach quickly

50 **arbitrement**: deciding battle

51 **My point…fought**: My life's final mark will be truly made, for good or bad, on this final battle

---
Key Quotations

CORDELIA	*O my dear father! Restoration hang* *Thy medicine on my lips, and let this kiss* *Repair those violent harms that my two sisters* *Have in thy reverence made!*
LEAR	*You do me wrong to take me out o' the grave.* *Thou art a soul in bliss; but I am bound* *Upon a wheel of fire, that mine own tears* *Do scald like molten lead.*
LEAR	*I am a very foolish, fond old man,* *Fourscore and upward, not an hour more nor less;* *And to deal plainly,* *I fear I am not in my perfect mind.*
LEAR	*your sisters / Have, as I do remember, done me wrong. / You have some cause,* *they have not.*
LEAR	*You must bear with me. Pray you now, forget and forgive; I am old and foolish.*

Commentary

- **This scene of great tenderness and love juxtaposes the suffering, violence and trauma of many of the preceding scenes.** The overarching sense of forgiveness and reconciliation offers the audience respite from the destruction that characterises so many of the scenes in this tragedy.

- In *King Lear's* opening scene Cordelia tells Lear, 'I cannot heave / My heart into my mouth.' As the fourth act ends, Cordelia remains true to her word. **Her love for her father is expressed succinctly, avoiding any use of empty rhetoric or flowery sentiment.** When Lear wonders if it is really Cordelia he sees, she answers simply: 'And so I am, I am.' Similarly, when Lear exclaims that she has cause to hate him, she expresses her forgiveness concisely ('No cause, no cause') to reflect the simple beauty of her love for her father.

- **Cordelia is the personification of goodness and compassion.** Her humility in asking for Lear's blessing and her capacity for forgiveness illustrate her innate goodness. When Lear first sees Cordelia he believes she is an angel ('Thou art a soul in bliss') who has come to him in death. Shakespeare stresses her saintly nature by presenting her in these heavenly terms. By presenting Cordelia as a figure of compassion with huge capacity for forgiveness Shakespeare again associates her with Christ.

- **Cordelia is a tender woman who acts as a balm to her father's mental distress.** She prays for Lear's health to be restored: 'O you kind gods, / Cure this great breach in his abused nature!' and whispers to him as he sleeps:

> 'O my dear father! Restoration hang
> Thy medicine on my lips, and let this kiss
> Repair those violent harms that my two sisters
> Have in thy reverence made!'

Her compassion for her father is in sharp relief to the inhuman cruelty Lear has experienced at the hands of Goneril and Regan.

- **Lear's humility illustrates how he has personally grown as he attains self-knowledge.** He acknowledges to Cordelia how he wronged her: 'I know you do not love me; for your sisters / Have, as I do remember, done me wrong. / You have some cause, they have not.' Lear feels tormented by what he has done. The image of the burning wheel illustrates this powerfully: 'I am bound / Upon a wheel of fire, that mine own tears / Do scald like molten lead.' His pride and arrogance have given way to guilt and admission of the wrongs he has committed.

- **Lear understands himself as an old man who has made terrible mistakes.** He humbly tells Cordelia:

> 'I am a very foolish, fond old man,
> Fourscore and upward, not an hour more nor less;
> And to deal plainly,
> I fear I am not in my perfect mind.'

Lear recognises that he is a confused old man, far from his prime. Again, at the end of the scene he tells Cordelia, 'You must bear with me. Pray you now, forget and forgive; I am old and foolish.' **Suffering has brought Lear to a point where he can now recognise his own flaws and mistakes.**

- Although confused for parts of this scene, **Lear's mental distress is subsiding.** He becomes increasingly in tune with reality: once he realises that Cordelia is not an angel he recognises her as his daughter. The Doctor's diagnosis that Lear's 'great rage' has ended appears to be correct.

Questions

1. How does Lear feel about the manner in which he treated Cordelia?
2. How does Cordelia treat her father in this scene?
3. What evidence is there that Lear's madness is subsiding?
4. What lessons do you think Lear has learnt about himself by this point of the play?
5. In what ways has Lear's manner changed from opening scene of *King Lear*?

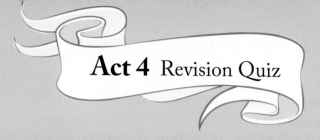

Act 4 Revision Quiz

1. At the start of Act 4, Gloucester plans to take his own life. How does he intend to do this?
2. Act 4 shows the growing rivalry and tension between Goneril and Regan. What are they competing with each other for?
3. How does Cordelia react to the news of Lear's suffering?
4. Cordelia says that she is not going to war for ambition. What is her motivation?
5. How does Edgar trick his father into believing that he has been saved by the gods?
6. Who kills Oswald?
7. When Lear is reunited with Cordelia, how does he behave?
   (a) *He scolds her for leaving him with Goneril and Regan*
   (b) *He asks her to prove that she loves him*
   (c) *He pretends he does not know her*
   (d) *He begs her forgiveness*
8. Who now commands Cornwall's army?
9. Who says each of the following?
   (a) *World, world, O world!*
   But that thy strange mutations make us hate thee,
   Life would not yield to age.
   (b) *Let the superfluous and lust-dieted man*
   That slaves your ordinance, that will not see
   Because he doth not feel, feel your power quickly;
   So distribution should undo excess,
   And each man have enough.
   (c) *O Goneril!*
   You are not worth the dust which the rude wind
   Blows in your face
   (d) *They flattered me like a dog and told me I had white hairs in my beard ere the black ones were there. To say 'ay' and 'no' to everything that I said 'ay' and 'no' to was no good divinity*
   (e) *I am bound*
   Upon a wheel of fire, that mine own tears
   Do scald like molten lead
10. Rewrite these quotations. In each case, write the speaker's name and fill in the blanks.
    (a) *The lamentable _____ is from the best,*
    The worst returns to _____
    (b) *I have no way, and therefore want no eyes:*
    I _____ when I saw
    (c) *As _____ to wanton boys, are we to the gods.*
    They kill us for their _____
    (d) *No blown _____ doth our arms incite,*
    But love, dear love, and our aged father's _____
    (e) *When we are born, we _____ that we are come*
    To this great stage of _____

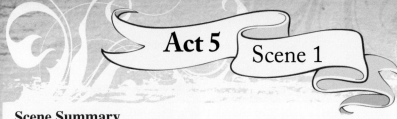

Act 5 Scene 1

Scene Summary

- The scene begins with Edmund wondering if Albany intends to send soldiers to war.
- Regan jealously questions Edmund about Goneril.
- Albany brings news that Lear and other rebels have joined forces with the French army.
- Goneril suspects Regan wants to keep her from Edmund.
- Edgar (disguised as a peasant) gives Albany the letter Goneril wrote to Edmund. Edgar says that if Albany wins the battle he should sound a trumpet and Edgar will produce a champion who will confirm the contents of the letter.
- Edmund, in soliloquy, wonders which sister (Goneril or Regan) he should remain romantically attached to. He also reveals to the audience his intention to have Lear and Cordelia murdered after the battle.

The British Camp, near Dover.
Enter, with drum and colours, EDMUND, REGAN, Officers,
Gentlemen and Soldiers

EDMUND
[*To an Officer*] Know of the Duke if his last purpose hold,[1]
Or whether since he is advised by aught[2]
To change the course. He's full of alteration
And self-reproving.[3] Bring his constant pleasure.[4]

[*Officer goes out*]

REGAN
Our sister's man is certainly miscarried.[5]

EDMUND
'Tis to be doubted,[6] madam.

REGAN
                    Now, sweet Lord,
You know the goodness I intend upon you;
Tell me, but truly, but then speak the truth,
Do you not love my sister?

EDMUND
                    In honoured[7] love.

REGAN
But have you never found my brother's[8] way

---

[1] **if his last...hold:** if he sticks to his most recent intention (to fight)
[2] **aught:** anything
[3] **He's full...self-reproving:** He's always changing his mind and reproaching himself
[4] **Bring...pleasure:** Bring me news of his final decision

[5] **miscarried:** come to harm / been killed. Regan is referring to Oswald

[6] **doubted:** feared

[7] **honoured:** honourable

[8] **brother's:** brother-in-law's i.e. Albany's

163

To the forfended place?[9]

EDMUND
                       That thought abuses[10] you.

REGAN
I am doubtful that you have been conjunct
And bosomed with her, as far as we call hers.[11]

ironic

EDMUND
No, by mine honour, madam.

REGAN
I never shall endure her. Dear my Lord,
Be not familiar[12] with her.

EDMUND
                         Fear me not.[13]
She and the Duke her husband – [14]

                 [Enter, with drum and colours,
ALBANY, GONERIL and Soldiers]

GONERIL
[Aside] I had rather lose the battle than that sister
Should loosen[15] him and me.

ALBANY
20 Our very loving sister, well be-met.
Sir, this I hear: the King is come to his daughter,
With others whom the rigours of our state
Forced to cry out.[16] Where I could not be honest,
I never yet was valiant.[17] For this business,
It touches us as France invades our land,
Not bolds the King, with others whom I fear
Most just and heavy causes make oppose.[18]

EDMUND
Sir, you speak nobly.

REGAN
                     Why is this reasoned?[19]

GONERIL
Combine together[20] 'gainst the enemy,
30 For these domestic and particular broils[21]
Are not the question here.

---

[9] **forfended place:** forbidden place i.e. Goneril's bed or body

[10] **abuses:** dishonours

[11] **I am doubtful...call hers:** I am suspicious that you have been intimate with her, and been 'hers' in every sense of the word

[12] **familiar:** intimate

[13] **Fear me not:** Don't have concerns about me
[14] **She and...husband:** It seems likely that Edmund breaks off here as he may see Albany and Goneril approaching

[15] **loosen:** come between

[16] **the rigours...cry out:** the strict government of our state forced into opposition
[17] **Where I could...valiant:** I was never able to valiantly (bravely) go into battle for a cause that I didn't feel was honest
[18] **It touches us...oppose:** It concerns me that the King of France has invaded our land. However, the invasion doesn't encourage Lear to oppose us; he and others have just and serious reasons for that
[19] **Why is this reasoned?:** Why are you giving us these reasons?

[20] **Combine together:** Join forces
[21] **domestic and particular broils:** national and personal disagreements

ALBANY
                    Let's then determine
With th' ancient of war²² on our proceedings.

EDMUND
I shall attend you presently at your tent.

REGAN
Sister, you'll go with us?

GONERIL
No.

REGAN
'Tis most convenient. Pray you, go with us.

GONERIL
[Aside] O, ho! I know the riddle.²³ *[Aloud]* I will go.
[As they are going out, enter EDGAR disguised]

²³ **riddle:** hidden intention

EDGAR
If e'er your Grace had speech with man so poor,
Hear me one word.

ALBANY
I'll overtake you.
[Exeunt all but ALBANY and EDGAR]
                    Speak.

EDGAR
Before you fight the battle, ope²⁴ this letter.²⁵
If you have victory, let the trumpet sound
For him that brought it; wretched though I seem,
I can produce a champion²⁶ that will prove
What is avouched²⁷ there. If you miscarry,²⁸
Your business of the world hath so an end,
And machination²⁹ ceases. Fortune love you!

²⁴ **ope:** open
²⁵ **letter:** i.e. the letter from Goneril to
Edmund that Edgar took from Oswald's
pocket
²⁶ **champion:** warrior that fights for a
particular cause or individual
²⁷ **avouched:** affirmed / written
²⁸ **miscarry:** lose
²⁹ **machination:** plots and intrigues

ALBANY
Stay till I have read the letter.

EDGAR
                    I was forbid it.
When time shall serve, let but the herald cry,
And I'll appear again.

ALBANY

         Why, fare thee well.
I will o'erlook thy paper.

[Exit EDGAR]
[Re-enter EDMUND]

EDMUND

The enemy's in view; draw up your powers.[30]
Here is the guess of their true strength and forces
By diligent discovery;[31] but your haste
Is now urged on you.

ALBANY

         We will greet the time.[32]

[Exit]

EDMUND

To both these sisters have I sworn my love;
Each jealous of the other, as the stung
Are of the adder.[33] Which of them shall I take?
60 Both? One? Or neither? Neither can be enjoyed,
If both remain alive. To take the widow
Exasperates, makes mad her sister Goneril;
And hardly shall I carry out my side,[34]
Her husband being alive. Now then we'll use
His countenance[35] for the battle, which being done,
Let her who would be rid of him devise
His speedy taking off.[36] As for the mercy
Which he intends to Lear and to Cordelia,
The battle done,[37] and they within our power,
70 Shall never see his pardon; for my state
Stands on me to defend, not to debate.[38]

[Exit]

---

[30] **draw up your powers:** prepare your forces
[31] **discovery:** reconnaissance
[32] **We will...time:** 1 We will be ready when the time is ripe 2 We will be prepared to do what the time requires
[33] **adder:** a type of snake
[34] **carry...side:** fulfil my side of the bargain (to satisfy Goneril's desire in return for power)
[35] **countenance:** authority
[36] **taking off:** death
[37] **the battle done:** after the battle is over
[38] **for my state...debate:** my position requires me to act rather than talk

---

Commentary

- **This scene builds towards the climactic battle between the forces of good and evil and underscores the factious alliance that exists between Lear's enemies.**

- Edmund wonders about Albany's commitment to go to war, seeing him as 'full of alteration / And self-reproving.' **Albany does indeed have mixed feelings about the battle.** On the one hand his sympathies lie with Lear and Cordelia whom he sees as having 'just and heavy' reasons for going to war. However, he also feels compelled to defend the kingdom against a French invasion. Ultimately, Albany decides to go to war. His motivation however sets him apart from the self-serving characters: Edmund, Goneril and Regan.

- **The audience anticipates that Goneril's treachery will be revealed to her husband** as Edgar gives Albany the letter Goneril wrote to Edmund. In this letter Goneril asks Edmund to kill Albany and take his place by her side.

- **The tension between Goneril and Regan illustrates how factious the alliance between Lear's enemies is.** Both sisters lust for Edmund and express their determination not to let the other have him. Regan is suspicious that Edmund may have been intimate with Goneril, while Goneril reveals her possessive feelings for Edmund in her asides.

- **Edmund's soliloquy reinforces the audience's image of him as a callous, exploitative character.** He coldly calculates whether Goneril or Regan best serves his thirst for power, knowing that 'Neither can be enjoyed, / If both remain alive.' Callously he takes delight in playing one off the other: 'To both these sisters have I sworn my love; / Each jealous of the other, as the stung / Are of the adder.'

- **Edmund's soliloquy also illustrates his ruthlessness.** He intends to use Albany's authority to spearhead the battle against the French but realises that he would be well served if Albany was to be killed after the battle. Edmund would prefer to see this done by Goneril:

> 'we'll use
> His countenance for the battle, which being done,
> Let her who would be rid of him devise
> His speedy taking off.'

With ruthless pragmatism Edmund also makes plans to kill Lear and Cordelia. Potentially they may pose a threat to his power, Edmund therefore decides to execute them and eliminate any opposition: 'for my state / Stands on me to defend, not to debate.' It is interesting that Edmund avoids directly committing acts of violence himself: he would rather that Goneril kill Albany, he sends a soldier to kill Cordelia, and, in Act 3, Scene 7, he leaves when Gloucester is to be tortured. Edmund tries to maintain an innocent appearance while controlling events behind the scenes.

Questions

1. What is Edmund's attitude to Albany in this scene?
2. Do you agree, that in this scene, Goneril and Regan are more concerned with their personal lives than the political situation? Explain your answer.
3. How does Albany feel about the battle ahead?
4. What does Edmund's soliloquy at the end of the scene reveal about his character?

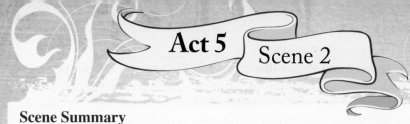
Scene Summary
- Edgar helps Gloucester to a place under a tree where he can rest.
- Edgar leaves and then returns with the news that the armies loyal to Lear have lost the battle. He tells Gloucester that Lear and Cordelia have been captured.
- Edgar urges Gloucester to hurry away with him. Gloucester says he wants to stay where he is but Edgar convinces him to leave.

A Field between the Two Camps.
Alarum within. Enter, with drum and colours, LEAR,
CORDELIA and Soldiers, over the stage; and exeunt

Enter EDGAR and GLOUCESTER

EDGAR
Here, father,[1] take the shadow of this tree
For your good host.[2] Pray that the right may thrive.
If ever I return to you again,
I'll bring you comfort.[3]

ironic

GLOUCESTER
            Grace go with you, sir!

[Exit EDGAR]
[Alarum and retreat[4] within. Re-enter EDGAR]

EDGAR
Away, old man! Give me thy hand; away!
King Lear hath lost, he and his daughter ta'en.[5]
Give me thy hand; come on.

GLOUCESTER
No farther, sir; a man may rot even here.

EDGAR
What, in ill thoughts again? Men must endure
10 Their going hence, even as their coming hither;[6]
Ripeness is all.[7] Come on.

GLOUCESTER
            And that's true too.

[Exeunt]

---

1 **father:** old man. Edgar has not yet revealed his true identity to Gloucester
2 **host:** shelter

3 **comfort:** comforting news

4 **Alarum and retreat:** Trumpet to start the battle begins and then signals that French forces are retreating

5 **ta'en:** taken / captured

6 **Men must...hither:** People must endure the suffering of death, just as much as they suffer the pain of being born
7 **Ripeness is all:** 1 Waiting for the right time (which is beyond our control) is all that matters 2 Being ready (in terms of maturity) for death is all that matters

Key Quotations

EDGAR   *Men must endure / Their going hence, even as their coming hither; / Ripeness is all.*

Commentary

- **This scene succinctly tells the audience that Cordelia's French army have lost the battle.** This is signalled by the 'Alarum and retreat' and Edgar's dire news that 'King Lear hath lost, he and his daughter ta'en.'
- **The terrible news prompts Gloucester to despair.** He tells Edgar that he has no desire to continue travelling and wishes to be left to die: 'No farther, sir; a man may rot even here.' However, Gloucester's metaphorical journey towards wisdom is not yet complete. Edgar successively gets Gloucester to continue by pointing out that to be human is to suffer and that we must wait until it is our time to die ('Ripeness is all').
- **Edgar remains resilient as he understands that the ups and downs of life are beyond human control; one must simply endure.** Being ready for death is what matters: 'Men must endure/ Their going hence, even as their coming hither; / Ripeness is all.' The final pithy phrase, 'Ripeness is all', stresses how important it is to wait until it is the right time to die.

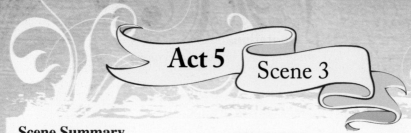

Act 5 — Scene 3

Scene Summary

- After being captured, Lear and Cordelia are imprisoned by Edmund.
- Lear tells Cordelia that together they can endure their imprisonment.
- Secretly, Edmund sends a captain to the prison to kill Lear and Cordelia.
- Albany demands to take charge of Lear and Cordelia. He asserts his superior rank over Edmund.
- Regan defends Edmund. Goneril does likewise.
- Goneril and Regan argue jealously over Edmund.
- Regan starts to feel sick because she has been poisoned by Goneril.
- Albany accuses Edmund of treason.
- Because she is ill, Regan is taken to Albany's tent.
- As per Edgar's previous instructions, Albany sounds a trumpet three times and calls for a champion to challenge Edmund. Edgar (in disguise) answers the call.
- Edgar and Edmund fight. Edgar mortally wounds Edmund.
- Albany produces Goneril's letter to Edmund which proves her treachery.
- Goneril storms off.
- Edgar reveals his identity and explains how he cared for Gloucester. Edmund says he is moved by his story.
- A gentleman arrives with the news that Goneril has killed herself with a knife, and that Regan is dead after being poisoned by Goneril.
- Edmund tries to stop the deaths of Lear and Cordelia which he ordered. Edmund is taken away.
- Lear arrives with Cordelia's lifeless body in his arms.
- Lear recognises Kent.
- Edmund dies offstage as a result of the wounds he received in his fight with Edgar.
- Albany says that all friends will be duly rewarded, all enemies punished.
- As Lear mourns for Cordelia, he dies.
- Kent says he will follow his master into the afterlife.

The British Camp near Dover.
Enter, in conquest, with drum and colours, EDMUND;
LEAR and CORDELIA, as prisoners; CAPTAIN and
Soldiers.

EDMUND
Some officers take them away – good guard,[1]
Until their greater pleasures first be known
That are to censure them.[2]

---

[1] **good guard:** guard them well

[2] **Until...censure them:** until we know the wishes of those in charge whose job it is to judge them

CORDELIA

               We are not the first
Who, with best meaning, have incurred the worst.[3]
For thee, oppressed King, am I cast down;[4]
Myself could else outfrown false Fortune's frown.[5]
Shall we not see these daughters and these sisters?

LEAR

No, no, no, no! Come, let's away to prison;
We two alone will sing like birds i' the cage.
When thou dost ask me blessing I'll kneel down,
And ask of thee forgiveness. So we'll live
And pray, and sing, and tell old tales, and laugh
At gilded butterflies,[6] and hear poor rogues
Talk of court news;[7] and we'll talk with them too,
Who loses and who wins, who's in, who's out;[8]
And take upon's the mystery of things,
As if we were gods' spies.[9] And we'll wear out
In a walled prison, packs and sects of great ones
That ebb and flow by the moon.[10]

EDMUND

                      Take them away.

LEAR

Upon such sacrifices,[11] my Cordelia,
The gods themselves throw incense. Have I caught thee?[12]
He that parts us shall bring a brand from heaven,
And fire us hence like foxes.[13] Wipe thine eyes;
The good years[14] shall devour them, flesh and fell,[15]
Ere they shall make us weep, we'll see 'em starve first.
Come.
[Exeunt LEAR and CORDELIA, guarded]

EDMUND

Come hither, Captain; hark.
Take thou this note. Go follow them to prison.
One step I have advanced[16] thee. If thou dost
As this instructs thee, thou dost make thy way
To noble fortunes.[17] Know thou this, that men
Are as the time is;[18] to be tender-minded
Does not become a sword.[19] Thy great employment
Will not bear question:[20] either say thou'lt do't,
Or thrive[21] by other means.

CAPTAIN

                   I'll do't, my Lord.

---

3 **with best...worst:** with the best intentions have suffered the worst

4 **cast down:** 1 dispirited 2 cast down by Fortune

5 **Myself...frown:** if I was by myself I could defy the untrustworthy nature of Fortune

6 **gilded butterflies:** fashionable courtiers

7 **court news:** news / gossip from the court

8 **who's in, who's out:** who is in or out of the King's favour

9 **gods' spies:** 1 God's spies 2 the spies of the gods. (The original texts include a capital letter for 'Gods' but no apostrophe. Lear later refers to 'gods' plural)

10 **And we'll...by the moon:** we'll last longer in our secured prison than the cliques ('packs') and factions ('sects') of those in power, whose fortunes change with the cycles of the moon

11 **such sacrifices:** 1 i.e. their renunciation of the world 2 i.e Cordelia's sacrifice in her attempts to help Lear

12 **caught thee:** 1 made you cry 2 reunited with you

13 **He that parts...foxes:** whoever splits us apart will need the fire of heaven to do so, just like foxes are smoked out of their burrows i.e. only the power of heaven can divide us now

14 **good years:** 1 'goodyear' = evil spirit 2 as long as Cordelia is with Lear she will experience 'good years'

15 **flesh and fell:** flesh and skin i.e. entirely

16 **advanced:** promoted

17 **noble fortunes:** great wealth

18 **men/Are...time is:** men's conduct is determined by the time in which they live

19 **to be...sword:** to be merciful is inappropriate for a man that carries a sword

20 **Thy great...question:** Your great task will not allow for debate or discussion

21 **thrive:** prosper

EDMUND
About it,[22] and write happy[23] when thou hast done.
Mark, I say, instantly; and carry it[24] so
As I have set it down.

CAPTAIN
I cannot draw a cart, nor eat dried oats.
40 If it be man's work, I'll do't.
[Exit]

[Flourish. Enter ALBANY, GONERIL, REGAN, another
CAPTAIN and Soldiers]

ALBANY
Sir, you have shown today your valiant strain,[25]
And Fortune led you well. You have the captives
That were the opposites[26] of this day's strife:
I do require them of you, so to use them
As we shall find their merits and our safety
May equally determine.[27]

EDMUND
                              Sir, I thought it fit
To send the old and miserable King
To some retention[28] and appointed guard,
Whose age has charms in it, whose title more,
50 To pluck the common bosom on his side,[29]
And turn our impressed lances[30] in our eyes
Which do command them. With him I sent the Queen,
My reason all the same; and they are ready
Tomorrow, or at further space, t' appear
Where you shall hold your session.[31] At this time
We sweat and bleed; the friend hath lost his friend
And the best quarrels, in the heat are cursed
By those that feel their sharpness.[32]
The question of Cordelia and her father
60 Requires a fitter place.

ALBANY
                              Sir, by your patience,
I hold you but a subject of this war,
Not as a brother.[33]

REGAN
                              That's as we list[34] to grace him.
Methinks our pleasure might have been demanded
Ere you had spoke so far.[35] He led our powers,

22	**About it:** be quick about it
23	**write happy:** call yourself a happy man (because of the reward Edmund has promised)
24	**carry it:** carry it out
25	**strain:** breeding / nature
26	**opposites:** opponents
27	**I do require...determine:** I need to take them from you, so that they can be treated in the way they deserve but which also ensures our safety
28	**retention:** place of detention
29	**Whose age...his side:** whose (Lear's) age may encourage sympathy as would his title, and may win the hearts of ordinary people
30	**impressed lances:** conscripted soldiers who carry lances
31	**session:** trial
32	**the best quarrels...sharpness:** the best causes are cursed by the passion of those who still feel the pain of battle
33	**Sir...brother:** Sir, if you don't mind me saying so, I think of you as subordinate in this war, not as an equal (or perhaps 'brother-in-law')
34	**we list:** I choose. Regan uses the royal 'we'
35	**Methinks...so far:** I think you could have asked me what I thought before you said so much

Bore the commission of my place and person;[36]
The which immediacy may well stand up
And call itself your brother.

GONERIL

             Not so hot![37]
In his own grace he doth exalt himself
More than in your addition.[38]

REGAN

             In my rights,
By me invested, he compeers the best.[39]

GONERIL

That were the most, if he should husband you.[40]

REGAN

Jesters do oft prove prophets.[41]

GONERIL

             Holla, holla!
That eye that told you so looked but asquint.[42]

REGAN

Lady, I am not well,[43] else I should answer
From a full-flowing stomach.[44] *[To EDMUND]* General,
Take thou my soldiers, prisoners, patrimony;[45]
Dispose of them, of me; the walls are thine.[46]
Witness the world, that I create thee here
My Lord and master.

GONERIL

             Mean you to enjoy him?[47]

ALBANY

The let-alone lies not in your good will.[48]

EDMUND

Nor in thine, Lord.

ALBANY

             Half-blooded fellow,[49] yes.

REGAN

[To EDMUND] Let the drum strike, and prove my title
thine.[50]

---

36   **Bore...person:** carried the authority of my rank and acted on my behalf

37   **Not so hot!:** not so fast!
38   **In his own...addition:** Edmund has proven himself in his own right, more so than by any power you have conferred on him

39   **In my rights...best:** by royal right he has been given power which makes him equal to the best man
40   **That were...you:** he would outrank anybody if he were to marry you. Some versions of the play give this line to Albany
41   **Jesters...prophets:** statements made in jest often turn out to be true

42   **That eye...asquint:** proverbial i.e. jealousy has stopped you seeing straight

43   **Lady, I am not well:** Regan is suffering the effects of poison given to her by Goneril
44   **full-flowing stomach:** with angry words
45   **patrimony:** her inheritance
46   **the walls are thine:** Regan imagines herself as a castle overcome by a storm. She is giving herself and her wealth to Edmund
47   **Mean you...him?:** Do you intend to take him as your lover?

48   **The let-alone...will:** You do not have the power to prevent it

49   **Half-blooded fellow:** Bastard

50   **Let the drum...thine:** Let the battle drum start up, and prove that my title is yours. Regan is asking Edmund to fight Albany

ALBANY
Stay yet, hear reason. Edmund, I arrest thee
On capital treason, and in thine attaint,[51]
This gilded serpent[52] *[Pointing to GONERIL]*
[To REGAN]   For your claim, fair sister,
I bar it in the interest of my wife:
'Tis she is sub-contracted[53] to this Lord,
And I her husband contradict your banns.[54]
If you will marry, make your loves to me;
90 My lady is bespoke.[55]

GONERIL
                    An interlude![56]

ALBANY
Thou art armed, Gloucester. Let the trumpet sound.
If none appear to prove upon thy person
Thy heinous,[57] manifest[58] and many treasons,
There is my pledge[59] *[Throws down his glove]*
                    I'll make it on thy heart,
Ere I taste bread, thou art in nothing less
Than I have here proclaimed thee.[60]

REGAN
                    Sick, O, sick!

GONERIL
[Aside] If not, I'll ne'er trust medicine.[61]

EDMUND
There's my exchange.[62] *[Throws down a glove]*
                    What[63] in the world he is
That names me traitor, villain-like he lies.
100 Call by thy trumpet. He that dares approach,
On him, on you – who not? – I will maintain
My truth and honour firmly.

ALBANY
                    A herald, ho!

[Enter a Herald]

Trust to thy single virtue, for thy soldiers,
All levied in my name, have in my name
Took their discharge.[64]

REGAN
My sickness grows upon me.

51 **attaint:** impeachment
52 **gilded serpent:** beautified snake

53 **sub-contracted:** already engaged
54 **banns:** public announcement of a proposed marriage

55 **bespoke:** spoken for (already engaged to Edmund)

56 **interlude:** farce. An interlude was a comic moment in a long play

57 **heinous:** hateful
58 **manifest:** readily apparent / obvious
59 **pledge:** token (symbol of his challenge to fight)
60 **I'll make it...thee:** I'll pierce your heart before I eat bread, to prove that you are nothing less than what I have called you

61 **medicine:** drugs

62 **exchange:** answer to Albany's challenge
63 **What:** Whoever

64 **Trust to thy...discharge:** we will have to trust your unaided strength because your soldiers, who were recruited in my name, have been discharged by my order

ALBANY
She is not well; convey her to my tent.

[Exit REGAN, supported]

Come hither, herald. Let the trumpet sound,
And read out this.

[A trumpet sounds]

HERALD
[Reads] 'If any man of quality or degree within the lists of
the army will maintain upon[65] Edmund, supposed Earl of
Gloucester, that he is a manifold[66] traitor, let him appear by
the third sound of the trumpet. He is bold in his defence.'

[First trumpet sounds]

HERALD
Again!

[Second trumpet]

HERALD
Again!

[Third trumpet]
[Trumpet answers within]
[Enter EDGAR,[67] armed]

ALBANY
Ask him his purposes, why he appears
Upon this call o' the trumpet.

HERALD
                    What are you?
Your name, your quality,[68] and why you answer
This present summons?

EDGAR
                  Know, my name is lost,
By treason's tooth bare-gnawn and canker-bit;[69]
Yet am I noble as the adversary
I come to cope.[70]

ALBANY
                  Which is that adversary?

---

65 **maintain upon:** accuse
66 **manifold:** in many ways

67 **EDGAR:** Although it isn't stated, Edgar is wearing yet another disguise

68 **quality:** noble rank

69 **Know...canker-bit:** Know this: my noble title has been destroyed by treason, as if eaten away by caterpillars
70 **cope:** encounter in combat

EDGAR
What's he that speaks for Edmund, Earl of Gloucester?

EDMUND
Himself. What say'st thou to him?

EDGAR
                    Draw thy sword,
That, if my speech offend a noble heart,
Thy arm may do thee justice. Here is mine. *[Draws his sword]*
Behold, it is the privilege of mine honours,
My oath, and my profession.[71] I protest,
Maugre[72] thy strength, youth, place and eminence,
130 Despite thy victor[73] sword and fire-new[74] fortune,
Thy valour and thy heart,[75] thou art a traitor,
False to thy gods, thy brother, and thy father;
Conspirant[76] 'gainst this high-illustrious prince;
And, from the extremest upward[77] of thy head
To the descent and dust below thy foot,
A most toad-spotted[78] traitor. Say thou 'No',
This sword, this arm, and my best spirits are bent[79]
To prove upon thy heart, whereto I speak,
Thou liest.

EDMUND
          In wisdom I should ask thy name;
140 But, since thy outside looks so fair and warlike,
And that thy tongue some say of breeding breathes,[80]
What safe and nicely[81] I might well delay
By rule of knighthood, I disdain and spurn.
Back do I toss these treasons to thy head;
With the hell-hated[82] lie o'erwhelm thy heart;
Which, for they yet glance by and scarcely bruise,[83]
This sword of mine shall give them instant way,[84]
Where they shall rest for ever. Trumpets, speak!
[Alarums. They fight. EDMUND falls]

ALBANY
[To EDGAR] Save him, save him![85]

GONERIL
150 This is mere practice,[86] Gloucester.
By the law of arms thou wast not bound to answer
An unknown opposite. Thou art not vanquished,
But cozened and beguiled.[87]

71 **the privilege...profession:** the right of my nobility ('honours'), the oath I took when I became a knight and my status as a knight ('profession')
72 **Maugre:** in spite of
73 **victor:** victorious
74 **fire-new:** brand new
75 **heart:** courage
76 **Conspirant:** conspirator
77 **extremest upward:** very top
78 **toad-spotted:** i.e. spotted with treason, just like a toad is spotted with poison
79 **bent:** determined

80 **thy tongue...breathes:** your speech shows some proof ('say') of nobility ('breeding')
81 **safe and nicely:** strictly according to the rules. Edmund is not obliged to fight a man of lower rank and Edgar's nobility has not been strictly proven
82 **hell-hated:** hated as much as hell
83 **they yet glance...bruise:** because they fail to hurt me properly and barely bruise
84 **instant way:** immediate passage (back to Edgar)
85 **save him:** Probably a call for Edgar to spare Edmund's life so that he can be questioned. Some critics see it as a call to save a threatened Edgar
86 **practice:** trickery
87 **Thou art...beguiled:** You are not beaten, but cheated and deceived

ALBANY

                      Shut your mouth, dame,
Or with this paper[88] shall I stop it! *[To EDGAR]* Hold, sir:
[To EDMUND] Thou worse than any name, read thine own evil.
[To GONERIL] No tearing, Lady; I perceive you know it.

GONERIL

Say, if I do, the laws are mine, not thine.[89]
Who can arraign[90] me for't?

ALBANY

                      Most monstrous! O!
[To EDMUND] Know'st thou this paper?

GONERIL

60 Ask me not what I know.

[Exit GONERIL]

ALBANY

[To an Officer] Go after her. She's desperate; govern her.[91]

[Exit Officer]

EDMUND

What you have charged me with, that have I done,
And more, much more; the time will bring it out.
'Tis past, and so am I. *[To EDGAR]* But what art thou
That hast this fortune on me?[92] If thou'rt noble,
I do forgive thee.

EDGAR

                    Let's exchange charity.
I am no less in blood than thou art, Edmund;
If more, the more thou hast wronged me.
My name is Edgar, and thy father's son.
70 The gods are just and of our pleasant vices[93]
Make instruments to plague us:[94]
The dark and vicious place[95] where thee he got[96]
Cost him his eyes.

EDMUND

                    Thou hast spoken right, 'tis true;
The wheel[97] is come full circle; I am here.

ALBANY

[To EDGAR] Methought thy very gait[98] did prophesy
A royal nobleness. I must embrace thee.
Let sorrow split my heart if ever I
Did hate thee or thy father.

---

88 **paper:** letter from Goneril to Edmund that Edgar found upon Oswald

89 **the laws...thine:** Goneril asserts that she is above the law as she is Queen
90 **arraign:** charge in court

91 **She's desperate...her:** She is in a state of despair; control her

92 **hast this fortune on me:** has been victorious over me. Edmund could also be suggesting that luck ('fortune') was on Edgar's side

93 **pleasant vices:** pleasurable sins
94 **Make instruments...us:** create ways of punishing us
95 **dark and vicious place:** i.e. the bed where Edmund was conceived
96 **got:** begot / fathered

97 **wheel:** the wheel of Fortune, which raised Edmund's position only to bring him low again

98 **gait:** walk

EDGAR

          Worthy Prince, I know't.

ALBANY

Where have you hid yourself?
180 How have you known the miseries of your father?

EDGAR

By nursing them, my Lord. List[99] a brief tale;
And when 'tis told, O, that my heart would burst!
The bloody proclamation to escape
That followed me so near[100] – O, our lives' sweetness,
That we the pain of death would hourly die
Rather than die at once![101] – taught me to shift[102]
Into a madman's rags, t'assume a semblance[103]
That very dogs disdained; and in this habit[104]
Met I my father with his bleeding rings,[105]
190 Their precious stones new lost; became his guide,
Led him, begged for him, saved him from despair,
Never – O fault! – revealed myself unto him
Until some half-hour past, when I was armed,
Not sure, though hoping of this good success,
I asked his blessing, and from first to last
Told him my pilgrimage.[106] But his flawed heart,
Alack, too weak the conflict[107] to support,
'Twixt two extremes of passion, joy and grief,
Burst smilingly.

EDMUND

          This speech of yours hath moved me,
200 And shall perchance do good; but speak you on;
You look as you had something more to say.

ALBANY

If there be more, more woeful, hold it in,
For I am almost ready to dissolve[108]
Hearing of this.

EDGAR

          This would have seemed a period[109]
To such as love not sorrow, but another
To amplify too much, would make much more,
And top extremity.[110]
Whilst I was big in clamour[111] came there in a man
Who, having seen me in my worst estate,[112]
210 Shunned my abhorred society,[113] but then, finding
Who 'twas that so endured, with his strong arms

---

99 **List:** Listen to

100 **The bloody...so near:** I was
   compelled to escape he that
   threatened my life so imminently
101 **That we...at once!:** that we would
   rather suffer the pain of death
   every hour rather than die once
102 **shift:** change
103 **semblance:** appearance
104 **habit:** outfit
105 **bleeding rings:** bleeding eye-
   sockets, like rings without jewels

106 **from first...pilgrimage:** from start
   to finish told him about my journey
107 **conflict:** i.e. conflict between his
   joy of finding Edgar and his pain
   upon hearing about Edgar's
   suffering

108 **dissolve:** melt

109 **period:** limit / highest point
110 **This would...extremity:** This story
   would appear to be the limit for
   someone that does not love sad
   tales; another sorrowful story would
   increase the sense of sadness too
   much and go beyond what could
   be tolerated
111 **big in clamour:** crying loudly in
   grief
112 **estate:** condition
113 **abhorred society:** hateful
   company

He fastened on my neck,[114] and bellowed out
As he'd burst heaven, threw him[115] on my father;
Told the most piteous tale of Lear and him
That ever ear received, which in recounting
His grief grew puissant[116] and the strings of life[117]
Began to crack. Twice then the trumpets sounded
And there I left him tranced.[118]

ALBANY
                    But who was this?

EDGAR
Kent, sir, the banished Kent, who in disguise
20 Followed his enemy[119] king and did him service
Improper for a slave.

[Enter a Gentleman, with a bloody knife]

GENTLEMAN
Help, help, O, help!

EDGAR
                    What kind of help?

ALBANY
                              Speak, man.

EDGAR
What means that bloody knife?

GENTLEMAN
                              'Tis hot, it smokes,[120]
It came even from the heart of – O, she's dead!

ALBANY
Who dead? Speak, man.

GENTLEMAN
Your Lady, sir, your Lady; and her sister
By her is poisoned; she confesses it.

EDMUND
I was contracted[121] to them both. All three
Now marry in an instant.[122]

EDGAR
30 Here comes Kent.
    [Enter KENT]

---

[114] **fastened on my neck:** hugged me round the neck
[115] **him:** himself

[116] **puissant:** powerful
[117] **strings of life:** heartstrings
[118] **tranced:** stupefied in grief

[119] **enemy:** hostile

[120] **smokes:** steams

[121] **contracted:** engaged
[122] **All three…instant:** All three of us will be united soon. There is wordplay on 'marry'

ALBANY
Produce their bodies, be they alive or dead.

[Exit Gentleman]

This judgement of the heavens, that makes us tremble
Touches us not with pity. *[To KENT]* O, is this he?
The time will not allow the compliment
Which very manners urges.[123]

KENT
                          I am come
To bid my King and master aye[124] good night.
Is he not here?

ALBANY
                     Great thing of us forgot!
Speak, Edmund, where's the King? And where's Cordelia?

[The bodies of GONERIL and REGAN are brought in]

See'st thou this object,[125] Kent?

KENT
240 Alack, why thus?

EDMUND
                     Yet Edmund was beloved:
The one the other poisoned for my sake,
And after slew[126] herself.

ALBANY
                     Even so. Cover their faces.

EDMUND
I pant for life. Some good I mean to do,
Despite of mine own nature. Quickly send –
Be brief in it – to the castle; for my writ[127]
Is on the life of Lear and on Cordelia;
Nay, send in time.

ALBANY
                     Run, run, O, run!

EDGAR
To who, my Lord? Who hath the office?[128]
Send thy token of reprieve.

[123] **The time...urges:** The time will not allow the ceremony that good manners requires of us

[124] **aye:** for ever

[125] **object:** spectacle

[126] **slew:** killed

[127] **writ:** order of execution

[128] **office:** authority

EDMUND

Well thought on. *[To Officer]* Take my sword,
Give it the captain.

EDGAR

         Haste thee, for thy life.

[Exit Officer]

EDMUND

He hath commission from thy wife and me
To hang Cordelia in the prison and
To lay the blame upon her own despair,
That she fordid herself.[129]

	[129] **fordid herself:** i.e. took her own life

ALBANY

The gods defend her! Bear him hence awhile.

[EDMUND is borne off]
*[Re-enter LEAR, with CORDELIA in his arms; followed by
an Officer]*

LEAR

Howl, howl, howl, howl![130] O, you are men of stones![131]
Had I your tongues and eyes,[132] I'd use them so
That heaven's vault[133] should crack. She's gone for ever!
I know when one is dead, and when one lives;
She's dead as earth. Lend me a looking-glass;[134]
If that her breath will mist or stain the stone,[135]
Why, then she lives.

[130] **Howl:** 1 A cry of anguish 2 A command for others to cry

[131] **men of stones:** like statues, unresponsive (possibly to a command to 'Howl')

[132] **tongues and eyes:** tongues for lamenting, eyes for weeping

[133] **heaven's vault:** the sky

[134] **looking-glass:** mirror

[135] **stone:** polished stone used as a mirror

KENT

         Is this the promised end?[136]

[136] **promised end:** doomsday / the end of the world

EDGAR

Or image[137] of that horror?

[137] **image:** representation

ALBANY

         Fall, and cease![138]

[138] **Fall, and cease!:** Albany is calling for the end of the world so moved is he by the image of Cordelia's body

LEAR

This feather stirs; she lives! If it be so,
It is a chance which does redeem all sorrows
That ever I have felt.[139]

[139] **It is a chance...felt:** it is a stroke of fortune that makes up for all of the sorrows that I have ever felt

KENT

         O my good master!

LEAR
Prithee, away!

EDGAR
'Tis noble Kent, your friend.

LEAR
A plague upon you, murderers, traitors all!
270 I might have saved her; now she's gone for ever!
Cordelia, Cordelia! Stay a little. Ha!
What is't thou say'st? Her voice was ever soft,
Gentle, and low, an excellent thing in woman.
I killed the slave that was a-hanging thee.

OFFICER
'Tis true, my Lords, he did.

LEAR
                    Did I not, fellow?
I have seen the day, with my good biting falchion[140]
I would have made them skip. I am old now
And these same crosses spoil me.[141] *[To KENT]* Who are
you?
Mine eyes are not o' the best, I'll tell you straight.[142]

KENT
280 If Fortune brag of two she loved and hated,
One of them we behold.[143]

LEAR
This is a dull sight.[144] Are you not Kent?

KENT
                              The same,
Your servant Kent: Where is your servant Caius?[145]

LEAR
He's a good fellow, I can tell you that;
He'll strike, and quickly too. He's dead and rotten.

KENT
No, my good Lord, I am the very man –

LEAR
I'll see that straight.[146]

KENT
That, from your first of difference and decay[147]

---

140 **falchion:** curved sword

141 **these same crosses spoil me:** the suffering of old age, prevents me from being the swordsman I once was

142 **I'll tell you straight:** I'll recognise you shortly

143 **If Fortune...behold:** If Fortune boasts of two people whom she loved and hated, then we can see one of them now (i.e. Lear – once loved and then hated by Fortune)

144 **dull sight:** 1 sad spectacle 2 Lear's failing vision

145 **Caius:** The only mention of the name Kent adopted while in disguise

146 **I'll see that straight:** I'll look into that in a moment

147 **first of difference and decay:** first sign of your change and decline (in fortune)

Have followed your sad steps –

LEAR
                 You are welcome hither.

KENT
Nor no man else.[148] All's cheerless, dark, and deadly.
Your eldest daughters have fordone[149] themselves,
And desperately are dead.

LEAR
              Ay, so I think.

ALBANY
He knows not what he says and vain is it
That we present us to him.[150]

EDGAR
             Very bootless.[151]

[Enter a Messenger]

MESSENGER
Edmund is dead, my Lord.

ALBANY
             That's but a trifle[152] here.
You lords and noble friends, know our intent:
What comfort to this great decay[153] may come
Shall be applied. For us we will resign
During the life of this old Majesty,
To him our absolute power.
[To EDGAR and KENT] You, to your rights,
With boot,[154] and such addition as your honours
Have more than merited. All friends shall taste
The wages of their virtue, and all foes
The cup of their deservings. O, see, see!

LEAR
And my poor fool[155] is hanged! No, no, no life!
Why should a dog, a horse, a rat, have life
And thou no breath at all? Thou'lt come no more,
Never, never, never, never, never!
Pray you, undo this button:[156] thank you, sir.
Do you see this? Look[157] on her! Look, her lips!
Look there, look there!
[He dies]

148 **Nor no man else:** I am nobody else (but Kent)
149 **fordone:** destroyed
150 **He knows...him:** He doesn't know what he is saying and it's pointless to try and explain things to him
151 **bootless:** useless
152 **trifle:** insignificant detail
153 **great decay:** decline of a great person (i.e. Lear)
154 **With boot:** and more
155 **poor fool:** A term of endearment for Cordelia. Some commentators argue that Lear confuses Cordelia with the Fool here; some suggest that Lear is referring only to the Fool
156 **button:** 1 a button on Lear's clothes perhaps suggesting that he feels suffocated 2 a button on Cordelia's clothes
157 **Look:** Possibly: 1 Lear believes that Cordelia is alive and he dies in a state of joy 2 Lear is overwhelmed by the painful reality of Cordelia's dead body before him 3 Lear is pointing to the noose marks around Cordelia's neck which resemble a mouth ('lips')

EDGAR

       He faints! My Lord, my Lord!

KENT

Break, heart, I prithee, break!

EDGAR

           Look up, my Lord.

KENT

Vex not his ghost;[158] O, let him pass![159] He hates him
That would upon the rack[160] of this tough world
Stretch him out longer.

EDGAR

         He is gone indeed.

KENT

The wonder is, he hath endured so long;
He but usurped[161] his life.

ALBANY

Bear them from hence. Our present business
Is general woe.[162] *[To KENT and EDGAR]* Friends of my
320 soul, you twain
Rule in this realm,[163] and the gored state sustain.[164]

KENT

I have a journey,[165] sir, shortly to go;
My master calls me, I must not say no.

EDGAR

The weight[166] of this sad time we must obey;
Speak what we feel, not what we ought to say.
The oldest hath borne most: we that are young
Shall never see so much, nor live so long.[167]
[Exeunt, with a dead march]

---

[158] **ghost:** soul / spirit
[158] **pass:** i.e. die / pass away
[160] **rack:** instrument of torture

[161] **usurped:** clung onto

[162] **general woe:** public mourning

[163] **Rule in this realm:** 1 Albany is restoring Kent and Edgar to their noble titles 2 Albany is inviting Kent and Edgar to share power with him
[164] **gored state sustain:** maintain order in the deeply wounded state
[165] **journey:** i.e. a journey into the afterlife

[166] **weight:** heavy burden / sorrow

[167] **The weight...so long:** Some versions of the text give these lines to Albany

———— Key Quotations ————

CORDELIA	*We are not the first*
	Who, with best meaning, have incurred the worst.
	For thee, oppressed King, am I cast down;
	Myself could else outfrown false Fortune's frown.
EDGAR	*The gods are just and of our pleasant vices / Make instruments to plague us*
LEAR	*Howl, howl, howl, howl! O, you are men of stones!*
	Had I your tongues and eyes, I'd use them so
	That heaven's vault should crack. She's gone for ever!
	I know when one is dead, and when one lives;
	She's dead as earth.
LEAR	*Did I not, fellow?*
	I have seen the day, with my good biting falchion
	I would have made them skip. I am old now
	And these same crosses spoil me.
KENT	*All's cheerless, dark, and deadly.*
LEAR	*And my poor fool is hanged! No, no, no life!*
	Why should a dog, a horse, a rat, have life
	And thou no breath at all? Thou'lt come no more,
	Never, never, never, never, never!
KENT	*Vex not his ghost; O, let him pass! He hates him / That would upon the rack of this tough world / Stretch him out longer.*
KENT	*I have a journey, sir, shortly to go; / My master calls me, I must not say no.*

———— Commentary ————

- **The final scene of *King Lear* is dramatically charged**, containing moments of hope and despair, and culminating in the intense suffering of Lear. The tension of the scene is drawn out as the audience worry for the lives of Lear and Cordelia, yet are offered glimmers of hope (from Albany and then Edmund) that they may yet be saved.
- Lear is radically changed from the first scene of the play. **He has come to recognise the meaninglessness of his arrogant pride.** The indignity of his pending imprisonment does not faze him. Instead he mocks the pomp and intrigue of the royal court, the court of which he was once the centre:

    'So we'll live
    And pray, and sing, and tell old tales, and laugh
    At gilded butterflies, and hear poor rogues
    Talk of court news; and we'll talk with them too,

Who loses and who wins, who's in, who's out;

And take upon's the mystery of things,

As if we were gods' spies.'

Lear now understands his own humanity. He has come to know and understand himself without the trappings of wealth, status and power that he once valued so much.

- After being reunited with Cordelia, Lear's mood in this first movement of the scene is buoyant. **Lear now knows what it is to be nothing:** having lost his power, status, wealth and the love of two of his children, Lear has suffered immeasurably. Now he is simply happy to have Cordelia's love and forgiveness. Suffering has allowed Lear to see what is important in life and to appreciate who he is.

- **Lear's arrogance has been replaced by humility.** He humbly repents to Cordelia, begging her for forgiveness. There is no trace of his former arrogant pride; the wrathful 'dragon' of the first scene now sees himself as an old man, no longer at the height of his powers. When Lear describes killing the soldier that murdered Cordelia, he does not mention his skill in overpowering a much younger man, instead he describes himself as weak in comparison to his younger self: 'I have seen the day, with my good biting falchion / I would have made them skip. I am old now / And these same crosses spoil me.'

- **Lear comes to understand his own humanity in the great chain of being.** In the first scene he acts as if he has god-like status. Later, during the storm he equates his humanity with the status of a beast: 'man is no more but…[a] forked animal' (Act 3, Sc 4). In this final scene, Lear appreciates the dignity and value of human life. He understands that Cordelia's life is worth so much more than a beast's: 'Why should a dog, a horse, a rat, have life / And thou no breath at all?'

- Lear's cry 'And my poor fool is hanged!' most likely refers to Cordelia who foolishly places her life in danger to save her father. **The language equates Cordelia's role with the Fool's, both of whom led Lear to wisdom.** However, some critics argue that Lear is including the Fool in his final expression of grief.

- **The intensity of Lear's grief is distressing and moving for the audience.** The spectacle of Lear with Cordelia in his arms is a heartrending moment. Lear's pain knows no bounds as he wails for his great loss: 'Howl, howl, howl, howl!...She's gone for ever!...She's dead as earth.' Although Lear dies a heartbroken man, he has achieved wisdom. He now understands the importance of love in the human experience; the tragedy is that Cordelia's death means he can no longer enjoy this love.

- **The jealous feud between Goneril and Regan reaches its dramatic climax.** Goneril kills Regan by poisoning her. She then takes her own life once Albany reveals her treachery by producing her letter to Edmund. Albany dubs his wife a 'gilded serpent' but the description could be applied to either sister, both of whom remain utterly false and self-interested to the end.

- Throughout *King Lear*, Edmund proves himself to be treacherous, callous and manipulative. **Some critics argue that he redeems himself somewhat at the end.** So moved is Edmund by Edgar's account of their father's death that, in his final moments, he calls for his execution order on Lear and Cordelia's lives to be revoked. **However, other critics believe that Edmund remains false and manipulative till the end** and that his final words reflect his instinct to divert blame from himself. Whichever way you read this moment, Edmund does not do enough to earn forgiveness for his crimes. Thus the news of his death arouses little pity: as Albany says, 'That's but a trifle here.'

- **Edgar is confirmed as a noble character, set to play an important role in healing the deep divisions of the kingdom.** He bravely comes forward to challenge Edmund and appropriately is looked to by Albany as a future leader. Throughout the play, Edgar's unshakeable belief in the gods and divine justice allows him to endure terrible suffering. This faith is reiterated in this final scene: 'The gods are just and of our pleasant vices / Make instruments to plague us.' Edgar's nobility is further confirmed in his generous offer of forgiveness to Edmund: 'Let's exchange charity.'

- **Kent remains steadfast and unwavering in his loyalty, even when facing death.** As Lear dies, Edgar looks to help him but is prevented by Kent who points to the unbearable extent of Lear's suffering: 'Vex not his ghost; O, let him pass! He hates him / That would upon the rack of this tough world / Stretch him out longer.' After, when Albany looks to Kent as a future leader and someone to help restore order in the kingdom, Kent declines. He is dying having spent all his strength in the service of his king. Kent expresses his intention to wait for death and follow Lear into the afterlife: 'I have a journey, sir, shortly to go; / My master calls me, I must not say no.'

Questions

1. How does the feud between Goneril and Regan conclude?
2. How is Edgar's statement, 'The gods are just and of our pleasant vices / Make instruments to plague us', relevant to the play as a whole?
3. Do you agree that Edgar maintains an unshakeable faith in divine justice to the end of the play? Refer to this scene in your answer.
4. (a) Describe Edmund's attempts to redeem himself in his final moments of life.
   (b) Do you think he successfully redeems himself? Why / why not?
5. Why does Kent prevent Edgar from coming to Lear's aid?
6. In what way does this scene illustrate Lear's personal growth throughout the course of the play?

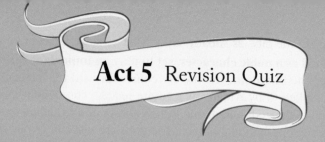

Act 5 Revision Quiz

1. Who gives Albany the letter in which Goneril looks for Edmund to kill her husband?
2. While Gloucester is resting under a tree Edgar brings him terrible news that prompts Gloucester to despair again. What terrible news does Edgar bring?
3. Edmund plans the murders of Lear and Cordelia. What is this plan?
4. What is the outcome of Edmund's plan to murder Lear and Cordelia?
5. How does Regan die?
6. How does Goneril die?
7. How does Edmund die?
8. Albany offers Kent a role in restoring order to the kingdom. What reason does Kent give for not accepting this offer?
9. Who says each of the following?

   (a) *We are not the first*
   Who, with best meaning, have incurred the worst.
   For thee, oppressed King, am I cast down;
   Myself could else outfrown false Fortune's frown.

   (b) *All's cheerless, dark, and deadly*

   (c) *Howl, howl, howl, howl! O, you are men of stones!*
   Had I your tongues and eyes, I'd use them so
   That heaven's vault should crack. She's gone for ever!
   I know when one is dead, and when one lives;
   She's dead as earth.

   (d) *The gods are just and of our pleasant vices*
   Make instruments to plague us

10. Rewrite these quotations. In each case, write the speaker's name and fill in the blanks.

    (a) *Men must endure*
    Their going hence, even as their _____ hither;
    _____ is all

    (b) *And my poor _____ is hanged! No, no, no life!*
    Why should a dog, a horse, a _____, have life
    And thou no _____ at all? Thou'lt come no more,
    Never, never, never, never, never!

    (c) *Vex not his _____; O, let him pass! He hates him*
    That would upon the _____ of this tough world
    Stretch him out _____

    (d) *I have a journey, sir, _____ to go;*
    My _____ calls me, I must not say no

Tragedy

Tragedy

Tragedy is a form of drama that deals with human suffering. There are many definitions of what constitutes tragedy. Broadly speaking, tragedy depicts a hero who thrives at the beginning of a story but then, because of a tragic act, experiences a reversal of fortune. In the course of the play, the tragic hero experiences great suffering and hardship. Through this experience he achieves wisdom and understanding. He dies a wiser man than he has lived (see Character Study of Lear p.197).

In *King Lear*, the tragic downfall of the play's hero, Lear, is mirrored in the downfall of Gloucester in the sub-plot (see 'Main Plot and Sub-Plot').

King Lear is a supreme expression of the tragic pattern. We can understand it as a tragedy as it contains the following tragic elements:

The Hero Enjoys an Elevated Social Status

King Lear begins the drama as an all-powerful king. He inspires love and loyalty in others such as Cordelia, Kent and Gloucester. And although Goneril and Regan do not love their father, they are initially respectful of the great power he wields. As King, Lear has the highest social position a man can attain.

The Hero is characterised by a Tragic Flaw

All tragic heroes are flawed individuals. King Lear's tragic flaw is his excessive pride. It is this that blinds him, causing him to make errors in judgement and rash decisions. Acting on his pride, Lear conducts the love-test and courts his daughters' flattery. When Cordelia refuses to pander to his ego during the love-test, Lear's pride blinds him to the true meaning of her words; he believes she is saying that she does not love him. He succumbs to fiery passion by rashly disowning his daughter and banishing Kent. Pride blinds Lear to the virtues and vices of those around him, as a result he rewards his two treacherous daughters Goneril and Regan and punishes those who really love him.

The Hero commits a Tragic Act

All tragic heroes commit a tragic act. This action is the direct result of his flawed humanity. In the case of *King Lear*, Lear makes many mistakes, all of which stem from his excessive pride and poor judgement. However, Lear's tragic act occurs in the first scene when he divides his kingdom in an unnatural way and then banishes Cordelia. Blinded by pride and arrogance, Lear wishes to retain the status of King, but abdicates his responsibilities as royal leader. He then misinterprets Cordelia's words and banishes the one daughter who truly loves him.

This sets in motion all of the disastrous events in the play. An audience of Shakespeare's time would have believed in a natural social order with the King at its head. This king was thought to be divinely appointed. By dividing his power amongst his daughters, Lear is defying this natural order. Similarly, Lear's banishment of Cordelia is an unnatural way to treat a daughter. These tragic actions bring Lear great suffering and lead to war, the deaths of his daughters and his personal tragic downfall.

The Hero experiences Tragic Reversal

As a result of his tragic act, a tragic hero necessarily experiences a dramatic reversal of fortune. The favourable circumstances that he enjoyed at the start of the play change utterly. King Lear was once a respected, supremely powerful ruler, a man with great wealth and respect. However, by relinquishing his royal responsibilities, Lear sets in motion a sequence of events that see him lose his power, respect and identity. Goneril and Regan reduce his train of knights; he finds himself homeless in the midst of a raging storm, and his favourite daughter Cordelia is murdered. By the end of the play he is left wretched, grief stricken and tortured by regret.

The Hero achieves Tragic Recognition

Through suffering, the tragic hero gains wisdom or tragic recognition. This is true of King Lear who comes to see the meaninglessness of his own pride and understands his own flawed humanity. Through suffering he learns compassion, humility and gains empathy for all who are poor and needy. Lear gains insight into the dignity of being human and appreciates the true nature of love. Despite this insight, Lear is powerless to change his situation and becomes a victim of his own tragic flaw.

The play inspires Pity and Fear

A tragic hero should inspire pity. By the end of the play, the audience pity King Lear as he succumbs to inconsolable grief. The heartrending image of him stooped over the dead body of Cordelia should evoke pity in any audience.

A tragedy should also excite fear. By the end of *King Lear* the audience feel fear for themselves. Lear's passion, arrogance and pride destroy him. The audience should realise that the same could happen to anybody.

The Development of King Lear as a Tragic Hero

Hero enjoys Elevated Social Status	◎ As King, Lear holds the highest office that an individual can ◎ Lear inspires loyalty and love in others, namely: Cordelia, Kent and Gloucester ◎ King Lear is respected by the members of the court. Even his ungrateful daughters, Goneril and Regan are respectful at the start of the play
Tragic Flaw	◎ Lear's tragic flaw is his excessive pride ◎ This blinds him to the virtues and vices of others ◎ Pride also encourages Lear's violent passion and rash judgement
Tragic Act	◎ Lear's tragic act is the unnatural division of his kingdom and the banishment of Cordelia ◎ This sets in train a sequence of events that leaves him suffering and eventually grief stricken and broken
Tragic Reversal	◎ King Lear experiences intense suffering as he comes to face his own folly ◎ This reaches its fullest expression in the Storm Scenes and when Cordelia dies

Tragic Recognition	◎ King Lear comes to see himself not as a 'dragon' but rather as 'a very foolish, fond old man'
	◎ He learns humility, compassion and empathy as he recognises the suffering of others
	◎ Lear gains insight into the true meaning of love and comes to understand the dignity of being human
Inspires Pity and Fear	◎ King Lear dies a heartbroken man. The spectacle of his grief as he holds Cordelia in his arms arouses huge pity in the audience
	◎ The audience pity King Lear as a man who has lost everything because of his flawed humanity
	◎ *King Lear* also excites fear in the audience who see their own potential for self-destruction

The Main Plot and Sub-Plot

King Lear is a finely crafted play. Shakespeare carefully echoes Lear's story (the main plot) in Gloucester's (sub-plot). Both men make gross errors of judgement, experience terrible suffering and eventually achieve wisdom and insight. The tragic downfall of each character results from his own flaws and instances of 'moral blindness'. Furthermore, the characters' downfalls are facilitated by cruel and ungrateful children. Similarly, each man has a loyal, loving and forgiving child.

Main Plot and Sub-plot	Lear	Gloucester
Moral Blindness / Tragically Flawed	Lear is flawed by his pride and arrogance. This leads him to divide his kingdom unnaturally and banish Cordelia, the daughter that truly loves him.	Gloucester's moral blindness is his lust. His 'sin' produces his evil child Edmund.
Both men are initially blind to the true natures of their children	Lear fails to appreciate the hollowness of Goneril's and Regan's flattery. He foolishly trusts his welfare to these women. Similarly, Lear misinterprets Cordelia's words in the first scene and fails to recognise her as truly loving.	Gloucester is manipulated by the charismatic Edmund. He foolishly places his trust in his 'bastard' son and comes to believe that Edgar is a villain.
Each has a good child	Cordelia – her honesty, compassion and ability to forgive establish Cordelia as a saint-like figure. This is reflected in the imagery of the play.	Edgar – his unwavering loyalty, compassion and capacity for forgiveness clearly establish Edgar as a reflection of Cordelia.

Main Plot and Sub-plot	Lear	Gloucester
Both men are mistreated by evil children	Goneril and Regan – their false flattery of Lear, efforts to provoke confrontation with him and neglect of their father, establish Lear's eldest daughters as cruel, self-serving women.	Edmund – the cruel way he manipulates Gloucester and blackens Edgar's name establish Edmund as a villain. He later betrays Gloucester and steals his wealth.
Both Lear and Gloucester are forgiven by their deserving children	Cordelia readily forgives Lear for disowning and disinheriting her.	Without reservation Edgar forgives his father for branding him a villain and seeking his death.
Lear and Gloucester experience intense suffering	Lear experiences great hardship during the storm and loses his great status as a powerful ruler. He undergoes mental suffering as he is taken to the brink of insanity. Lear is also tormented by his guilt.	Because Gloucester's moral flaw (lust) is physical in nature, his suffering is primarily physical. The cruel torture he receives at the hands of Cornwall and Regan is horrendous. Like Lear, he suffers great guilt for his rash actions.
Both men develop compassion as a result of their intense suffering	Lear comes to pity the Fool, Poor Tom and all who suffer deprivation.	Gloucester expresses pity and concern for Poor Tom and develops a sense of social justice in solidarity with the poor.
Lear and Gloucester achieve wisdom and insight by the end of the play	Lear comes to appreciate the emptiness of his own pride and understands the true meaning of love. Lear also sees the dignity of humanity and appreciates its place in the great chain of being.	Gloucester overcomes despair and learns humanity's capacity to endure suffering. He stops seeing himself as a victim of the gods and learns to take responsibility for his own fate.

Characters

King Lear

King Lear is a fascinating and complex character. When he enters the stage in the first scene of the play, his arrogance, pride and 'hideous rashness' are immediately apparent. The tragedy of the play grows out of the poor decisions King Lear makes in the opening minutes of the drama.

As the play continues we come to sympathise with Lear as an old man whose mistakes have left him vulnerable to the cruelties of his two eldest daughters. Despite this, the audience should not be blinded to the fact that Lear's suffering grows out of his own folly and poor judgement; we appreciate Lear as the architect of his own downfall.

As Lear suffers and is taken to the brink of insanity, he grows in wisdom and moral integrity. He comes to know himself and also develops compassion and empathy for others. By the end of the play the spectacle of Lear's suffering and loss is a deeply moving experience.

Excessively Proud (at first)

The tragic mistakes that Lear makes have their roots in his excessive pride. It is his inflated sense of self-importance that compels Lear to conduct a 'love-test' as he attempts to measure the extent of his daughters' love for him by their testimonies of love. Lear's pride invites the hollow, disingenuous flattery of Goneril and Regan, whose empty rhetoric panders to his ego yet masks their self-serving intentions.

It is this same pride that encourages Lear to see himself as a powerful 'dragon' (traditionally a symbol for England), a man to be feared. After Kent bravely questions Lear in the first scene, Lear proudly draws on this self-image as he warns Kent, 'Come not between the dragon and his wrath!'

Lear's pride leaves him vulnerable. In the play Goneril and Regan exploit Lear's pride as a means of provoking a confrontation and undermining him. Regan insults Lear's pride by ensuring that his messenger (Kent in disguise) is placed in the stocks long enough for Lear to see him; this sparks outrage in the King. Similarly, Goneril and Regan, in a gross parody of the love-test, erode Lear's train of knights, successively enraging their father and driving him out into the storm.

Only as Lear suffers does he come to see the emptiness of his own pride and learn humility (see 'Learns Humility' below).

Fiery, Rash and Exercises Poor Judgement (at first)

It is Lear's pride that blinds him to the virtues and vices of those around him. It is his pride that encourages his poor judgement. The most obvious example of this occurs in the play's opening scene. When Cordelia refuses to massage Lear's ego and pander to his excessive pride, Lear misunderstands her believing that she doesn't love him. He becomes enraged, disinheriting his favourite daughter summarily. His hyperbolic language illustrates his fiery passion:

> 'The barbarous Scythian,
> Or he that makes his generation messes
> To gorge his appetite, shall to my bosom
> Be as well neighboured, pitied and relieved,
> As thou my sometime daughter' (Act 1, Sc 1).

In this scene, Lear fails to see Cordelia for the loving daughter she is and is blind to Goneril's and Regan's conniving natures.

His mistreatment of Kent also points to Lear's poor judgement and rash behaviour. Despite the fact that Kent loyally tries to protect Lear's interests by offering sound advice, Lear misinterprets Kent's intervention, seeing it as a challenge to his authority. Lear banishes Kent on pain of death. The violence of Lear's language underscores his 'hideous rashness': 'The bow is bent and drawn, make from the shaft' (Act 1, Sc 1).

Later in the play Lear's fiery and rash nature is still evident. Although he is correct to see Goneril as a villain, his language again signals Lear's lack of control and violent temper. He curses Goneril, saying,

> 'Into her womb convey sterility!
> Dry up in her the organs of increase,
> And from her derogate body never spring
> A babe to honour her!' (Act 1, Sc 4).

As the play continues, Lear gains insight into his own proud nature. He eventually learns to check his anger and see others for who they really are (see 'Learns Humility' below).

Egocentric (at first)

Lear's inflated sense of self-importance grows out of his excessive pride. At the start of the play Lear states his intention to 'still retain / The name, and all th' addition to a king' (Act 1, Sc 1). Lear wishes to abdicate his responsibilities as King but still maintain the authority, status and pomp of kingship.

Similarly, when Lear first enters the storm he can only understand the plight of others in terms of his own suffering. When he comes across Poor Tom shivering in the cold, Lear immediately sees a reflection of his own situation and assumes that Poor Tom has been mistreated by his daughters: 'What, has his daughters brought him to this pass? / Couldst thou save nothing? Didst thou give 'em all?' (Act 3, Sc 4). His pity for Poor Tom is expressed in terms that relate to himself. It is only later as he grows in wisdom does Lear see beyond himself and develop true empathy for the suffering of others.

Lear's egocentricity and puffed pride leave it difficult for him to accept that he is a flawed individual responsible for his own downfall. At first he views himself simply as an innocent victim of his cruel daughters: 'To shut me out! Pour on; I will endure. / In such a night as this! O Regan, Goneril! / Your old kind father, whose frank heart gave all' (Act 3, Sc 4). Lear is certainly a victim of Goneril's and Regan's cruelty, greed and deception. However, only after suffering does Lear recognise that he too has a part in bringing about his own suffering and downfall (see 'Learns Humility' below).

Achieves 'Reason in Madness'

Lear's 'madness' is a very human response to the trauma and suffering he experiences. His erratic behaviour points to the imbalance of his mind. We see him tearing off his clothes on the heath, conducting an imaginary trial of his daughters and treating Poor Tom as if he were a learned scholar.

Lear is very aware of the threat to his sanity as suffering starts to take its toll: 'O, let me not be mad, not mad, sweet heaven! / Keep me in temper; I would not be mad!' (Act 1, Sc 5). He recognises his loosening grip on reality as he teeters on the edge of madness: 'O, how this mother swells up toward my heart! / *Hysterica passio*, down, thou climbing sorrow! / Thy element's below!', 'O, Fool I shall go mad!' (Act 2, Sc 4)

However, as Lear's sanity is threatened, his understanding of himself and his world grows. This apparent paradox is pithily noted by Edgar who says, 'O, matter and impertinency mixed! Reason in madness!' (Act 4, Sc 6).

It is during moments of madness that Lear achieves many of his insights. Just before he runs merrily from Cordelia's men announcing that he will 'die bravely, like a smug bridegroom' (Act 4,

Sc 6), Lear reflects philosophically on the human condition and the folly of human pride: 'When we are born, we cry that we are come / To this great stage of fools.' Similarly, Lear's expressions of empathy and social solidarity are often said during moments of apparent 'madness' (see 'Emptiness of Pomp and Wealth' below).

To achieve wisdom Lear needs to be undone; his 'madness' is an expression of this. It is an understandable reaction to losing status, power and respect and to Goneril and Regan's mistreatment of him. However, it is during this process that Lear achieves wisdom and insight, 'Reason in madness'.

Learns Humility

As he journeys towards self-discovery Lear comes to recognise the emptiness of his excessive pride and learns humility. At the start of the play Regan notes that Lear 'hath ever but slenderly known himself' (Act 1, Sc 1); she sees that Lear is lacking in self-knowledge. However, as the play progresses and Lear loses the power, wealth and status he once enjoyed, his identity as a powerful and respected leader is destroyed. He has to uncover who Lear the man is and come to know himself. This process of self-discovery is a humbling experience.

Lear's pride starts to unravel shortly after Goneril reduces his train of knights. Lear quickly realises the mistake he has made in giving so much of his kingdom to Goneril. He berates himself for this mistake: 'O Lear, Lear, Lear! / Beat at this gate, that let thy folly in / And thy dear judgement out!' (Act 1, Sc 4). Lear comes to realise that his pride allowed Goneril to mistreat him; he is starting to understand his own folly and poor judgement.

Lear's first admission of guilt occurs in the next scene: referring to Cordelia he tells the Fool 'I did her wrong' (Act 1, Sc 5). Although he doesn't dwell on his mistreatment of his daughter in this scene and still sees himself as a victim, this important admission is a humbling step on the road to wisdom.

Lear comes to see that his daughters' mistreatment of him is perhaps deserved in light of his mistreatment of Cordelia. It was Lear who courted Goneril's and Regan's false praise, and it was his excessive pride that blinded him to Cordelia's true nature. Lear therefore sees that he deserves to suffer: 'Judicious punishment! 'Twas this flesh begot / Those pelican daughters' (Act 3, Sc 4). It was thought in Shakespeare's time that the young pelicans fed on the flesh of their parents. The image here is of Lear being devoured by his daughters. Lear now sees that his poor judgement allowed this situation to occur.

As Lear suffers his sense of humility and remorse grows. He expresses great shame for disowning Cordelia and seems tortured by regret: 'I am bound / Upon a wheel of fire, that mine own tears / Do scald like molten lead' (Act 4, Sc 7). Gone is the 'dragon' of the first scene, instead Lear now sees himself as 'a very foolish, fond old man' (Act 4, Sc 7). With great humility he begs Cordelia's forgiveness: 'You must bear with me. Pray you now, forget and forgive; I am old and foolish' (Act 4, Sc 7). His arrogant pride has now given way to humility.

Grows in Compassion

Another aspect of Lear's personal growth is his renewed sense of compassion. Only by suffering can he truly understand the plight of the poor and the needy. We see this in his concern for the Fool. As Lear is taken to a hovel to shelter from the storm, he urges the Fool to enter before him: 'Poor Fool and knave, I have one part in my heart / That's sorry yet for thee' (Act 3, Sc 2). The storm also encourages Lear to express concern and compassion for Poor Tom.

Similarly, as Lear endures all of the discomfort and suffering that the storm brings, he sympathises with poor people everywhere:

> 'Poor naked wretches, whereso'er you are
> That bide the pelting of this pitiless storm,

How shall your houseless heads and unfed sides,
Your looped and windowed raggedness, defend you
From seasons such as these?' (Act 3, Sc 4).

At the start of the play Lear's concern was for himself. Only by suffering does he develop compassion and sympathy for others.

Comes to Recognise the Emptiness of Pomp and Wealth

After acknowledging the suffering that deprivation brings, Lear sees that wealth and pride have blinded him to his royal obligations to the poor:

'O, I have ta'en
Too little care of this! Take physic, pomp;
Expose thyself to feel what wretches feel,
That thou mayst shake the superflux to them,
And show the heavens more just' (Act 3, Sc 4).

The growth in his empathy allows him to appreciate the corrupting influence of wealth. This is reflected in the clothing imagery of the play. When Lear tears off his own clothes during the storm (Act 3, Sc 4) he is symbolically stripping back the trappings of power, status and wealth and attempting to understand his own humanity.

Lear comes to see that wealth allows the rich to hide their vices, whereas poor people are often condemned for minor sins: 'Through tattered clothes small vices do appear; / Robes and furred gowns hide all' (Act 4, Sc 6)

Continuing this metaphor, Lear says, 'Plate sin with gold, / And the strong lance of justice hurtless breaks; / Arm it in rags, a pigmy's straw does pierce it' (Act 4, Sc 6). Lear's suffering allows him to develop a new sense of social justice and see through the hypocrisy and corruption that can often accompany wealth.

Comes to Understand his own Humanity in the Great Chain of Being

In the first scene Lear acts as if he has god-like status, summarily disowning Cordelia and banishing Kent. Later, during the storm, he radically changes his view of himself as he equates his status with that of a beast: 'man is no more but…[a] forked animal' (Act 3, Sc 4).

Lear tends to swing between these extremes throughout much of the play. Only towards the end of the play does Lear find the balance between these two ideas. Lear comes to appreciate that a human being, even a king, never has the status of a god: 'they told me I was everything; 'tis a lie, I am not ague-proof' (Act 4, Sc 6). But he also learns the dignity and value of human life as he recognises that Cordelia's life is worth so much more than a beast's: 'Why should a dog, a horse, a rat, have life / And thou no breath at all?' (Act 5, Scene 3).

Dies a Heartbroken, yet Wiser Man

Lear's final moments in the play are a profound expression of grief and loss. The spectacle of Lear carrying Cordelia's dead body onstage is deeply moving. He cries out: 'Howl, howl, howl, howl! O, you are men of stones! / Had I your tongues and eyes, I'd use them so / That heaven's vault should crack. She's gone for ever!' (Act 5, Sc 3), unable to come to terms with his great loss.

Lear's suffering is compounded as he tries to hold onto the hope that Cordelia is still alive. He desperately holds a feather and mirror over her mouth for signs of her breath. The crushing realisation that she is utterly gone is too much for him to bear: 'Why should a dog, a horse, a rat, have life / And thou no breath at all? Thou'lt come no more, / Never, never, never, never, never!' (Act 5, Sc 3). Now that Cordelia is gone, Lear appreciates the importance of love in the human experience; the tragedy is that Cordelia's death means he can no longer enjoy this love.

Although Lear must bear responsibility for his own tragedy and it is he who set the train of events in motion, we still pity Lear's flawed humanity that brought him such intense suffering. Like Kent, the audience would not like to see Lear's suffering prolonged: 'Vex not his ghost; O, let him pass! He hates him / That would upon the rack of this tough world / Stretch him out longer' (Act 5, Sc 3).

Although it does nothing to lessen Lear's suffering, he does achieve wisdom by the end of the play. The once arrogant, rash, proud, egocentric king has learned compassion, humility and empathy. He also understands his humanity in the context of the chain of being. The audience can only watch with pity as he dies a heartbroken man.

Lear

- ◎ Excessively Proud (at first)
- ◎ Fiery, Rash and Exercises Poor Judgement (at first)
- ◎ Egocentric (at first)
- ◎ Achieves 'Reason in Madness'
- ◎ Learns Humility
- ◎ Grows in Compassion
- ◎ Comes to Recognise the Emptiness of Pomp and Wealth
- ◎ Comes to Understand his own Humanity in the Great Chain of Being
- ◎ Dies a Heartbroken, yet Wiser Man

Cordelia

Cordelia exemplifies the best of human nature. Her devotion to her father, remarkable capacity for forgiveness and saintly humility mark her out as a model of virtue. As such, she acts as a foil to her cruel, self-serving and false sisters.

Some see Cordelia as stubborn for her inflexible idealism in the opening scene. However, others view her as a strong woman who remains true to her principles throughout the play.

Virtuous

From the first scene of *King Lear*, Cordelia sets herself apart from her sisters as a woman of great courage and integrity. Goneril and Regan display their skill with words as they falsely flatter their father to secure a larger share of the kingdom. However, Cordelia says she has no time for this 'glib and oily art'. Instead she remains true to her principles, choosing to 'love and be silent'. This is a stand against Lear's foolish pride and against her sisters' self-serving, hypocritical natures.

As a character of great virtue, Cordelia understands the true nature of love, that it can be neither quantified nor measured. As such the weight of her love for her father cannot be reduced to mere words: 'I cannot heave / My heart into my mouth', 'I am sure, my love's / More ponderous than my tongue' (Act 1, Sc 1).

Further evidence of Cordelia's virtue can be found as she explains her motivation for supporting France's war in Britain. She says: 'No blown ambition doth our arms incite, / But love, dear love, and our aged father's right' (Act 4, Sc 4). Unlike Goneril and Regan, Cordelia is motivated by love and duty to her father.

Stubborn?

If Cordelia can be criticised, it is perhaps for her inflexibility in the first scene, where she refuses to humour Lear. Lear is an old man, no longer at the height of his powers. Perhaps if Cordelia had taken part in the love-test, to please her father, then much of the catastrophe could have been averted. However, some look on Cordelia's apparent stubbornness as further proof of her idealism and noble nature. By not taking part in the love-test she remains true to herself; it is this that invites our admiration.

Forgiving and Generous

Lear's treatment of Cordelia is reprehensible. His ego and pride lead him to disown Cordelia. However, rather than blaming her father, Cordelia expresses only concern for his wellbeing, wishing that he could stay somewhere other than with Goneril or Regan: 'I prefer him to a better place' (Act 1, Sc 1).

Indeed, never in the play does Cordelia blame or even say anything ill of her father. Instead she looks to forgive him. When she learns of Lear's fragmenting mental state, she sends out a party to find him and cries out for him to be healed: 'All you unpublished virtues of the earth, / Spring with my tears! Be aidant and remediate / In the good man's distress!' (Act 4, Sc 4). Her generosity of spirit is evident when she says she would gladly give away all of her wealth if it would cure Lear: 'He that helps him take all my outward worth' (Act 4, Sc 4).

Composed

Despite the depth of feeling she has for her father, Cordelia is a composed individual with control over her emotions. Following the love-test, Cordelia is treated most unfairly. However, she never expresses anger or resentment and instead speaks before the assembled court with great dignity and poise. She tells Lear:

>   'make known
>   It is no vicious blot, murder or foulness,
>   No unchaste action, or dishonoured step,
>   That hath deprived me of your grace and favour' (Act 1, Sc 1).

Here Cordelia clearly has a sense of her own worth; with dignity and control she insists that her reputation should not be tarnished by any 'vicious blot'.

Later in the play Cordelia is reported to exhibit great composure upon hearing the news of Lear's suffering. Although upset about Lear's plight Cordelia proves to be 'a queen / Over her passion' (Act 4, Sc 3) who suppresses her passion and deals with her upset privately and alone.

Cordelia's composure and restraint is in marked contrast to Lear. In this way she acts as a foil to Lear showing up one of Lear's flaws: his tendency to be led by his emotions.

Saintly and Compassionate

Shakespeare makes it clear that Cordelia is a force for good, describing her in heavenly terms that give her an almost religious significance: 'she shook / The holy water from her heavenly eyes' (Act 4, Sc 3). Similarly, when Lear is reunited with Cordelia he thinks she is an angel ('Thou art a soul in bliss') who has come to him in death (Act 4, Sc 7). Shakespeare stresses her saintly nature by presenting her in these heavenly terms.

Cordelia's compassion and saintliness are further underlined by associating her with healing. She looks to cure Lear of his 'bereaved sense' (Act 4, Sc 4) as she tenderly kisses him:

>   'O my dear father! Restoration hang
>   Thy medicine on my lips, and let this kiss
>   Repair those violent harms that my two sisters
>   Have in thy reverence made!' (Act 4, Sc 7).

Cordelia's compassion here is a moving reminder of her innate goodness.

Cordelia is also saintly in her humility. Upon being reunited with Lear, her first action is to ask for Lear's blessing: 'O, look upon me, sir, / And hold your hands in benediction o'er me!' (Act 4, Sc 7). After being so grossly mistreated by Lear she holds no grudge and instead forgives readily. Cordelia again proves her humility after she and Lear are captured. She is philosophical about their misfortune, her concern being wholly for Lear rather than herself:

'We are not the first
Who, with best meaning, have incurred the worst.
For thee, oppressed King, am I cast down;
Myself could else outfrown false Fortune's frown' (Act 5, Sc 3).

Cordelia	◎ Virtuous
	◎ Stubborn?
	◎ Forgiving and Generous
	◎ Composed
	◎ Saintly and Compassionate

Goneril

Goneril is evil to her core. Her falsity, contempt for others and ruthlessness point to Goneril's lack of humanity. As the plot develops, Goneril becomes an increasingly despicable character. She firstly reneges on her responsibilities to her father, then becomes a would-be adulterer, and finally a murderer. Her malicious, self-serving nature is the antithesis of Cordelia's.

False

As with Regan, the love-test shows Goneril to be a hypocritical liar. Without hesitation she testifies to her love for her ageing father: 'Sir, I love you more than words can wield the matter'. Although she does not want for gushing statements of flattery, Goneril tells Lear that she loves him more than words can express: 'A love that makes breath poor, and speech unable; / Beyond all manner of so much I love you' (Act 1, Sc 1). However, after Goneril has secured half of Lear's kingdom she does not hesitate to disparage her father, calling Regan's attention to his advanced years, 'poor judgement' and 'unruly waywardness'. Goneril sees her father as a nuisance and is keen to address this problem as she sees it; her language in this scene has a malicious overtone: 'We must do something, and i' the heat' (Act 1, Sc 1). Her two-faced nature establishes Goneril as a distasteful character early on. However, her behaviour becomes progressively more abhorrent as the play continues.

Contemptuous

Goneril becomes increasingly contemptuous of Lear. She refers to her father as an 'Idle old man, / That still would manage those authorities / That he hath given away!' (Act 1, Sc 3) and portrays him as a petulant child who must be praised and scolded: 'Old fools are babes again, and must be used / With checks as flatteries' (Act 1, Sc 3). Goneril tries to justify her mistreatment of her father by depicting him as a burdensome and foolish old man. In the eyes of the audience her contempt for Lear makes her even more repugnant, and underscores her filial ingratitude.

Goneril's contempt is not reserved solely for Lear. She looks down on her husband as overly mild mannered, a man composed of 'milky gentleness' (Act 1, Sc 4). Her bitter disdain for Albany reaches its fullest expression in their heated argument in Act 4, Scene 2. She refers to Albany as her 'mild husband' and tells Edmund that Albany's 'cowish terror of his spirit' prevents him from acting decisively. She later caustically mocks Albany for his failure to go to war: 'Milk-livered man! / That bear'st a cheek for blows' (Act 4, Sc 2). She contemptuously derides Albany as ineffectual; instead she is drawn to Edmund's ruthless decisiveness. Goneril clearly values the idea of a strong and powerful man and is contemptuous of men who do not meet this standard.

Calculating

In a calculated way Goneril looks to humiliate Lear and erode his regal dignity. This is a ploy to drive a wedge between her and her father. She tells Oswald to act rudely to Lear, effectively undermining Lear's status as King: 'Put on what weary negligence you please' (Act 1, Sc 3). This strategy is furthered when she reduces her father's train of knights by half. Goneril ensures that her efforts to undermine Lear are continued by writing to Regan and urging her to do the same: 'I'll write straight to my sister, / To hold my very course' (Act 1, Sc 3). She follows Lear to Gloucester's castle, to ensure that her strategy is carried out. Together, both Goneril and Regan successively undermine Lear's dignity and power, but it is perhaps Goneril who leads in this regard.

Unscrupulous and Ruthless

Goneril never displays any moral scruples in the play. Her ruthlessness means that she embraces evil to consolidate her power and get what she wants. Her contribution to the torture of Gloucester illustrates this as it is Goneril who first suggests blinding him: 'Pluck out his eyes!' (Act 3, Sc 7).

Similarly her plans to kill Albany point to her ruthless nature. She has no moral qualms about asking Edmund to commit this murder. She writes to Edmund, 'You have many opportunities to cut him off' (Act 4, Sc 6). Driven by lust for Edmund, Goneril is unwilling to let anything stand in her way, certainly not her 'mild husband' (Act 4, Sc 2).

This ruthlessness extends to her very own sister. In an effort to rid herself of a competitor for Edmund's affections, Goneril poisons Regan. As Regan complains of illness, Goneril in an aside callously remarks, 'If not, I'll ne'er trust medicine' (Act 5, Sc 3). Her complete lack of moral scruples coupled with a ruthless nature contribute to her inhumanity and utter disregard for others.

Monstrous

Goneril's inhumanity is reflected in the use of animal imagery. Throughout the play she is described in animalistic terms that stress her inhumanity: 'Detested kite!', 'sea-monster', 'serpent's tooth' (Act 1, Sc 4), 'tiger' (Act 4, Sc 2), 'gilded serpent' (Act 5, Sc 3). These animals are all predatory, vicious and aggressive. The association with snakes also emphasises Goneril's evil nature by connecting her with the devil.

Goneril	◎ False
	◎ Contemptuous
	◎ Calculating
	◎ Unscrupulous and Ruthless
	◎ Monstrous

Regan

Although younger than Goneril, Regan's wickedness rivals that of her sister's. She is a strikingly evil individual characterised by cruelty, falsity, ingratitude and malice.

False

During the love-test, Lear's daughters are invited to flatter him in order to secure a share of his kingdom which he intends to divide. Like Goneril, Regan seizes this opportunity. By lavishing Lear with false praise and massaging his inflated ego, Regan disguises the cruel and ungrateful daughter that she is. Kent and Cordelia recognise the falseness of her flattery. Kent compares it to the sound of an empty vessel: loud yet hollow.

We see Regan's falsity when she swears her love to Lear, telling him that she can only experience joy and happiness while in his company:

'I profess
Myself an enemy to all other joys,
…I am alone felicitate
In your dear Highness' love' (Act 1, Sc 1).

However, Regan's words are utterly untrue. This is seen later in the play when Regan cruelly disregards her father and fails to live up to the image of the loving daughter she so eagerly portrayed (*see below*).

Ungrateful

Regan's mistreatment of Lear shows her to be an ungrateful daughter. Towards the end of the first scene she conspires with Goneril against her father. Instead of expressing their gratitude for inheriting Lear's kingdom, they instead see their father as a liability, somebody whom they have to 'do something' about.

As the play continues, Regan is openly ungrateful to her father, 'the lunatic King' as she calls him (Act 3, Sc 7). Regan reduces her father's entourage of knights, disregarding the terms of Lear's abdication. Lear protests: 'I gave you all –.' Regan callously replies: 'And in good time you gave it' (Act 2, Sc 4). Regan knows that Lear will not accept having just one knight, yet she callously encourages Lear's rage by reducing his train of knights. Lear responds to this undermining of his social status by going out into the storm. Regan feels no compulsion to care for her father and instead tells Gloucester:

'O, sir, to wilful men
The injuries that they themselves procure
Must be their schoolmasters' (Act 2, Sc 4).

Lear bitterly acknowledges Regan's ingratitude, wondering what has created her callous nature: 'let them anatomize Regan; see what breeds about her heart. Is there any cause in nature that makes these hard hearts?' (Act 3, Sc 6). The answer to Lear's question lies with himself. Regan's ingratitude is perhaps modelled on Lear's mistreatment of Cordelia. Like her father she fails to live up to the responsibilities placed upon her.

Malicious

Regan is also a vindictive character, maliciously causing pain to others. Throughout the Eye-Gouging Scene (Act 3, Sc 7), Regan takes cruel delight in torturing Gloucester. After Cornwall blinds Gloucester in one eye, Regan calls out for more torment: 'One side will mock another – the other too!' She then looks to amplify Gloucester's pain by mocking him for trusting Edmund. The torture is finished only when Gloucester is thrown out of his own castle upon Regan's instruction that he must, 'smell / His way to Dover.'

Rival to Goneril

From the beginning of the play Regan is a rival to her older sister Goneril. During the love-test, Regan looks to top her sister's flattery of Lear:

'I am made of the self-same mettle that my sister is,
And prize me at her worth. In my true heart
I find she names my very deed of love;
Only she comes too short' (Act 1, Sc 1).

She tells her father that Goneril's testimony of love 'comes too short'; as she attempts to secure a larger portion of Lear's kingdom.

This rivalry continues throughout the play as both sisters compete for the affection of Edmund. Regan unscrupulously tries to open her sister's letter to Edmund as she tries to discover Goneril's feelings for Edmund. Later she feels threatened by Goneril and jealous of her sister's relationship with Edmund: 'She gave strange oeillades and most speaking looks / To noble Edmund' (Act 4, Sc 5). Regan deepens her rift with Goneril by warning her sister off Edmund:

'Edmund and I have talked,
And more convenient is he for my hand
Than for your Lady's…
I pray desire her call her wisdom to her' (Act 4, Sc 5).

As the play develops Regan becomes increasingly led by her jealous passion, lust for Edmund and rivalry with her sister. It is this very lust and rivalry with her sister that leads to her death as she is eventually poisoned by Goneril.

Regan	◎ False
	◎ Ungrateful
	◎ Malicious
	◎ Rival to Goneril

Kent

From the first scene to the last, Kent is unwavering in his loyalty to Lear. The strength of Kent's devotion testifies to King Lear's former greatness as Kent is so inspired to serve and love his king. Kent is a consistently courageous character; his actions and outspoken nature all grow out of his deep commitment to Lear.

Unwavering in His Loyalty

Kent expresses his utter to devotion to Lear in the first scene of the play, seeing that the purpose of his life is to serve Lear: 'My life I never held but as a pawn / To wage against thy enemies, nor fear to lose it, / Thy safety being the motive' (Act 1, Sc 1). In the same scene Kent makes clear his love for Lear as he testifies to the profound importance Lear has in his life:

'Royal Lear,
Whom I have ever honoured as my king,
Loved as my father, as my master followed,
As my great patron thought on in my prayers –' (Act 1, Sc 1)

Kent's unwavering loyalty determines all of his actions. Despite being banished and threatened with death, Kent risks his life by returning to Lear in disguise so that he can serve and protect his master. Similarly, Kent is moved to anger when Lear is disrespected. When Oswald treats Lear in a particularly offhand manner, Kent trips him, loyally protecting his master's dignity (Act 1, Sc 4).

Kent's loyalty is best displayed in the final moments of the play. After seeing Lear die, Kent refuses to take up Albany's offer to help rule the kingdom. He is dying having spent all his strength in the service of his king. Kent poignantly expresses his intention to wait for death and follow Lear into the afterlife: 'I have a journey, sir, shortly to go; / My master calls me, I must not say no' (Act 5, Sc 3).

The disloyalty and treachery of Goneril and Regan is understood more acutely when viewed next to Kent's devotion. In this way Kent acts as foil to Lear's two ungrateful daughters.

Plain Spoken / Blunt

Despite his utter devotion to his king, Kent's loyalty does not blind him to Lear's faults. In fact it is his sense of loyalty that prompts Kent to confront Lear during the first scene:

> 'Be Kent unmannerly,
> When Lear is mad…
> To plainness honour's bound,
> When majesty stoops to folly. Reserve thy state,
> And, in thy best consideration check
> This hideous rashness' (Act 1, Sc 1)

Kent's 'plainness' incurs Lear's wrath, but Kent would rather speak bluntly and be the target of this anger than allow Lear to blindly make a foolish mistake: 'See better, Lear, and let me still remain / The true blank of thine eye' (Act 1, Sc 1).

Kent's blunt language is also evident in his interactions with Oswald. With unrestrained fury he expresses his complete contempt for Oswald, calling him a 'filthy, worsted-stocking knave; a lily-livered, action-taking whoreson, glass-gazing, super-serviceable finical rogue …and the son and heir of a mongrel bitch' (Act 2, Sc 2). Kent justifies his treatment of Oswald to Cornwall, telling him, 'anger hath a privilege' (Act 2, Sc 2).

Kent's blunt manner and passion leads him to speak disrespectfully to Cornwall. Kent compares him to the stupid god Ajax, whose name is associated with a lavatory. As punishment Kent is placed in the stocks.

It is worth noting that Kent's anger here echoes Lear's. However, unlike Lear, Kent's anger does not blind his integrity and honour.

Perceptive

Despite his blunt manner, Kent is a shrewd judge of character. He is quick to see through Goneril's and Regan's hollow flattery of their father and recognises the sincerity of Cordelia's love. He tells Lear: 'Thy youngest daughter does not love thee least; / Nor are those empty-hearted whose low sound / Reverbs no hollowness' (Act 1, Sc 1). Similarly, he quickly sees Cornwall as a character unworthy of respect.

Kent's devotion to Lear does not blind him to Lear's faults. It is because of his loyalty that he feels duty bound to confront Lear in the first scene. He is willing to endure 'the dragon and his wrath' as he perceptively sees Lear's treatment of Cordelia as an act of 'hideous rashness'.

Compassionate and Caring towards Lear

Kent's devotion prompts his compassion for his King. He empathises readily with Lear's suffering and acts in a consistently caring manner. As Kent leads Lear to a hovel to take shelter from the storm, Lear asks: 'Wilt break my heart?' Kent replies, 'I had rather break mine own' (Act 3, Sc 4). Kent compassionately watches over Lear throughout the storm scenes.

Later when Lear is given refuge in a farmhouse, Gloucester urges Kent to take the King to Dover to escape an assassination attempt. Kent is reluctant to move Lear as he sees that the King needs rest: 'This rest might yet have balmed thy broken sinews'. His concern is always for his master.

As Lear dies stooped over the body of Cordelia, Kent is deeply moved by Lear's grief and death: 'Break, heart, I prithee, break!' (Act 5, Sc 3). He prevents Edgar from trying to revive Lear so acutely aware is he of Lear's suffering: 'Vex not his ghost; O, let him pass! He hates him / That would upon the rack of this tough world / Stretch him out longer' (Act 5, Sc 3).

Philosophical

Kent is a philosophical individual. While he is placed in the stocks, he appeals to Fortune to favourably control events: 'Fortune, good night. Smile once more, turn thy wheel!' (Act 2, Sc 2). He takes comfort in the idea that human fate cannot be altered as it is inextricably bound to the influence of the stars: 'It is the stars, / The stars above us, govern our condition' (Act 4, Sc 3).

However, Kent's appeals to the stars and Fortune do not chime with the message of the play. Ultimately *King Lear* shows how human beings are responsible for their own actions.

Provides important Information for the Audience

Apart from being a character in his own right, Kent serves a practical dramatic function. Throughout the play he provides important information about events offstage for the audience. While in the stocks he reads a letter from Cordelia, making the audience aware that Cordelia is preparing to intervene and come to Lear's aid. Kent also reports on the 'division…'twixt Albany and Cornwall' (Act 3, Sc 1) and on the arrival of the French forces.

Kent	◎ Unwavering in His Loyalty
	◎ Plain Spoken / Blunt
	◎ Perceptive
	◎ Compassionate and Caring towards Lear
	◎ Philosophical
	◎ Provides important Information for the Audience

The Fool

The Fool is a colourful and loyal character in the play, whose caustic, often cryptic, comments underscore Lear's flawed humanity. The Fool functions as the voice of Lear's conscience. His role is to guide Lear on the path to self-discovery. The Fool's sudden disappearance from the drama occurs just as Lear becomes able to recognise his own poor judgement.

A Loyal Companion

As Lear suffers the ingratitude of his daughters, the Fool remains a loyal and true companion. He accompanies Lear throughout the Storm Scenes, suffering alongside his master. As a loyal servant he looks to take care of his king, urging him to swallow his pride and find shelter with Goneril and Regan: 'Good nuncle, in, and ask thy daughters' blessing' (Act 3, Sc 2). Throughout Lear's dark moments, the Fool looks to diffuse Lear's pain through humour. However, his wit is barbed as it pokes fun at Lear's errors in judgement and foolish mistakes.

A Guide for Lear on the Path to Self-Discovery

Goneril describes the Fool as an 'all-licensed fool' (Act 1, Sc 4), recognising his freedom to speak freely without being reprimanded. It is precisely this licence to say what he feels that makes the Fool an excellent character to hold a mirror up to Lear and show him his flaws. This unvarnished truth is not always welcome; as the Fool himself says, 'Truth's a dog must to kennel' (Act 1, Sc 4). However, this harsh truth is essential for Lear as he comes to understand his own flaws.

Insightful

The Fool does not shy away from the task of reminding Lear of his own foolishness: 'Thou shouldst not have been old till thou hadst been wise' (Act 1, Sc 5). When Lear asks, 'Dost thou call me fool, boy?' The Fool replies, 'All thy other titles thou hast given away; that thou wast born with' (Act 1, Sc 4). His acerbic wit pinpoints the reason for Lear's tragic suffering.

The Fool mocks Lear for abdicating his power to his daughters: 'Thou hadst little wit in thy bald crown, when thou gavest thy golden one away' (Act 1, Sc 4). The Fool understands that Goneril and Regan will be blind to Lear's welfare once he has nothing to offer them: 'Fathers that wear rags / Do make their children blind' (Act 2, Sc 4). He chides Lear for giving his daughters power over him: 'thou madest thy daughters thy mothers; for when thou gavest them the rod, and put'st down thine own breeches' (Act 1, Sc 4). These observations and criticisms are vital for Lear to see himself clearly and understand his own humanity.

The Object of Lear's Pity

As it is the Fool that points out Lear's foolishness to him, it is perhaps fitting that it is the Fool who inspires Lear's pity. As Lear is taken to a hovel to shelter from the storm, he urges the Fool to enter before him as he starts to recognise suffering in others: 'Poor Fool and knave, I have one part in my heart / That's sorry yet for thee' (Act 3, Sc 2).

Disappears Mysteriously

The Fool is last seen in Act 3, Scene 6. His disappearance from the play is never fully explained. Some critics suggest that this is because the same actor would play the parts of both the Fool and Cordelia. Both roles are also symbolically linked in that they hold a mirror up to Lear, directing his journey towards self-awareness. In the final scene, as Lear carries Cordelia's body, he cries 'my poor fool is hanged!' This perhaps stresses the similar roles Cordelia and the Fool play in terms of Lear's personal growth and journey towards wisdom.

The Fool's disappearance is also important thematically. As Lear grows in wisdom and insight there is no more need for the Fool. In earlier scenes the Fool acted as Lear's conscience; Lear now has to see his own faults and mistakes for himself.

	◎ A Loyal Companion
	◎ A Guide for Lear on the Path to Self-Discovery
The Fool	◎ Insightful
	◎ The Object of Lear's Pity
	◎ Disappears Mysteriously

Gloucester

Like Lear, Gloucester undergoes a profound change throughout the course of the play. At the start of the play we see a man who is glib about the 'sport' he had during Edmund's conception. As a superstitious and gullible elderly man he is easily duped by the charismatic Edmund. Midway through the play, Gloucester is set upon by the evil characters in *King Lear*. As he suffers, he grows in moral integrity. In the final two acts of the play the audience watch as he swings between despair and stoicism (ability to endure suffering), before finally achieving wisdom.

Morally Blind (at the start)

In the first scene, Gloucester tells Kent about his 'illegitimate' son, Edmund. Gloucester laughs at the circumstances of Edmund's conception and speaks about Edmund's mother in a dismissive and insensitive manner: 'yet was his mother fair; there was good sport at his making, and the whoreson must be acknowledged' (Act 1, Sc 1). An audience during Shakespeare's time would have understood Gloucester's lust and sexual behaviour as sinful. They would have seen justice in the fact that it is Edmund (the product of Gloucester's 'sin') that treacherously betrays his father. This is echoed by Edgar who describes the bed in which Edmund was conceived as a 'dark and vicious place' (Act 5, Sc 3). At the start of the play Gloucester is morally blind in his inability to see his own lustful behaviour as sinful; it is this blindness that contributes to his own downfall.

Rash (at the start)

Gloucester's decision making is rash and the product of a fiery, passionate nature. He fails to properly examine the evidence against Edgar, and without pause or reflection declares Edgar a villain: 'O villain, villain! His very opinion in the letter! Abhorred villain! Unnatural, detested, brutish villain! Worse than brutish!…Abominable villain!' (Act 1, Sc 2).

Just as Lear is quick to disown Cordelia, Gloucester readily proclaims Edgar a fugitive:

'All ports I'll bar; the villain shall not 'scape;
…Besides, his picture
I will send far and near, that all the kingdom
May have the due note of him' (Act 2, Sc 1).

With scarcely a pause, Gloucester then disinherits Edgar and hastily promises to make Edmund his sole inheritor: 'of my land, / Loyal and natural boy, I'll work the means / To make thee capable.' (Act 2, Sc 1).

However, Gloucester learns to regret his rash decisions. After he is physically blinded he cries out for Edgar, clearly filled with regret for mistreating his son:

'O dear son Edgar,
The food of thy abused father's wrath!
Might I but live to see thee in my touch,
I'd say I had eyes again!' (Act 4, Sc 1).

Like Lear, Gloucester's rash actions grow out of his poor judgement. Blind to the true natures of others, Gloucester has to live with the consequences of the terrible mistakes he makes. His rashness, like his moral blindness, helps to bring about his downfall.

Gullible

Gloucester is easily duped by Edmund. Although Edmund is a convincing and capable liar, Gloucester does little to interrogate the evidence against Edgar and is swayed merely by Edmund's account and a forged letter.

Later, Gloucester is deceived a second time; this time by Edgar. Blinded and traumatised after being tortured by Cornwall and Regan, Gloucester is tricked into believing that he has thrown himself from a high cliff at Dover and been miraculously saved. It should be noted that in this second instance, Edgar deceives his father to cure him of his despair; as Edgar says, 'Why I do trifle thus with his despair / Is done to cure it' (Act 4, Sc 6).

Superstitious

Gloucester is a superstitious man. He looks to the stars and the gods to explain human behaviour, ignoring the fact that our moral choices are our own. In light of Kent's banishment, Lear's treatment of Cordelia and his mistaken belief that Edgar is plotting against him, Gloucester argues that planetary discord influences the affairs of people: 'These late eclipses in the sun and moon portend no good to us; though the wisdom of Nature can reason it thus and thus, yet nature finds itself scourged by the sequent effects' (Act 1, Sc 2).

Similarly, after he is blinded and realises Edmund's betrayal, Gloucester tries to blame the gods for his misfortune: 'As flies to wanton boys, are we to the gods. / They kill us for their sport' (Act 4, Sc 1). At this point of the play, he cannot see that his own lustful behaviour, rashness and gullibility brought about his suffering.

Edmund mocks his father's superstitious nature, calling it 'excellent foppery' (Act 1, Sc 2) and perceptively notes how misguided are those like Gloucester who look to astrological or divine influences to explain their misfortunes:

> 'we make guilty of our disasters the sun, the moon, and the stars, as if we were villains by necessity, fools by heavenly compulsion, knaves, thieves, and treachers, by spherical predominance, drunkards, liars and adulterers, by an enforced obedience of planetary influence' (Act 1, Sc 2).

Compassionate and Noble

Despite his flaws, Gloucester is a noble and compassionate figure who tries to do good. When Kent is placed in the stocks, Gloucester protests on his behalf. Later, he nobly states his intention to aid Lear despite the fact this could put his life in danger: 'We must incline to the King. I will look him, and privily relieve him….If I die for it, as no less is threatened me, the King my old master must be relieved' (Act 3, Sc 3).

As he himself suffers he learns to empathise with those around him. He expresses concern for the old man and, fearing for the man's life, urges him to leave: 'Away, get thee away; good friend, be gone. / Thy comforts can do me no good at all; / Thee they may hurt' (Act 4, Sc 1).

Through suffering Gloucester's compassion grows. He learns to recognise social injustice and argues for a radical redistribution of wealth to help the poor and the needy: 'So distribution should undo excess, / And each man have enough' (Act 4, Sc 1).

Swings between Despair and Stoicism (towards the end)

As Gloucester deals with the trauma of being blinded and is faced with his own failings, he begins to despair. He expresses a desire to take his own life because he believes that the gods torture him for their own amusement (see 'Superstitious' above). Only after Edgar tricks him into believing that the gods have saved him from a terrible fall, does Gloucester agree to stoically endure the misfortunes of life: 'I'll bear / Affliction till it do cry out itself / 'Enough, enough' and die' (Act 4, Sc 6).

However, later as Gloucester continues to suffer he starts to despair again. While resting under a tree, he at first refuses to get up, saying that he would rather 'rot' than continue (Act 5, Sc 2). However, Edgar again lifts him out of despair by pointing to humanity's capacity to endure: 'Men must endure / Their going hence, even as their coming hither; / Ripeness is all.' Gloucester's reply ('And that's true too'), shows how he finally accepts that suffering is part of the human condition and leaves despair behind.

Acquires Wisdom through Suffering (at the end)

In the first scene of the play Gloucester's moral blindness is shown to the audience. His sexual 'sin' that resulted in Edmund is a physical one; it is therefore fitting that Gloucester's suffering is primarily physical too. The torture that he experiences at the hands of Cornwall and Regan inflicts irreparable damage to his body. However, it is this suffering that allows him to acquire self-knowledge. Gloucester recognises the irony that he only develops moral vision after he loses his eyesight: 'I stumbled when I saw' (Act 4, Sc 1).

He comes to understand that his situation is the result of his own failings and that he is not a put-upon victim of the gods (see above). It is this that compels him to endure rather than give into despair.

Gloucester expresses guilt for rashly disowning Edgar and suffers intensely for his hasty actions. With regret he cries out for his loyal son: 'O dear son Edgar…/ Might I but live to see thee in my touch, / I'd say I had eyes again!' (Act 4, Sc 1).

Gloucester develops compassion for those around him and learns to empathise with those who live in deprivation (see 'Compassionate and Noble' above). This sense of empathy is confirmed in Edgar's account of Gloucester's death:

> 'But his flawed heart,
> Alack, too weak the conflict to support,
> 'Twixt two extremes of passion, joy and grief,
> Burst smilingly' (Act 5, Sc 3).

Gloucester, torn between the joy of reuniting with Edgar and the pain of hearing Edgar's suffering, dies. However, Gloucester learns to endure until the end. He resists despair and waits until it is his time to die, Gloucester comes to understand that 'ripeness is all' (Act 5, Sc 2).

	◎ Morally Blind (at the start)
	◎ Rash (at the start)
	◎ Gullible
Gloucester	◎ Superstitious
	◎ Compassionate and Noble
	◎ Swings between Despair and Stoicism (towards the end)
	◎ Acquires Wisdom through Suffering (at the end)

Edmund

Edmund is an extraordinarily evil character. He shows himself to be devious, treacherous, manipulative and lacking in any moral scruples. Edmund's cleverness and charm make him a somewhat attractive villain, and a plum role for an actor to play. However, this does not take away from the fact that he is a callous and ruthless individual who causes huge suffering to those around him.

Motivated by a Desire for Greater Social Standing and Wealth

Embittered about his status as Gloucester's 'bastard' son, Edmund is driven by the ambition to improve his social standing and enrich himself. His powerful soliloquy in Act 1, Scene 2, offers a fascinating insight into his mindset as he explains and attempts to justify his future treachery. Edmund argues that he has as much worth as any 'legitimate' son, his mind and body being just as sound:

> 'my dimensions are as well compact,
> My mind as generous, and my shape as true,
> As honest madam's issue? Why brand they us
> With base? With baseness? Bastardy? Base, base?'

His bitterness and anger here are reflected in his repetitive language.

Edmund goes on to say that children born outside of marriage are the result of passion as opposed to 'legitimate' children who are 'Got 'tween asleep and wake'. Edmund suggests that this gives 'bastards' an edge, making them more vital and energetic than 'a whole tribe of fops'. Edmund is clearly looking to justify the heinous crimes he is about to commit. His undermining of the sacred bonds of marriage would have been condemned by an audience during Shakespeare's time.

He finishes his soliloquy with an impassioned cry as he proudly asserts his desire to overcome his brother: 'Edmund the base / Shall top the legitimate. I grow; I prosper; / Now, gods, stand up for bastards!' His call for the gods to side with 'bastards' would have been considered truly blasphemous when *King Lear* was first performed. This would have cemented Edmund as villain in the minds of the audience.

Clever and Treacherous

Edmund is a clever villain. His self-serving and unscrupulous scheming allows him to consolidate his position throughout the play. He is only undone in the play's final scene.

Edmund's first clever ploy is to frame his brother Edgar. Edmund forges a letter addressed to himself, and signs it with his brother's name. The letter proposes a conspiracy against Gloucester to take his wealth and kill him. After Gloucester reads it, Edmund craftily protests on Edgar's behalf to avert suspicion. Later Edmund wounds himself claiming that Edgar did it. He blackens Edgar's name, turning Gloucester against his own son. Edmund then dupes Gloucester into believing that Edgar is a 'murderous coward'. Edmund then successfully encourages his father to write him into the will (Act 2, Sc 1). His clever manipulation of his own family allows him to rise in his father's esteem.

Later in the play, Edmund encourages Gloucester to confide in him. Gloucester tells him of his pity for Lear and about a letter he has received informing him of the arrival of the French forces. After Gloucester leaves, Edmund expresses his intention to betray his father. He justifies his scheme with his self-serving philosophy: 'The younger rises when the old doth fall' (Act 3, Sc 3). Edmund's success as a villain depends upon his devious treachery. It is this that offers him the chance to 'top the legitimate'.

Callous and Ruthless

Edmund lacks any respect for the lives of others. This is clear in his attitude towards Albany. Edmund intends to use Albany's authority to spearhead the battle against the French but sees the advantage of having Albany killed after the battle. Edmund plans to stand by and allow Goneril kill Albany so that he can become King himself:

> 'we'll use
> His countenance for the battle, which being done,
> Let her who would be rid of him devise
> His speedy taking off' (Act 5, Sc 1).

With similar ruthlessness, Edmund does not hesitate to plan the murders of Lear and Cordelia. He instructs a captain to kill them in the prison. Edmund sees this as an expedient way of shoring up his power, and by his own admission gives no thought to the rights or wrongs of his actions: 'for my state / Stands on me to defend, not to debate' (Act 5, Sc 1).

Edmund fails to extend sympathy to anybody, not even the two women with whom he has become intimate. He casually mocks the jealous rivalry between Goneril and Regan: 'To both these sisters have I sworn my love; / Each jealous of the other, as the stung / Are of the adder' (Act 5, Sc 1).

Attempts to Redeem Himself?

All of Edmund's relations with others are characterised by cold disdain as he looks to exploit those around to further his own aims. Some critics argue that Edmund presents a more humane side when he faces death by trying to save the lives of Lear and Cordelia.

However, such a radical transformation seems implausible. A more likely interpretation is that

Edmund remains false and manipulative to the end and that his final words reflect his instinct to divert blame from himself. Thus the news of his death arouses little pity: as Albany says, 'That's but a trifle here' (Act 5, Sc 3).

Edmund

◎ Motivated by a Desire for Greater Social Standing and Wealth

◎ Clever and Treacherous

◎ Callous and Ruthless

◎ Attempts to Redeem Himself?

Edgar

Edgar is a fascinating character in *King Lear*. He undergoes a profound change from the helpless victim of his brother's manipulative strategies to a man of action and a potential future leader in the kingdom. Edgar is also sometimes considered the philosopher of the play, reflecting on the role of fate and the influence of the gods in human lives.

Gullible (at first)

Edgar's gullibility at the start of the play allows Edmund to blacken Edgar's name and take his inheritance. He is initially presented as an easy victim for Edmund to exploit. He naïvely trusts his cynical brother; Edmund himself notes this trusting, honest nature:
    'a brother noble,
    Whose nature is so far from doing harms,
    That he suspects none; on whose foolish honesty
    My practices ride easy!' (Act 1, Sc 2).
Edgar trusts his brother enough to blindly follow his instructions to at first hide and then flee.

Optimistic

Throughout the play, Edgar never loses his optimism and resilience in the face of adversity. Unlike Gloucester, he is more resilient to thoughts of despair. Even when he is compelled to live as Poor Tom, taking the 'the basest and most poorest shape / That ever penury, in contempt of man, / Brought near to beast' (Act 2, Sc 3) Edgar remains hopeful. Edgar believes that even those in the most wretched state of destitution can hope for their situation to improve. Pithily he argues that 'The worst returns to laughter' (Act 4, Sc 1).

Possesses Unshakeable Faith

Edgar's optimism stems from his faith in divine justice. This gives him incredible resilience in the face of adversity. He looks beyond the human world, taking comfort in the wills of the 'clearest gods'. Edgar sees Edmund's death as evidence of divine justice: 'The gods are just and of our pleasant vices / Make instruments to plague us' (Act 5, Sc 3). This notion of justice is central to the play as characters are eventually punished for their sins and power is returned to the forces of good. Edgar sees this just order as divinely inspired.

Stoical

Edgar's faith and optimism give him a great inner strength and stoicism. He readily disregards his own pain when he witnesses the intensity of Lear's suffering: 'How light and portable my pain seems now, / When that which makes me bend makes the King bow' (Act 3, Sc 6). Edgar celebrates humanity's capacity to endure suffering and to continue in the face of it; to counteract his father's despair he tells him: 'Men must endure / Their going hence, even as their coming hither; / Ripeness is all' (Act 5, Sc 2).

Uses Deception for Good

Unlike his brother Edmund, Edgar uses deception for good rather than evil. Edgar disguises himself as Poor Tom initially to hide his identity and avoid capture. The disguise later allows him to protect Gloucester and help him towards insight. Where Edmund lies to Gloucester to enrich himself and usurp his father, Edgar deceives his father to cure him of despair. As he explains himself: 'Why I do trifle thus with his despair / Is done to cure it' (Act 4, Sc 6).

Gloucester laments that people are as insignificant as flies to the gods: 'As flies to wanton boys, are we to the gods. / They kill us for their sport' (Act 4, Sc 1). Edgar dissuades his father of this fatalistic despair through trickery. He fools his father into believing he is at the edge of a cliff. After Gloucester 'jumps' Edgar tells him that it is the gods who saved him: 'happy father, / Think that the clearest gods, who make them honours / Of men's impossibilities, have preserved thee' (Act 4, Sc 6). Deception protects his father from taking his own life, but also helps Gloucester to realise that he is not a victim of the gods.

It is the same logic that prevents Edgar from revealing his identity to his father until the end. Some critics see this as evidence that Edgar is trying to take revenge on his father. However, a more likely reading is that Edgar realises that Gloucester has to first come to wisdom himself before Edgar can be truly reunited with him.

Forgiving

Edgar displays an immense capacity for forgiveness. Despite the fact that Gloucester makes Edgar an outlaw and disinherits him, Edgar readily forgives Gloucester and does everything he can to help his father. Motivated by love, Edgar goes to great lengths to cure Gloucester of his despair. Such concern signals Edgar's naturally forgiving nature and compassion for his father.

Similarly, after he defeats Edmund in a duel, Edgar extends a forgiving hand to his brother ('Let's exchange charity' (Act 5, Sc 3)). This is done despite the great malice that Edmund has directed at him and their father.

Compassionate

Edgar's compassion causes him to empathise with the suffering of others. He is readily moved by the pain of those around him. When he sees Lear's intense suffering, Edgar weeps, almost revealing his true identity: 'My tears begin to take his part so much / They mar my counterfeiting' (Act 3, Sc 6). Similarly, he finds it difficult to maintain the persona of Poor Tom when he first sees the pitiful figure of his blinded father and laments the pain Gloucester must endure: 'World, world, O world! / But that thy strange mutations make us hate thee, / Life would not yield to age' (Act 4, Sc 1).

A Man of Action

However, despite his compassion and capacity for forgiveness, Edgar is also a man of action, ready to use violence when it is justified. This is made clear when he comes across Oswald and kills him in defence of his father. Similarly, he assertively challenges Edmund and mortally wounds him.

A Man of Great Moral Integrity

Edgar develops as a character over the course of the play. He was once the gullible victim of his charismatic brother, easily put upon and forced into hiding. By the end of the play he emerges as a man of great moral integrity and strength. It is Edgar who unmasks Edmund revealing him as a villain. Edgar then righteously asserts himself as Gloucester's son: 'I am no less in blood than thou art, Edmund; / If more, the more thou hast wronged me' (Act 5, Sc 3). And it is Edgar who challenges and mortally wounds Edmund, one of the play's chief villains. It is this integrity and nobility of spirit that allows him to emerge as a capable force for good and it is this that perhaps inspires Albany to look to Edgar as a figure to lead within the kingdom. From the gullible victim of the earlier scenes, Edgar has grown to become a significant figure commanding the respect of those around him. Because of his nobility and potential to be a future leader it seems fitting that Edgar is given the final lines in the play.*

Some edition attribute these final lines to Albany

Edgar	◎ Gullible (at first)
	◎ Optimistic
	◎ Possesses Unshakeable Faith
	◎ Stoical
	◎ Uses Deception for Good
	◎ Forgiving
	◎ Compassionate
	◎ A Man of Action
	◎ A Man of Great Moral Integrity

Albany

Albany is an interesting character in that he develops in moral stature throughout the course of the play. At first he is a weak individual, very much dominated by his wife. However, he grows increasingly uncomfortable with Goneril's actions and eventually stands up to her, effectively severing his relationship with her. By the end of the play, Albany is a commanding figure who looks for allies to heal the rifts and restore order to the kingdom.

Weak and Dominated (at first)

In the first act Albany is very much dominated by his wife. Goneril reduces Lear's train of knights and Lear is outraged. When Albany comes on stage he appears not to understand the reason for Lear's incredulity, probably because Goneril did not consult with him. Albany does not wish to cause Lear anguish, but he does nothing to aid Lear other than weakly suggesting that Goneril may have gone 'too far'. Goneril readily disregards his opinion, seeing Albany as a man characterised by 'milky gentleness' (Act 1, Sc 4). It is this attitude towards her husband that encourages her to pursue Edmund.

Grows in Spirit

Later in the play Goneril dismissively refers to Albany as her 'mild husband' (Act 4, Sc 2) but Oswald replies Albany is 'never man so changed'. This change in Albany grows out of his increasing disillusionment with the mistreatment of Lear. When he meets Goneril he criticises her in the harshest terms: 'You are not worth the dust which the rude wind / Blows in your face' (Act 4, Sc 2) and lambasts her for treating Lear so unkindly:

'That nature, which contemns its origin,

Cannot be bordered certain in itself.
She that herself will sliver and disbranch
From her material sap, perforce must wither
And come to deadly use.'

He sees her behaviour as grossly unnatural. Just like a severed branch will wither and die, he sees her inevitably bringing about her own self-destruction.

This argument effectively ends their relationship. Albany now looks on the good characters within the play with increasing sympathy, while Goneril grows closer to Edmund.

A Force for Good (towards the end)

In the final act of *King Lear*, Albany clearly sympathises with Lear's plight. However, he is placed in a difficult situation as the French forces invade. He feels compelled to defend the kingdom from a foreign invader but at the same time he realises that Lear and Cordelia have a legitimate grievance that is both 'just and heavy' (Act 5, Sc 1). Ultimately, Albany does go to war. However, his sympathy for Lear and Cordelia, and his reluctance to engage in battle, set him apart from Edmund, Goneril and Regan.

Once the battle is won he exerts a righteous authority, demanding that Edmund give him custody of Lear and Cordelia. However, some critics of Albany argue that had he pursued this issue with greater insistence, Albany could have prevented Cordelia's death.

Nonetheless, Albany looks to break his ties with Edmund and acts as a force for good. He is quick to put Edmund in his place, identifying him as a social inferior: 'I hold you but a subject of this war, / Not as a brother' (Act 5, Sc 3). Albany has no hesitation in issuing a challenge to Edmund and calling on Edgar (disguised) to represent him.

In the final moments of the play it is Albany who authoritatively tries to recruit Edgar as a future leader to help restore order in the kingdom.

	◎ Weak and Dominated (at first)
Albany	◎ Grows in Spirit
	◎ A Force for Good (towards the end)

Cornwall

Like his wife Regan, Cornwall is a harsh, brutal character. Cornwall aligns himself with evil, in particular Edmund. As the play progresses, his cruel nature expands and he reveals himself to be a pitiless and violent villain.

Aligns Himself with Evil

From early on in the play, Cornwall aligns himself with evil. He is the first character to form an alliance with Edmund. After Edmund blackens Edgar's name and hoodwinks his father, Cornwall forms a bond with Edmund, telling him 'You we first seize on' (Act 2, Sc 1). Later when Edmund betrays Gloucester to Cornwall by showing him his father's letter, Cornwall reward Edmund's treachery by making *him* Earl of Gloucester.

Disloyal and Disrespectful

Cornwall has no loyalty to King Lear. He seeks to provoke Lear's anger by placing Kent in the stocks; this is an act of significant disrespect as Kent (in disguise) is Lear's personal messenger.

Later in the scene, Lear leaves the castle during a violent storm. It is Cornwall who says that the doors should be locked, effectively abandoning Lear to the wild weather. Such callous indifference shows Cornwall's utter lack of respect for his king.

Vicious

In Act 3, Scene 5, Cornwall vengefully swears to Edmund that he will punish Gloucester for supporting Lear: 'I will have my revenge ere I depart his house.' He makes good on this dark promise in the eye-gouging scene (Act 3, Sc 7). This is Cornwall's most dramatic moment in the play where he shows the most brutal aspect of his nature by taking a lead role in the torture of Gloucester. It is Cornwall that gouges out Gloucester's eyes and then stamps on them. He matches the violence of his actions with the bitterness of his language: 'Out, vile jelly! / Where is thy lustre now?' In the same scene Cornwall is quick to attack the servant loyal to Lear for his brave intervention. His callous disregard for the man's life is readily apparent: 'Throw this slave / Upon the dunghill.' There is perhaps some justice in the fact that Cornwall is mortally wounded by this servant and dies soon after.

Cornwall	◎ Aligns Himself with Evil
	◎ Disloyal and Disrespectful
	◎ Vicious

Imagery

The rich imagery of *King Lear* brings the themes of the play into sharp focus. Shakespeare uses poetic language to metaphorically explore key ideas. The play's imagery also enriches the audience's understanding of the characters. In particular, three recurring images are woven into the text:

- Animals
- Blindness and Seeing
- Clothing

Animals

There are over one hundred and fifty references to animals in *King Lear* including thirty-four references to dogs, nineteen to horses, fourteen to birds, six to wolves, five to foxes, four to snakes, three to rats and two to worms. The function of this imagery is to explore humanity's place in the world and to highlight the inhuman behaviour of many of the characters.

Throughout the play Goneril and Regan are consistently associated with vicious creatures. Albany declares them 'Tigers, not daughters' (Act 4, Sc 2) and equates their behaviour with animals of prey: 'Humanity must perforce prey on itself, / Like monsters of the deep' (Act 4, Sc 2). Albany's use of animal imagery is a condemnation of Goneril and Regan's inhumanity as they abandon all morality. Lear too uses ugly animal imagery to criticise his daughters. He calls Goneril a 'Detested kite!' and describes her face as a 'wolvish visage' (Act 1, Sc 4); her ingratitude feels 'sharper than a serpent's tooth' (Act 1, Sc 4). Later, Lear labels Goneril and Regan 'pelican daughters' (Act 3, Sc 4). The image here is of young birds cannibalising their parent.

Gloucester too describes Lear's two eldest daughters in animalistic terms. He tells them:

> 'I would not see
> Thy cruel nails pluck out his poor old eyes;
> Nor thy fierce sister in his anointed flesh
> Stick boarish fangs' (Act 3, Sc 7).

In all of these examples the animal imagery underscores Goneril's and Regan's cruelty and inhumanity. By comparing the characters' barbarous behaviour to animal savagery, Shakespeare is pointing to the vileness that humanity is capable of. The point of the imagery is not to show how humans are similar to animals but rather to distinguish between them. The shock Goneril and Regan's behaviour provokes in the audience is a recognition of how unnatural and essentially wrong their actions are. The animal imagery reinforces this idea.

Animal imagery is also used to represent the characters' attempts try to understand humanity's place in the world. It provokes the question: what is a man, and where is his place in the chain of being? At some points of the play, Lear sees humanity as having no greater dignity than an animal. He declares that 'man is no more but such a poor bare, forked animal' (Act 3, Sc 4). This is prompted by the spectacle of Poor Tom's suffering, who ascribes animal status to his own humanity, saying that he has been 'hog in sloth, fox in stealth, wolf in greediness, dog in madness, lion in prey' (Act 3, Sc 4).

Echoing this Gloucester says that the sight of Poor Tom 'made [him] think a man a worm' (Act 4, Sc 1). Gloucester also despairs that in comparison to the gods humanity is as insignificant and powerless as a fly: 'As flies to wanton boys, are we to the gods. / They kill us for their sport' (Act 4, Sc 1). Like Lear, Gloucester at this point of the play cannot recognise the dignity and importance of humanity. This insight comes later.

Both Lear and Gloucester are seeking to make sense of their own suffering. In this process they initially fail to differentiate between the status of humanity and animals. However, towards the end of the play, both characters grow in insight. Lear again draws on animal imagery as he recognises the true value of human life and the greater dignity that comes with being human. As he pitifully grieves over Cordelia's body he cries, 'Why should a dog, a horse, a rat, have life / And thou no breath at all?' (Act 5, Sc 3). Lear has come to see that a human's life is more important than an animal's; he now appreciates humanity's greater status in the chain of being.

Blindness and Seeing

Blindness is present in the play as a powerful metaphor, and, in the case of Gloucester, in a very literal way. Shakespeare uses blindness imagery to highlight the moral blindness of the characters, principally Lear and Gloucester. As the play continues, both men attain insight; Shakespeare employs seeing imagery to point to their development of wisdom and understanding.

From that start of the play, Lear is presented as a man blinded by his inflated pride. In his short-sightedness Lear abdicates his regal responsibilities but still retains the title of King. Just as he is blind to his own folly, Lear cannot recognise the true natures of his daughters: he welcomes hollow flattery from Goneril and Regan and misunderstands Cordelia's plain spoken words. Shakespeare underscores the idea that Lear's judgement is blinded through the language in this scene. When Lear disowns Cordelia he shouts, 'Out of my sight!' Perceptively, Kent recognises Lear's inability to see his daughters' true natures and says, 'See better, Lear'.

The Fool points to Lear's blindness and lack of self-awareness using similar imagery. While Kent is in the stocks the Fool tells him:

> 'All that follow their noses are led by their eyes, but blind men; and there's not a nose among twenty but can smell him that's stinking. Let go thy hold when a great wheel runs down a hill, lest it break thy neck with following it' (Act 2, Sc 4)

Here the Fool argues, that although Lear lacks self-awareness, even the blind can perceive that Lear's downfall is imminent ('can smell him that's stinking'). The Fool says that those who blindly follow Lear will be ruined alongside him.

As Lear starts to understand his own folly and the emptiness of his overblown pride, the imagery changes to one of seeing. In Act 4, Scene 6, amidst his 'madness', Lear recognises Gloucester: 'I remember thine eyes well enough' and 'If thou wilt weep my fortunes, take my eyes. / I know thee well enough, thy name is Gloucester'. Lear says that 'A man may see how this world goes with no eyes'. These images of seeing echo Lear's own growing understanding. As the fog of his moral blindness lifts, Lear can now recognise his own folly and humanity.

Gloucester's downfall follows the same tragic trajectory as Lear's. He too is morally blind at the start of the play. He fails to see the significance of his lust that produced Edmund. This blindness leaves him vulnerable to be manipulated. Gloucester lacks the insight into human nature to recognise Edmund's scheming. There is great irony when he is presented with a forged letter by Edmund, only to comment that he will not need 'spectacles' to read it (Act 1, Sc 2). His lack of vision means that he fails to see Edgar as the loyal son he is and instead disowns him, branding him a villain.

Gloucester is punished in a very literal way for his moral blindness and inability to see his sons for who they are: his eyes are gouged out. The dramatic spectacle of Gloucester being blinded is intensified by the other characters' language. Goneril cries, 'Pluck out his eyes' and Cornwall cruelly says, 'Out, vile jelly! / Where is thy lustre now?' (Act 3, Sc 7).

Blinded and in shock, Gloucester ironically develops moral vision. He starts to see his own folly, 'I stumbled when I saw' (Act 4, Sc 1). He tells Lear that now he is blinded he understands the world at a deeper emotional level: 'I see it feelingly' (Act 4, Sc 6).

Gloucester comes to see Edgar's true nature, the imagery of blindness and seeing is continued as he cries out for Edgar:

> 'O dear son Edgar,

> The food of thy abused father's wrath!
> Might I but live to see thee in my touch,
> I'd say I had eyes again!' (Act 4, Sc 1).

As with Lear, the fog of Gloucester's spiritual blindness lifts as he grows in insight. Both men come to recognise their own flaws, accept ownership of their own fates and understand their own humanity. They develop compassion as they see the suffering of others. Importantly, both men see their children for who they truly are and recognise the depth of love in their loyal children (Cordelia and Edgar). However, this ability to see comes too late for them to avoid their own tragedies.

Clothing

In *King Lear*, the clothing imagery emphasises the themes of power and corruption. Through this imagery Shakespeare illustrates how a person's high status and wealth may mask their vices and corrupt nature. Only by removing the trappings of power can an individual gain true insight and fully appreciate their own humanity.

As Lear starts to appreciate the greed and falseness of Goneril and Regan, he uses a clothing metaphor to highlight their excesses: 'If only to go warm were gorgeous, / Why, nature needs not what thou gorgeous wear'st, / Which scarcely keeps thee warm' (Act 2, Sc 2). Later in the play, Lear sees wealth as masking the vices of the rich; again clothing imagery is used to highlight this point:

> 'Through tattered clothes small vices do appear;
> Robes and furred gowns hide all. Plate sin with gold,
> And the strong lance of justice hurtless breaks;
> Arm it in rags, a pigmy's straw does pierce it' (Act 4, Sc 6).

As Lear appreciates that wealth lends itself to hypocrisy and corruption, he develops a new found compassion for the poor. He imagines their clothes as offering them little protection from the buffeting of the storm:

> 'Poor naked wretches, whereso'er you are
> That bide the pelting of this pitiless storm,
> How shall your houseless heads and unfed sides,
> Your looped and windowed raggedness, defend you
> From seasons such as these?' (Act 3, Sc 4)

Lear chastises himself for embracing pomp and neglecting his royal duty to those who live in poverty: 'O, I have ta'en / Too little care of this! Take physic, pomp; / Expose thyself to feel what wretches feel' (Act 3, Sc 4).

He comes to understand that wealth and status may blind a person morally. Lear sees that an individual can only gain true insight and fully appreciate their own humanity if they remove the trappings of power. This is made clear when Lear first encounters Poor Tom who shivers in the storm (Act 3, Sc 4). There is much emphasis on Tom's nakedness; Lear recognises him as an 'Unaccommodated man' and a 'bare, forked animal'. In solidarity with Tom's suffering and in an effort to discover the meaning of his own humanity, Lear tears off his own clothes. The point here being that pomp (symbolised by clothing) must be discarded if a person is to gain self-awareness.

After Lear's madness subsides and he has uncovered his own humanity, it is fitting that his clothes are restored to him. Cordelia is told that, 'In the heaviness of his sleep / We put fresh garments on him' (Act 4, Sc 7). Lear's status as King is reaffirmed by his clothes. The play argues that only those who deserve power, who can wield it without corruption, should wear the crown. Lear has had to suffer and rediscover his identity for him to understand his kingly duties. Now that he has gained insight he can wear the robes of office again.

Clothing imagery is also important in terms of the disguises adopted throughout the play. Kent disguises himself as Caius (Lear's servant) and Edgar disguises himself as Poor Tom. Both of these characters use disguise, not for malevolent trickery, but instead for good. Both Kent and Edgar 'dress down', signalling their humility. Kent pretends to be a serving-man, while Edgar dresses as a Bedlam beggar:

> 'I will preserve myself, and am bethought
> To take the basest and most poorest shape
> That ever penury, in contempt of man,
> Brought near to beast. My face I'll grime with filth,
> Blanket my loins, elf all my hair in knots,
> And with presented nakedness outface
> The winds and persecutions of the sky' (Act 2, Sc 3)

Neither Kent nor Edgar are motivated by greed, status or power, but rather by love.

Like Lear, Edgar grows as an individual after stripping back the trappings of power. Formerly, as the privileged son of an Earl, Edgar was naïve enough to be duped by his brother. By laying himself bare (symbolised by his nakedness) he grows in strength and resolve to the point where Albany offers him a leadership role in the restored kingdom.

In contrast to this, Oswald uses clothing as a means of social advancement; by 'dressing up' he adopts false social airs beyond his station. Kent berates him calling him a 'three-suited...worsted-stocking...knave' and tells him, 'a tailor made thee' (Act 2, Sc 2). Kent looks to put Oswald in his place. The clothing imagery is relevant in that Oswald does not deserve greater power or status; he is motivated by selfishness, a sharp contrast to Edgar and Kent.

One of the central themes of *King Lear* is power and social status. Shakespeare recognises that wealth and status (symbolised by clothing) can corrupt (e.g. Goneril, Regan, Edmund, Oswald). The evil characters cannot live up to the responsibilities of power and the duties of office. The saying, 'Clothes do not make the man' seems fitting here. At the start of the play Lear is blinded by the pomp of his great office; only by relearning what it means to be King and who he is, does he become fit to wear the crown again.

Imagery	Function
Animals	◎ Highlights the vileness that humanity is capable of ◎ Is used as characters come to understand humanity's place in the chain of being
Blindness and Seeing	◎ The imagery points to both Lear's and Gloucester's moral blindness ◎ Both men initially fail to recognise their own flaws, are blinded to the true natures of their children and are unable to question their own judgement ◎ The imagery reflects Lear's and Gloucester's growth in insight. As Lear suffers mentally during the storm and Gloucester experiences the trauma of being blinded both men 'see' more clearly ◎ Towards the end of the play both men come to recognise their own flawed humanity and see their children for who they are
Clothing	◎ *King Lear*'s clothing imagery highlights the themes of power and corruption ◎ Lear comes to know himself by stripping back the trappings of power. This is symbolised in the clothing imagery ◎ The disguises adopted by Kent and Edgar point to their humility and goodness. This is contrasted by clothing adopted by Oswald ◎ Edgar, like Lear, learns by 'dressing down' and as a result grows as an individual ◎ Ultimately the clothing imagery highlights that only those who deserve power should wield it. Power in the wrong hands leads to corruption

Themes

> **Justice**
> **Divine Justice**
> **Human Justice**
> **Madness**
> **Love**

Justice

At the end of *King Lear*, Albany declares, 'All friends shall taste / The wages of their virtue, and all foes / The cup of their deservings.' He confidently asserts that justice will ensure that everybody will get what they deserve: the virtuous will be rewarded; the wicked will be punished. However, an audience may wonder if this is an accurate reflection of what actually happens to many of the characters in the play.

There is certainly a logic and justice to the fact that Edmund dies at the hands of the brother that he wronged. The deaths of Goneril and Regan, although horrible, also seem a just end to the cruelty they meted out. However, how do we make sense of Cordelia's death? There is little fairness in someone so pure and virtuous dying so violently. Similarly, Kent has loyally served by Lear's side, displaying moral resilience; is it fair he faces imminent death at the end of the play? Gloucester is portrayed as a man who suffers for the 'sin' of lust, but there seems little justice in the excessive suffering he experiences. The same could be said of Lear, whose mental torment and then loss of his beloved daughter seems an unjust and disproportionate punishment for his folly in the first scene. If justice means that individuals get what they deserve, how can we understand what happens to the good characters in the play? *King Lear* also draws attention to social inequality, asking questions about social justice and the possibility of human justice.

In *King Lear*, Shakespeare explores the idea of justice in terms of divine justice and justice in the human realm.

Divine Justice

King Lear explores the concept of divine justice. Different characters offer radically opposing views on the influence of the gods in human affairs. It is important to realise that not one individual character functions as a mouthpiece for Shakespeare, but rather the play presents a multitude of views of divine justice through the characterisation.

Throughout the play, Lear makes appeals to the gods and the stars. He swears 'by the sacred radiance of the sun, / The mysteries of Hecate, and the night; / By all the operation of the orbs' and calls upon 'Apollo' and 'Jupiter' (Act 1, Sc 1). He appeals to the heavens: 'O heavens…If you do love old men…Send down, and take my part!' (Act 2, Sc 4). In his arrogance, Lear expects the gods to take his side, but such a prayer is futile. As Kent says, 'Thou swear'st thy gods in vain' (Act 2, Sc 4). Shakespeare shows the pointlessness of praying blindly, of asking the gods for favours that are not deserved.

During the storm Lear comes to believe that justice does not grow out of divine influence but rather comes from the actions of people. He calls for greater social justice, for people to make the world a fairer place and 'show the heavens more just' (Act 3, Sc 4). Lear comes to see his own suffering as a 'Judicious punishment' (Act 3, Sc 4). However, he does not endorse a religious reason for this and instead locates justice in the actions of people rather than the agency of the gods (see 'Human Justice' below).

In contrast, Edgar testifies to the just intervention of the gods in human affairs: 'The gods are just, and of our pleasant vices / Make instruments to plague us' (Act 5, Sc 3). However, he does recognise human beings as the architects of their own fates as he tells Edmund that Gloucester's suffering has its roots in the 'sin' of lust: 'The dark and vicious place where thee he got / Cost him his eyes' (Act 5, Sc 3). Edgar sees a connection between human actions and divine justice.

Gloucester's attitude to the gods changes. In the midst of despair he blames his suffering on the vagaries of the gods: 'As flies to wanton boys, are we to the gods. / They kill us for their sport' (Act 4, Sc 1). In this moment, Gloucester sees the actions of the gods as inherently unjust. However, after he is tricked by Edgar into believing that the gods have saved him, Gloucester revises his view, seeing the gods as benevolent: 'You ever-gentle gods, take my breath from me. / Let not my worser spirit tempt me again / To die before you please!' (Act 4, Sc 1). It is interesting however, that Gloucester's renewed faith in divine justice is the result of a trick. Some critics argue that *King Lear* suggests that there is no divine order to the world, that ultimately the human condition is one of suffering. Humanity must simply endure the ups and downs of life: 'Men must endure / Their going hence, even as their coming hither; / Ripeness is all' (Act 5, Sc 2).

In contrast with the views of the other characters, Kent believes astrology and fate bring a just balance to life. While he is placed in the stocks, he appeals to Fortune to favourably control events: 'Fortune, good night. Smile once more, turn thy wheel!' (Act 2, Sc 2). He takes comfort in the idea that human fate cannot be altered as it is inextricably bound to the influence of the stars: 'It is the stars, / The stars above us, govern our condition' (Act 4, Sc 3).

Ultimately *King Lear* presents a multitude of views about the possibility of divine justice. The play creates a dialogue about this issue. The character of Lear finds justice in the world but does not give it divine significance. In contrast Gloucester and Edgar affirm the just influence of gods in the world. Kent however believes that justice and order have their genesis in astrological events and in Fortune. Perhaps the idea of cosmic justice is most strongly challenged by the final scene of the play. The injustice of Cordelia's death and the intensity of Lear's suffering undermine faith in a divine or cosmic order. Even Kent admits that, 'All's cheerless, dark, and deadly.' This final scene asks the question of the audience: where are the gods in a world beset by evil and suffering? Ultimately, is the world an unfair place where man brings about his own disastrous downfall?

Human Justice

King Lear also explores the idea of justice within the human realm. The play exposes the injustice of social inequality and the hypocrisy that so often accompanies wealth. Also, in one of the most pessimistic notes of the play, *King Lear* points to the ineffectuality of legal systems in promoting justice in the world.

Social injustice is a key idea within *King Lear*. As Lear suffers himself, he starts to appreciate that a system of privilege unfairly creates deprivation for many. During the storm Lear is prompted by the spectacle of Poor Tom's nakedness and declares:

'Poor naked wretches, whereso'er you are
That bide the pelting of this pitiless storm,
How shall your houseless heads and unfed sides,
Your looped and windowed raggedness, defend you
From seasons such as these? O, I have ta'en
Too little care of this! Take physic, pomp;
Expose thyself to feel what wretches feel,
That thou mayst shake the superflux to them,
And show the heavens more just' (Act 3, Sc 4)

Lear is ashamed of the way he ignored the plight of the poor in the past ('O, I have ta'en / Too little care of this!) and the vanity or pride that accompanies wealth: 'Take physic, pomp; / Expose thyself to feel what wretches feel'.

In Act 4, Scene 6, Lear comes to see that there is little difference between the rich and the poor bar their social circumstances. He tells Gloucester, 'See how yond justice rails upon yond simple thief. Hark, in thine ear: change places and, handy-dandy, which is the justice, which is the thief?' He understands that the office of power does not necessarily reflect the merit of the person who occupies it: 'a dog's obeyed in office'. Lear sees that wealth and privilege may obscure the sins of the rich; the poor cannot afford such luxury: 'Through tattered clothes small vices do appear; / Robes and furred gowns hide all.'

As he suffers, Gloucester comes to a similar conclusion as Lear. He recognises the grossly disproportionate manner in which wealth is distributed in society:

> 'Let the superfluous and lust-dieted man
> That slaves your ordinance, that will not see
> Because he doth not feel, feel your power quickly;
> So distribution should undo excess,
> And each man have enough' (Act 4, Sc 1).

He espouses a radical doctrine of wealth redistribution, where the assets of a society should be used to meet the needs of people so that 'each man have enough.'

King Lear exposes the inequalities and injustices of social structures. The play takes a jaundiced view of legal systems, offering a number of 'trials' within the play.

Lear's 'love-test' is a trial of sorts, whereby Lear tries to judge the strength of his daughters' love for him. Lear's inability to judge correctly leads to the unjust punishing of Cordelia and Kent: Cordelia is disowned, while Kent is banished.

Another trial of sorts occurs when Cornwall places Kent on trial for his 'bluntness'. As punishment, Kent is placed in the stocks. Kent is certainly fiery and disrespectful in this scene but he is motivated by loyalty to Lear. Here again justice isn't seen to be done as Kent is punished for loyally defending the honour of the King – albeit in an overly passionate manner.

Gloucester is placed on 'trial' by Cornwall, Goneril and Regan. Charged with treason he is severely punished by having his eyes gouged out. Although, as Edgar later points out, Gloucester is punished for the sin of 'lust', his punishment seems disproportionate to his crime. The cruelty and unfairness of this highlights the injustice of the world.

An obvious exploration of the meaning of human justice occurs during Lear's 'mock trial' of Goneril and Regan. With Lear as chief justice and Poor Tom and the Fool taking the role of assistant judges, Lear imagines arraigning Goneril and Regan. He calls for Regan's heart to be dissected to find the source of her cruel nature: 'let them anatomize Regan; see what breeds about her heart. Is there any cause in nature that makes these hard hearts?' (Act 3, Sc 6). The mock-trial points to the absurdity of human justice. Lear as judge, fails to interrogate himself and explore his own role in bringing about his own downfall. The mad nature of the trial combined with its inability to successfully apportion blame offers a jaundiced view of legal systems.

Through all of these examples of trials within the text, *King Lear* suggests that when human beings try to exercise justice and pass judgement on others there is no guarantee that the outcome will be just, fair or right. In fact, the idea that one flawed human can condemn another is shown in itself to be absurd. Lear imagines a 'beadle' (early type of police officer) whipping a 'whore' for a sexual crime, when in reality he 'hotly lusts to use her in that kind'. In Lear's view, those who can afford it may avoid justice, whereas the poor have to pay for their crimes: 'Plate sin with gold, / And the strong lance of justice hurtless breaks; / Arm it in rags, a pigmy's straw does pierce it' (Act 4, Sc 6).

Although *King Lear* offers a pessimistic view of the possibility of justice, the ideas explored certainly resonate in the modern world. Issues of social inequality and corruption are as relevant now as they were during Shakespeare's time.

Justice		
Divine Justice	◎ Different views on the possibility of divine justice are offered by the various characters	
	◎ Lear at first makes vain appeals to the gods. He comes to see that his fate results from his own actions rather than divine influence	
	◎ Gloucester changes his view of the gods seeing them at first as uncaring and cruel but then comes to understand them as benevolent	
	◎ Edgar connects divine justice with human action. He argues that human actions prompt the agency of divine justice	
	◎ Rather than appealing to the gods, Kent believes in the just order of astrology and Fortune	
	◎ The play's final scene arguably undermines the idea of cosmic or divine justice through the unjust death of Cordelia and the disproportionate suffering that Lear experiences	
Human Justice	◎ *King Lear* exposes social injustice, highlighting deprivation and abuses of power	
	◎ The play offers a jaundiced view of legal systems and suggests the absurdity of human justice	

Madness

Madness is central to *King Lear* and is associated with both social disorder and insight in the play. King Lear's madness represents the extent of his psychological suffering but is also a mental state that allows him to achieve wisdom.

Lear's madness is a very human response to the trauma and suffering he experiences at the hands of his daughters. His unpredictable behaviour reflects his mental imbalance: we see him tearing off his clothes on the heath, conducting an imaginary trial of his daughters and treating Poor Tom as if he were a learned scholar. His madness occurs as his arrogant, volatile self is humbled by the erosion of his pride.

Lear is very aware of the threat of madness as his identity as King is undermined. He tells the Fool: 'O, let me not be mad, not mad, sweet heaven! / Keep me in temper; I would not be mad!' (Act 1, Sc 5). He experiences fear as his grip on reality loosens: 'O, how this mother swells up toward my heart! / *Hysterica passio*, down, thou climbing sorrow! / Thy element's below!', 'O, Fool I shall go mad!' (Act 2, Sc 4)

Lear's madness is certainly a very real psychological response to stress but it also has a symbolic function within the play. His fragmenting mind reflects the division within his kingdom. As King, Lear's selfhood is bound up with the state; the disorder within Britain is therefore echoed by his mental turmoil. The Fool draws a parallel between Lear's impaired mind and the division of his kingdom: 'Thou hast pared thy wit o' both sides, and left nothing i' the middle' (Act 1, Sc 4). The Fool mocks Lear for splitting his mind along with his kingdom: 'When thou clovest thy crown i' the middle, and gavest away both parts, thou borest thy ass on thy back o'er the dirt' (Act 1, Sc 4). Here the Fool puns on the word 'crown' meaning both 'head' and a symbol of kingly power; the implication being that Lear foolishly has divided both. Lear's madness therefore symbolises the chaos that ensues once the social order is upturned. This idea is compounded by the presence of the storm as a backdrop to Lear's madness.

Lear's madness also serves as a vehicle for him to achieve insight. As Edgar listens to Lear rant during the storm, he pithily notes, 'O, matter and impertinency mixed! Reason in madness!' (Act 4, Sc 6). He recognises that although Lear is losing touch with reality, through madness Lear is developing an imaginative vision of evil, human folly and the world.

It is during moments of madness that Lear achieves many of his philosophical insights. Just before he runs merrily from Cordelia's men announcing that he will 'die bravely, like a smug bridegroom', Lear comments on the folly and pain that comes with being human: 'When we are born, we cry that we are come / To this great stage of fools' (Act 4, Sc 6). Similarly, Lear's empathy for 'poor naked wretches' and his recognition of the emptiness of 'pomp' (Act 3, Sc 4) happen as his mental state deteriorates. Again, it is during a moment of madness that Lear imaginatively conceives how wealth hides the sins of the rich: 'Through tattered clothes small vices do appear; / Robes and furred gowns hide all' (Act 4, Sc 6).

It is also in the midst of madness that Lear comes to understand his own humanity. As his mental state starts to deteriorate Lear begins to recognise his mistreatment of Cordelia: 'I did her wrong' (Act 1, Sc 5). He expresses great shame and becomes tortured by regret: 'I am bound / Upon a wheel of fire, that mine own tears / Do scald like molten lead' (Act 4, Sc 7). As he see his own mistakes, Lear revises his vision of himself. Gone is the 'dragon' of the first scene, instead Lear comes to see himself as 'a very foolish, fond old man' (Act 4, Sc 7). It is through madness that Lear achieves this vision of his own flawed nature. Madness therefore has an ennobling and humanising effect on him. Lear truly achieves 'Reason in madness'.

Madness is also present in the play through the character of Edgar who adopts the persona of a mad Bedlam Beggar, Poor Tom. His feigned madness allows Shakespeare to extend the scope of his social commentary to include those judged insane and dispossessed by society. The figure of Poor Tom reminds the audience about the intolerable suffering experienced by social pariahs:

> 'Poor Tom, that … eats cow-dung for sallets, swallows the old rat and the ditch-dog, drinks the green mantle of the standing pool, who is whipped from tithing to tithing, and stock-punished and imprisoned' (Act 3, Sc 4).

Here madness is emblematic of misfortune and hardship, and intensifies the message of social justice espoused by Lear and Gloucester: 'distribution should undo excess, / And each man have enough' (Gloucester, Act 4, Sc 1).

In the modern world, 'madness' is treated in a much more sensitive fashion than it was during Shakespeare's time. This is reflected in the changed vocabulary around mental health. However, the theme of madness still resonates with a modern audience. It offers a fascinating depth to Lear's character, has an important symbolic function in the play and deepens our understanding of the play's progressive social commentary.

Madness	
Lear's madness	◎ A psychological response to trauma and stress ◎ Symbolises the social disorder created by the unnatural division of the kingdom ◎ Serves as a vehicle for Lear to gain insight into the world and himself: 'Reason in madness'
Poor Tom's 'madness'	◎ Allows Shakespeare to extend the scope of his social commentary

Love

King Lear asks questions about the meaning of love. The play offers the audience different visions of love, some pure, some corrupted. Shakespeare points to the destructive potential of love when it is founded on lust and on material gain. This is certainly the case with Goneril and Regan. However, *King Lear* also presents visions of true love: Cordelia and Kent's loving devotion to Lear, and Edgar's love for Gloucester, present a much more hopeful pattern. Ultimately the play suggests that true, uncorrupted love is immeasurable, healing and redemptive.

In the first scene of the play, King Lear mistakenly believes that he can quantify his daughters' love for him. He arrogantly conducts the 'love-test', inviting the flattery of his daughters by which he will measure their loving devotion. It is Cordelia who shows the audience the absurdity of this test as she explains that love cannot be quantified. As such the weight of her love for her father cannot be reduced to mere words: 'I cannot heave / My heart into my mouth', 'I am sure, my love's / More ponderous than my tongue' (Act 1, Sc 1).

As a virtuous character, Cordelia understands that love is immeasurable. Her love for her father is pure and absolute. Because of the strength of her devotion Cordelia remains deeply committed to Lear even after she is disowned by him. It is the purity of her love that allows her to forgive Lear unreservedly. Cordelia is constant in her concern for his wellbeing. As she explains, love for her father is what motivates her actions, even that of going to war: 'No blown ambition doth our arms incite, / But love, dear love, and our aged father's right' (Act 4, Sc 4).

As a loving daughter, Cordelia never blames or speaks ill of her father. Instead she looks to forgive him. When she learns of Lear's fragmenting mental state, she sends out a party to find him and cries out for him to be healed: 'All you unpublished virtues of the earth, / Spring with my tears! Be aidant and remediate / In the good man's distress!' (Act 4, Sc 4). Her love rises far above the selfish greed of her sisters when she says she would gladly give away all of her wealth if it would cure Lear: 'He that helps him take all my outward worth' (Act 4, Sc 4).

In Cordelia's case, love is presented as healing. She wishes to cure Lear of his 'bereaved sense' as she tenderly kisses him:

> 'O my dear father! Restoration hang
> Thy medicine on my lips, and let this kiss
> Repair those violent harms that my two sisters
> Have in thy reverence made!' (Act 4, Sc 7)

Through the character of Cordelia, Shakespeare articulates a hopeful vision of the redemptive power of love, and illustrates that true love is immeasurable and absolute.

Kent's love for Lear is also positively framed within the play. Like Cordelia, he is lovingly devoted:

> 'Royal Lear,
> Whom I have ever honoured as my king,
> Loved as my father, as my master followed,
> As my great patron thought on in my prayers' (Act 1, Sc 1).

As a loving follower of Lear, Kent feels that it is his duty to help prevent Lear from making any mistakes. He tries to show Lear that the decision to disown Cordelia is one of 'hideous rashness'. However, Lear's arrogance blinds him to the truth of Kent's observations and Lear is unable to see that Kent is acting out of love.

Kent is constant in his loving devotion to Lear. Despite being banished and threatened with death, Kent takes a great risk by returning to Lear in disguise and acting as his servant. Kent's love for his master is best displayed at the end of the play. After Lear dies, Kent refuses Albany's offer to help rule the kingdom. Kent himself is dying having expended himself in service to Lear. He touchingly expresses his intention to wait for death and follow Lear into the afterlife: 'I have a journey, sir, shortly to go; / My master calls me, I must not say no' (Act 5, Sc 3). His love for Lear transcends death itself. Through Kent, Shakespeare shows how powerful and unwavering true love can be. Again, love is shown as immeasurable and absolute.

King Lear also presents the audience with a number of examples of the evil characters' corruption of love. These serve as comparisons that deepen our appreciation of true love in the play. Most obviously, the false testimonies of love offered by Goneril and Regan in the first scene contrast with the purity of Cordelia's love. Goneril and Regan lavish Lear with false praise: 'A love that makes breath poor, and speech unable; / Beyond all manner of so much I love you' (Goneril), 'I profess / Myself an enemy to all other joys, / …I am alone felicitate / In your dear Highness' love' (Regan). The subsequent cruelty that Regan and Goneril show their father, demonstrates the insincerity of their expressions of love. Goneril and Regan are motivated by greed. Shakespeare shows that when love is corrupted by materialism, it is deeply destructive. Their false expressions of love for their father allows the audience, and indeed Lear, to appreciate the purity of Cordelia's love all the more.

Goneril's and Regan's feelings for Edmund is another example of love being corrupted. Just as their false testimonies of love for their father grow out of greed, their feelings for Edmund are based on lust. Both Goneril and Regan become bitter rivals for Edmund's affections. Regan's lust for Edmund drives her to jealousy: 'She gave strange oeillades and most speaking looks / To noble Edmund' (Act 4, Sc 5). Similarly, Goneril, in an effort to rid herself of a competitor for Edmund's affections, poisons and kills Regan. Shakespeare shows that lust is divisive and destructive, and although it may appear like love at times, it is not genuine love at all.

The theme of love is also explored in the play's sub-plot. Here again we see the destructive influence of lust. As Gloucester tells Kent about his 'illegitimate' son, Edmund, he laughs at his own lechery: 'yet was his mother fair; there was good sport at his making, and the whoreson must be acknowledged' (Act 1, Sc 1). During Shakespeare's time, the audience would have seen Gloucester's lust and sexual behaviour as sinful. As Edmund is the product of this 'sin', Gloucester's lust sets in motion a train of events that lead to his own downfall. This is echoed by Edgar who connects Gloucester's blindness with lust; he tells Edmund: 'The dark and vicious place where thee he got / Cost him his eyes' (Act 5, Sc 3). As with the cases of Goneril and Regan, Gloucester's story emphasises that romantic relationships should never be founded on lust.

However, the sub-plot also mirrors the main plot by offering the audience a vision of true love: that of Edgar for his father. Like Cordelia's love for Lear, Edgar's love for Gloucester is unwavering even after he is made an outlaw by him. Motivated by love, Edgar readily forgives Gloucester and goes to great lengths to help Gloucester. Out of kindness he tricks his father into believing that he has been saved by the gods, to lift him out of despair: 'Why I do trifle thus with his despair / Is done to cure it' (Act 4, Sc 6). Again, Shakespeare presents a vision of pure love that is unwavering and healing.

Love is a universal theme that transcends time and culture. *King Lear* is a fascinating endorsement of how love can redeem humanity but also warns against its corruption by greed and lust.

Love	
Cordelia's love for Lear	◉ Offers a vision of love that is immeasurable, absolute and healing
Kent's love for Lear	◉ Displays the power of loving devotion
Goneril and Regan's false love for Lear	◉ Acts as a contrast to Cordelia's love ◉ Illustrates how love can be corrupted by greed
Goneril and Regan's lust for Edmund	◉ Shows the destructive power of lust
Gloucester's lust	◉ Show the destructive power of lust
Edgar's love for Gloucester	◉ Echoes Cordelia's love for Lear ◉ Presents a vision of pure love that is redemptive

The Life of William Shakespeare

The exact details of William Shakespeare's life are unclear. However some facts are known from court and clercal records.

Shakespeare's exact date of birth is unknown but records reveal that he was baptised on the 26 April 1564. Due to a scholar's mistake, his birthday is commemorated on the 23 April. This date has appealed to commentators as it is also the same date on which he died (23 April 1616).

Shakespeare was born at Stratford-upon-Avon to John Shakespeare and Mary Arden. He was the third child of eight, although three of his siblings died before reaching adulthood.

None of his school records survive, but Shakespeare probably attended the local grammar school: the King's New School. It is thought that he left school at the age of 15.

In 1582, he married Anne Hathaway. He was 18; she was 26. Six months later, Anne gave birth to a daughter, whom they named Susanna. She was followed two years later by the twins: Hamnet and Judith. Sadly, Hamnet, Shakespeare's only son, died at the age of 11; the cause is unknown.

Biographers refer to the years 1585-1592 as 'The Lost Years' as there are no records of Shakespeare's life for this period. Shakespeare is mentioned in the London theatre records in 1592. Various legends suggest Shakespeare's reasons for leaving Stratford-upon-Avon. The most persistent is that Shakespeare fled to avoid prosecution for deer poaching at the Charlecote estate. This is unlikely as Charlecote did not have a deer park for another 100 years! Other biographers believe that he worked as a school teacher pointing to the record of a William Shakeshaft in Lancashire. However, Shakeshaft was a relatively popular name at the time.

What is known for certain is that Shakespeare worked as an actor, and wrote plays and poetry. He joined a theatre group called The Lord Chamberlain's Men. In 1603, King James I became the company's royal patron and it changed its name to The King's Men. Shakespeare also owned a share in the Globe Theatre in London which made him a wealthy man.

Shakespeare wrote about 37 plays, including the tragedies: *Romeo and Juliet*, *Julius Caesar*, *Hamlet*, *Othello*, *King Lear*, *Macbeth* and *Coriolanus*. His celebrated comedies include *The Tempest*, *A Midsummer's Night Dream*, *Much Ado About Nothing* and *The Merchant of Venice*. His dramas are performed regularly throughout the world today.

Shakespeare died in 1616. He left the bulk of his wealth to his daughter Susanna. Famously, Shakespeare left his wife his 'second best bed'. Some commentators see this as an insult to his wife, others argue that this is a reference to the matrimonial bed and therefore a symbolic gesture.

Shakespeare was buried at the Holy Trinity Church. His epitaph warns against his body being moved:

'Good friend, for Jesus' sake forbear,
To dig the dust enclosed here.
Blessed be the man that spares these stones,
And cursed be he that moves my bones.' [modern spelling]

Ordinary Level Exam Tips

- ◎ **Answer the question:** This may seem obvious, but it is vital that you remain focused on what exactly the question is asking.
- ◎ **Structure your answer:** Take a few minutes to plan the shape of your answer. Sequence your ideas in a logical order.
- ◎ **Make points. Don't narrate the plot:** Although there are times when you will need to explain what has occurred in a scene, it is important that you don't simply retell the story.
- ◎ **Use paragraphs in your answer:** Although you are not required to write a long essay, you should use paragraphs where it is appropriate.
- ◎ **Quote and refer:** The examiner is keen to see that you have an in-depth knowledge of the play. Illustrate this by using quotations and by making appropriate references.
- ◎ **Watch your timing:** Most students spend approximately an hour on the Single Text question.

Ordinary Level Exam Topics

- ◎ **Key scenes**: Focus on scenes that are tense or exciting, act as turning points, illuminate the characters' personalities and are of thematic importance.
- ◎ **Characters:** Think about how characters are portrayed, the relationship between central characters, the dramatic importance of key characters.
- ◎ **Staging** / **directing** the play.
- ◎ Your **personal response** to the play
- ◎ **Themes**

Ordinary Level – Past Exam Questions

2010

Answer **all** of the questions.

1. (a) How does Cordelia upset her father at the beginning of the play? (10)
   (b) Do you think that King Lear was wise to banish Kent? Explain your answer. (10)
2. Do you like Edmund? Explain your answer with reference to the text. (10)
3. Answer **ONE** of the following: [Each part carries 30 marks]
   (i) Based on your reading of the play, write a piece beginning with **ONE** of the following statements:
       – *this is a story about foolishness*
       – *this is a story about love*

OR

   (ii) 'Sisters! Sisters! Shame of ladies!'
        This is Cordelia's comment on her sisters, Goneril and Regan. Describe the character and conduct of the two sisters. Support your answer with reference to the play.

OR

   (iii) Which of the characters would you like to play in your school's production of *King Lear*? Give reasons for your choice. Support your answer with reference to the play.

See sample answer on p.231

2006

Answer **all** of the questions.

1. In the opening scene of the play Lear says:
   'Tell me, my daughters…Which of you shall we say doth love us most…?'
   (a) Describe King Lear's reaction when Cordelia refused to take part in the Love Test he organised for his daughters at the start of the play. (10)
   (b) In your opinion did Cordelia do the right thing in refusing to take part? Explain your view. (10)
2. Apart from the Love Test, what do you think was the most important moment in the play? Give reasons for your answer, supporting them by reference to the text. (10)
3. Answer **ONE** of the following: [each part carries 30 marks]
   (i) The most important lesson the play teaches us is that:
       – *Young people have a duty to respect their elders, no matter what*
       – *People are not to be trusted*
       – *Everybody makes mistakes*
       Choose **one** of the above statements and explain how the play teaches you that lesson.

OR

   (ii) Imagine that the Fool kept a diary of the time he spent with King Lear. Write out **two** entries he might make about his experience during that time.

OR

   (iii) Your local library is holding an event called *My Favourite Play* where readers explain what they particularly liked about their chosen play. You are to take part and you choose to introduce *King Lear* to the audience.

2002

Answer **all** of the questions.

1. (a) Briefly describe how King Lear behaved during the storm. (10)
   (b) In your opinion, was the storm scene a very dramatic scene?
       Briefly explain your answer. (10)

(c) Gloucester paid dearly for helping King Lear when Lear was sent out by his daughters into the storm. Briefly describe the scene when Gloucester was punished by Cornwall and Regan. (10)

2. Answer **ONE** of the following: [Each part carries 30 marks]

  (i) 'A good play should teach us something about life.'
What did your reading of *King Lear* teach you about relationships and about how people should treat one another?

OR

  (ii) The motion for a class debate is:
'In the play, *King Lear*, love is stronger than hate.'
Write the speech you would make for or against this motion.

OR

  (iii) 'Regan and Goneril – The sisters from hell!'
Using your knowledge of their behaviour in the play, *King Lear*, write a report for a tabloid newspaper under the above headline

2001

Answer **all** of the questions.

1. Describe the scene in which King Lear dies. (15)
2. With which character in *King Lear* do you feel most sympathy? Explain your answer. (15)
3. Answer **ONE** of the following [Each part carries 30 marks]

  (i) You are taking part in a school debate with the following motion;
'There is too much pointless violence in Shakespeare.'
Argue for *or* against this motion with particular reference to *King Lear*.

OR

  (ii) Do you think that Lear was completely responsible for the disaster which happens to him? Give reasons for your opinion.

OR

  (iii) In your opinion was Gloucester a good father to his sons, Edgar and Edmund? Give reasons for your opinion.

Ordinary Level – Sample Questions

Sample Questions A

Answer **all** of the questions.

1. (a) How does Edmund turn Gloucester against Edgar? (10)
   (b) What is your view of Gloucester as a character? (10)

2. Describe what happens to King Lear during the Storm scenes. (10)

3. Answer **ONE** of the following: [Each part carries 30 marks]
   (i) Discuss the similarities between Lear's story and Gloucester's story in the play.

   OR

   (ii) Which of the characters in *King Lear* do you admire the most? Explain by commenting on how the character behaves during the play.

   OR

   (iii) *King Lear* continues to be one of the most performed and popular of Shakespeare's plays. Do you think it deserves to remain so popular? Give reasons for your answer by referring to the text and/or your experience of watching the play performed.

Sample Questions B

Answer **all** of the questions.

1. (a) In the last scene of the play, Edgar calls Edmund a 'traitor'. Explain how Edmund has earned this description. (10)
   (b) What do you think is Edmund's motivation for his behaviour throughout the play? Make reference to the play in your answer. (10)

2. Do you think Cordelia is honest, stubborn or a combination of both? Base your answer on your knowledge of the play. (10)

3. Answer **ONE** of the following: [Each part carries 30 marks]
   (i) Imagine you are King Lear. Write two diary entries: one, as you first go out into the storm, and a second after you are reunited with Cordelia. You should base your diary entries on your knowledge of the play.

   OR

   (ii) Imagine you are a director. Choose one important moment from *King Lear* and describe how you would show it on stage or on film. Explain your reasons for showing it this way, pointing out the effect you would like it to have on the audience.

   OR

   (iii) Write a piece, based on your knowledge of the play, beginning with one of the following statements:
   I think King Lear brings about his own downfall
   I feel very sorry for King Lear
   I think King Lear learns valuable lessons throughout the course of the play

Ordinary Level 2010 – Sample Answers

1. **(a) How does Cordelia upset her father at the beginning of the play? (10)**
   1 (a)

   At the start of 'King Lear', Cordelia upsets her father by refusing to take part in the love-test. King Lear plans to divide his kingdom amongst his three daughters: Goneril, Regan and Cordelia. Lear says that he will give the largest portion of his land to the daughter who shows him the most love. Goneril and Regan both compete for this by falsely flattering their father. However, Cordelia refuses to do likewise.

   As an honourable and honest young woman, Cordelia is uncomfortable with the love-test. She knows that her love is so great that she cannot truly express it in words: 'I am sure, my love's / More ponderous than my tongue.' When Lear asks Cordelia to speak, her initial reply is 'Nothing.' She then tells her father: 'I cannot heave / My heart into my mouth. I love your Majesty / According to my bond; no more nor less.' Cordelia is telling Lear that she cannot articulate the true depth of her love and that she loves her father like a dutiful daughter should. However, because Lear is so proud and arrogant he misinterprets her words thinking that she does not love him at all. He becomes enraged and disowns her, refusing to give her any dowry.

   I think that Cordelia is a much better woman than her sisters. She is honest to Lear and remains calm when he loses his temper. I admire the way she stands up for herself insisting that Lear explain that she has no 'vicious blot' or flaw in her character. However, I think she was a little too stubborn. Although she is not responsible for King Lear's folly and fiery temper, she could have shown a little more compassion for an elderly man.

   (b) Do you think that King Lear was wise to banish Kent? Explain your answer. (10)
   1 (b)

   I think Lear is very unwise to banish Kent. When Lear disowns Cordelia and rewards Goneril and Regan, Kent tries to help Lear recognise the terrible mistake he is making. However, Lear is too proud and arrogant to understand Kent's intention. Kent warns Lear to 'check / This hideous rashness'. He asks Lear to see that Cordelia truly loves him and explains that Goneril and Regan's flattery is meaningless: 'Thy youngest daughter does not love thee least; / Nor are those empty-hearted whose low sound / Reverbs no hollowness'.

   Lear's angry response is extremely threatening. He warns Kent, 'Come not between the dragon and his wrath!' and roars, 'The bow is bent and drawn, make from the shaft.'

   Lear fails to understand that Kent is a loyal earl. He does not listen when Kent tells him, 'My life I never held but as a pawn / To wage against thy enemies'. Instead Lear thinks that Kent is challenging his authority and banishes Kent from the kingdom on pain of death.

   It is quite clear that Lear is making a huge mistake and does not understand the depth of Kent's loyalty. Later in the play Kent proves his devotion to Lear by disguising himself as a servant just to be close to his king. This is an act of great bravery as Kent is putting his life at risk by not leaving the kingdom. When Lear dies, Kent plans to loyally follow his master into the afterlife: 'I have a journey, sir, shortly to go; / My master calls me, I must not say no.'

   Blinded by his pride, Lear's decision to banish such a devoted and loyal follower as Kent is very unwise.

2. **Do you like Edmund? Explain your answer with reference to the text. (10)**
2. I do not like Edmund as he is a manipulative and evil character. However, I must admit that Edmund's intelligence and drive make him fascinating to watch on stage.

The manner in which Edmund mistreats his father and brother is shockingly evil. By forging a letter in his brother's name, Edmund turns Gloucester against Edgar. Edmund then wounds himself claiming that Edgar hurt him. This treachery makes Edmund a thoroughly vile individual.

Edmund celebrates his own intelligence and uses it for evil: 'Let me, if not by birth, have lands by wit; / All with me's meet that I can fashion fit.' He believes that all means are acceptable if they get him what he wants. I find this despicable.

Edmund is particularly cruel when he betrays Gloucester to Cornwall. He shows Cornwall a letter proving that Gloucester is in touch with the French forces and plans to help Lear. Edmund is motivated by a desire to increase his social status and wealth. Cornwall gives him both by making him the new Earl of Gloucester. Although some may sympathise with Edmund because he is labelled a 'bastard' I don't feel this justifies his terrible actions. Edmund's betrayal of his father has dire consequences: Gloucester's eyes are gouged out and he is removed from his own castle to 'smell / His way to Dover.'

Edmund is exploitative of Goneril and Regan. He encourages both women romantically. However, he is simply trying to see which sister will bring him the greatest advantage:

'To both these sisters have I sworn my love;
Each jealous of the other, as the stung
Are of the adder. Which of them shall I take?
Both? One? Or neither?'

This manipulative side of his personality makes him very sinister.

Perhaps Edmund's most despicable action is when he orders the murders of Lear and Cordelia. Although, his plot fails to kill Lear, Cordelia's death prompts Lear to die of a broken heart. Some might argue that Edmund redeems himself by trying to prevent the execution order being carried out. However, I believe that Edmund is a self-serving villain to the end; his attempts to save Lear and Cordelia are just an effort to fool others and avoid condemnation. In the end Edmund is a villainous, evil, manipulative and sinister character. Although he is fascinating to watch on stage, I dislike him strongly.

3. **Answer ONE of the following: [Each part carries 30 marks]**
   (ii) 'Sisters! Sisters! Shame of ladies!'
   This is Cordelia's comment on her sisters, Goneril and Regan. Describe the character and conduct of the two sisters. Support your answer with reference to the play.
   3 (ii)

Both Goneril and Regan are vile characters throughout the play. Their falsity, ingratitude, cruelty and self-interest make them thoroughly despicable. Their deaths at the end evoke little sympathy in either the other characters or the audience.

Goneril and Regan are shown to be utterly false in the first scene of the play. When Lear invites his daughters to testify to the strength of their love for him in the love-test, both Goneril and Regan use empty flattery to try to win Lear's approval. Goneril tells Lear: 'Sir, I love you more than words can wield the matter, / Dearer than eye-sight, space and liberty'. Regan tries to top her sister's words saying that Goneril 'comes too short'. She tells her father: 'I profess / Myself an enemy to all other joys… / And find I am alone felicitate / In your dear Highness' love.'

Cordelia points out that Goneril and Regan are well practised in the 'glib and oily art' (smooth-talking) but there is no substance to the things they say. We see this in the appalling way that Goneril and Regan mistreat their father once they have gained his wealth and power. The sisters know that Lear's weakness is his pride; they provoke a confrontation with Lear by undermining and insulting him. Goneril tells her servant Oswald to treat Lear rudely. Regan insults Lear encouraging Cornwall to place Lear's servant (Kent, in disguise) in the stocks. Goneril and Regan reduce Lear's train of knights from one hundred to one, leaving Lear with no entourage. Goneril and Regan know that this will unsettle their father. Unsurprisingly Lear flies into a rage and goes out into the storm alone. Neither Goneril nor Regan seem the least bit concerned about him. Clearly their expressions of love in the first scene were completely untrue. Both women are despicable in the underhand way in which they treat their father.

The sisters' cruelty is not reserved solely for Lear. Their treatment of Gloucester is horrifying. When Gloucester is taken captive for helping Lear, Goneril immediately calls out, 'Pluck out his eyes!' Regan encourages her husband Cornwall to do that very thing and then cruelly orders that Gloucester, now blind, should be cast out of his own castle: 'Go thrust him out at gates, and let him smell / His way to Dover.' Goneril is equally callous towards her own husband. She has no reservation in writing to Edmund asking him to kill Albany. Both sisters are clearly vicious and ruthless and will stop at nothing to get their own way.

The manner in which Goneril and Regan are suspicious of, and treat, each other is equally awful. Both women lust after the charismatically evil Edmund. This makes them jealous of each other and bitter rivals. Regan unscrupulously tries to open her sister's letter to Edmund as she looks to discover Goneril's feelings for Edmund. Later she feels threatened by Goneril and jealous of her sister's relationship with Edmund: 'She gave strange oeillades and most speaking looks / To noble Edmund'. Regan warns Goneril to stay away from Edmund.

Goneril is equally jealous of Regan, so much so that she kills her sister by poisoning her, just so that she has no rival for Edmund's affections. Both sisters are selfish and callous in the treatment of the other.

After Goneril's plot against Albany is made known Goneril stabs herself and dies. I think that she would rather die than face the consequences of her own villainy. Like her sister, she never repents for any of the vile things that she does throughout the play.

Shakespeare emphasises Goneril and Regan's inhumanity by using animal imagery to describe them. Goneril and Regan are consistently associated with vicious creatures. Albany calls them 'Tigers, not daughters' and says that they behave like animals of prey: 'Humanity must perforce prey on itself, / Like monsters of the deep'.

Lear too uses ugly animal imagery to criticise his daughters. He calls Goneril a 'Detested kite!' and describes her face as a 'wolvish visage'; her ingratitude feels 'sharper than a serpent's tooth'. Later, Lear labels Goneril and Regan 'pelican daughters' as he imagines them as birds that feed on the flesh of their parent.

Gloucester too describes Lear's two eldest daughters in animalistic terms. He tells them:

> 'I would not see
> Thy cruel nails pluck out his poor old eyes;
> Nor thy fierce sister in his anointed flesh
> Stick boarish fangs'.

In all of these examples Goneril and Regan's behaviour is shown to be savage. Both women subscribe to the 'law of the jungle', as they always try to serve their own interests best.

Because of their hypocrisy, cruelty and selfishness, I find the character and conduct of Goneril and Regan to be utterly despicable.

Higher Level Exam Tips

- ◎ **Answer the question:** This may seem obvious but it is vital that you remain focused on what exactly the question is asking.
- ◎ **Structure your answer:** Take a few minutes to plan the shape of your essay. Sequence your ideas in a logical order.
- ◎ **Include an introduction:** Address the question directly and outline your general response.
- ◎ **Make points. Don't narrate the plot:** Although there are times when you will need to explain what has occurred in a scene, it is important that you don't merely retell the story.
- ◎ **Use topic sentences:** It should be clear to the examiner what the overall point of each paragraph is. This is usually done in the opening sentence of each paragraph.
- ◎ **Make one point per paragraph.** Each paragraph should deal with one main idea that is discussed by referring to the play.
- ◎ **Quote and refer:** The examiner is keen to see that you have an in-depth knowledge of the play. Illustrate this by using quotations and making appropriate references.
- ◎ **Include a conclusion:** This should 'wrap up' your essay by drawing all your main points together.
- ◎ **Watch your timing:** Most students spend approximately one hour on the Single Text question.

Higher Level Exam Topics

- ◎ **Characters:** Think about how characters are portrayed, the relationship between central characters and the dramatic importance of key characters.
- ◎ **Themes**
- ◎ **Key scenes:** Focus on scenes that are tense or exciting, act as turning points, illuminate the characters' personalities and/or seem of thematic importance.
- ◎ **Soliloquies:** These are intimate moments when a character reflects on their situation out loud to the audience.
- ◎ **Imagery**, **symbolism** and **language**
- ◎ Your **personal response** to the play

Higher Level – Past Exam Questions
Each question is worth 60 marks.

2010

(i) 'In *King Lear* honour and loyalty triumph over brutality and viciousness.'
Write your response to this statement supporting your answer with suitable reference to the text.

OR

(ii) 'In *King Lear* the villainous characters hold more fascination for the audience than the virtuous ones.'
Discuss this statement with reference to at least one villainous and one virtuous character. Support your answer with suitable reference to the text.   **See sample answer on p.236**

2006

(i) 'In the play, *King Lear*, the stories of Lear and Gloucester mirror one another in interesting ways.'
Write a response to this view of the play, supporting your answer by reference to the text.

OR

(ii) 'Reading or seeing *King Lear* is a horrifying as well as an uplifting experience.'
Write a response to this view, supporting the points you make by reference to the text.

2002

(i) 'Powerful images heighten our experience of the play, *King Lear*.'   **See sample answer on p.238**
Write your response to this statement. Textual support may include reference to a particular performance you have seen of the play.

OR

(ii) 'Cordelia plays a very important role in the play, *King Lear*.'
Discuss this view of Cordelia, supporting your answer by reference to the play.

2001

(i) What, in your view, are the most important changes that take place in the character of Lear during the play, *King Lear*? Support your points by reference to the play.

OR

(ii) 'Scenes of great suffering and of great tenderness help to make *King Lear* a very memorable play.'
Discuss this statement, supporting your answer by reference to the play, *King Lear*.

Higher Level – Sample Questions

1. 'Despite his flaws, King Lear invites the audience's sympathy.'
   Discuss this statement, supporting your answer by reference to the play, *King Lear*.
2. Discuss the role of the Fool in Shakespeare's play *King Lear*. Support your points by reference to the play.
3. 'Through a process of intense suffering, Lear becomes a wiser man by the end of the play.'
   Write your response to this statement. Textual support may include reference to a particular performance you have seen of the play.
4. '*King Lear* presents a frightening vision of evil and human cruelty.'
   Write a response to this view of the play, supporting your answer by reference to the text.
5. King Lear says, 'I am a man / More sinned against than sinning.' Do you agree with this self-assessment?
   Explain your answer by making reference to the play *King Lear*.
6. 'Madness is a central theme of *King Lear*.'
   Write your response to this statement supporting your answer with suitable reference to the text.
7. '*King Lear* is a fascinating exploration of the destructive consequences of excessive pride.'
   Discuss this view of Shakespeare's *King Lear*. Support your answer by making reference to the text.
8. 'The audience of *King Lear* are moved by powerful moments of both hope and despair.'
   Discuss this statement with reference to at least one moment of hope and one moment of despair. Support your answer with suitable reference to the text.
9. '*King Lear* explores the meaning of love.'
   Write your response to this statement supporting your answer with suitable reference to the text.
10. 'Goneril, Regan and Edmund embody the worst that humanity is capable of.'
    Write your response to this statement supporting your answer with suitable reference to the text.

Higher Level – Sample Answers

2010

(ii) **'In *King Lear* the villainous characters hold more fascination for the audience than the virtuous ones.'**
Discuss this statement with reference to at least one villainous and one virtuous character. Support your answer with suitable reference to the text.

(ii) Shakespeare creates incredible and memorable characters in 'King Lear'. The audience are offered a spectrum of humanity on stage, from the saintly goodness of Cordelia to the malevolent, depravity of Goneril and Regan. Although I find the good characters interesting, the evil characters do more to capture my imagination and sustain my fascination. This is because the spectacle of human evil is powerful and frightening, and therefore more thrilling than the vision of goodness. I am therefore more fascinated by Lear's evil daughters, Goneril and Regan than I am by Cordelia.

Although she is remarkable for her good and loving nature, Cordelia fails to fully capture my imagination. Cordelia is a paragon of virtue. She sets herself apart from her sisters as a woman of great courage and integrity. While her sisters falsely flatter Lear to secure a larger portion of his kingdom, Cordelia remains true to her principles, choosing to 'love and be silent'. She has no time for the 'glib and oily art', the smooth talking of her sisters.

As a shining example of goodness, Cordelia understands the true nature of love, that it can be neither quantified nor measured. As such her love for her father cannot be reduced to mere words: 'I cannot heave / My heart into my mouth', 'I am sure, my love's / More ponderous than my tongue'. However, after seeing the play, I did not find myself reflecting on Cordelia as a character. I appreciate her goodness but she fails to fascinate me.

The only aspect of Cordelia's character that I do find fascinating is the inflexibility of her idealism. Although her virtue is admirable, I feel that she is somewhat stubborn in her refusal to humour Lear during the love-test. Lear is an old man, no longer at the height of his powers. Perhaps if Cordelia had taken part in the love-test, to please her father, then much of the catastrophe could have been averted.

Aside from this aspect of her character, Cordelia is largely defined by her goodness. This is perhaps most evident in her forgiving nature. Despite the fact that Lear's misplaced pride leads him to disown her, Cordelia is constant in her concern for his wellbeing. Just before she is sent away by Lear, she expresses her wish that Lear could reside with someone other than her sisters: 'I prefer him to a better place'.

Never in the play does Cordelia blame or speak ill of her father. Instead she looks to forgive him. When she learns of Lear's fragmenting mental state, she sends out a party to find him and cries out for him to be healed: 'All you unpublished virtues of the earth, / Spring with my tears! Be aidant and remediate / In the good man's distress!' Her generosity of spirit is evident when she says she would gladly give away all of her wealth if it would cure Lear: 'He that helps him take all my outward worth'.

Cordelia's goodness is furthered underlined by her religious significance. Although this is an important aspect of the play, it is not something that interests me as much as the spectacle of human evil. Shakespeare associates Cordelia with the divine by describing her in heavenly terms: 'she shook / The holy water from her heavenly eyes'. Similarly, after being reunited with Cordelia, Lear thinks she is an angel ('Thou art a soul in bliss') who has come to him in death. Shakespeare makes Cordelia a Christ-like figure by stressing her saintly nature. This chimes with her great capacity for forgiveness.

This idea is furthered through her association with healing. She seeks to cure Lear of his 'bereaved sense' as she tenderly kisses him:

> 'O my dear father! Restoration hang
> Thy medicine on my lips, and let this kiss
> Repair those violent harms that my two sisters
> Have in thy reverence made!'

Her compassion here is a moving reminder of her innate goodness.

As a Christ-like figure, Cordelia displays extraordinary humility. Upon being reunited with Lear, her first action is to ask for Lear's blessing: 'O, look upon me, sir, / And hold your hands in benediction o'er me!' After being so grossly mistreated by Lear she holds no grudge and instead gives her forgiveness readily. Cordelia's Christ-like nature is an interesting facet of who she is but it doesn't make her fascinating.

Cordelia is a well-drawn character, whose dramatic function is to help lead Lear towards wisdom and to serve as a foil to her evil sisters. However, as an individual she fails to hold my fascination. Goneril and Regan, as vile as they are, are far more interesting. Their inhuman cruelty shows the worst of humanity. I find this unsettling but ultimately thrilling.

Both Goneril and Regan reveal their hypocritical natures during the love-test. Without hesitation they each testify to their love for their ageing father. Goneril tells Lear, 'Sir, I love you more than words can wield the matter'. While Regan tries to top her sister: 'I find she names my very deed of love; / Only she comes too short'. In truth both sisters are simply looking to pander to their father's ego in order to secure a larger portion of his kingdom. Although it is Cordelia who does the right thing during the love-test, I find myself more interested in the self-serving motives of Goneril and Regan. Although I don't approve of their behaviour, it makes for great drama, bringing wonderful conflict to the stage.

Both Goneril and Regan are utterly callous in their mistreatment of their father. Goneril encourages Oswald to treat Lear with contempt to erode his status as King: 'Put on what weary negligence you please'. Goneril understands her father's pride is his weakness; by undermining this she successfully provokes a confrontation with her father as she looks to erode his status as King. This strategy is continued as she reduces his train of knights. This provokes Lear's rage and prompts him to leave her castle.

Regan is equally vile in her treatment of her father. She too reduces his train of knights. When Lear pathetically protests, 'I gave you all –.' Regan coldly replies: 'And in good time you gave it'. After Lear goes out into the storm, Regan, with characteristic callousness, orders the castle gates closed against him, effectively abandoning Lear to the violent storm. Goneril and Regan's reprehensible treatment of Lear is disquieting but also a fascinating contrast to the loyalty and goodness of Cordelia.

Goneril and Regan's inhumanity is most dramatically represented during the spectacle of the eye-gouging scene. As Gloucester is brought before them and bound, Goneril cries, 'Pluck out his eyes!' and it is Regan that calls for his second eye to be gouged: 'One side will mock another – the other too!' The torture is finished only when Gloucester is thrown out of his own castle; the horror is compounded by Regan's cruel remark that Gloucester must, 'smell / His way to Dover.' This moment of evil truly displays the depth of the sisters' depravity and the utter evil that humanity is capable of. Their despicable behaviour is grossly fascinating for an audience.

The deaths of Goneril and Regan are also a source of fascination for the audience. Both sisters are bitter rivals for the affections of Edmund. So much so that Goneril poisons her sister, callously murdering her, simply to facilitate her lust for Edmund. Goneril then takes her own life after her treacherous plan to murder Albany is revealed. I find Goneril's motives here fascinating. Driven by lust she kills her sister. Her reasons for taking her own life are less clear. Some critics argue that she is ashamed once her treachery is publicly revealed. However, I believe that her suicide is a way of avoiding punishment and condemnation. Again, villainy, although disquieting, is fascinating to watch.

Ultimately, the villainous characters are more fascinating than the virtuous ones. Although the good characters serve an important dramatic function, the evil ones frighten, thrill and shock the audience. It is villainy that offers so much of the dramatic tension on stage. An exploration of the evil characters' motivations offers an audience a fascinating look at the roots of evil. This is what finally endures in the audience's imagination.

2002

(i) **'Powerful images heighten our experience of the play, *King Lear*.'**
Write your response to this statement. Textual support may include reference to a particular performance you have seen of the play.

(i) Shakespeare's use of powerful imagery in 'King Lear' is a hugely important element of the drama. The imagery adds great poetry to the language and helps to illuminate the play's key themes. For me, two patterns of imagery are particularly memorable: animal imagery and images of blindness.

'King Lear' is rich in animal imagery including thirty-four references to dogs, nineteen to horses, fourteen to birds, six to wolves, five to foxes, four to snakes, three to rats and two to worms. 'King Lear' examines humanity's place in the natural order; the play is also a condemnation of inhumanity. The animal imagery facilitates this exploration. Throughout the play Goneril and Regan's unnatural behaviour illustrates what is worst in humanity. They falsely flatter Lear to enrich themselves; they provoke their father by exploiting his weaknesses; they callously abandon Lear to a ferocious storm; they contribute to the horrendous torture of Gloucester; and they bitterly compete for Edmund's affections. In the end Goneril kills Regan and then herself. Animal imagery is used to highlight the unnaturalness of this behaviour and suggests that Goneril and Regan have stooped to the level of beasts.

Animal imagery is used by many of the characters to describe Goneril and Regan. They are labelled 'Tigers, not daughters' by Albany who then compares them with animals of prey: 'Humanity must perforce prey on itself, / Like monsters of the deep'. Here Albany is condemning both women for their cruel inhumanity. He abhors their abandonment of morality and their embracement of the 'law of the jungle'.

Similarly, Goneril and Regan are criticised by their father through the use of ugly animal imagery. Lear calls Goneril a 'Detested kite!' and describes her face as a 'wolvish visage'. Later, Lear dubs them 'pelican daughters' as he imagines his two eldest daughters as young birds cannibalising their parent.

Just before he is blinded, Gloucester too describes Goneril and Regan in animalistic terms. He tells them: 'I would not see / Thy cruel nails pluck out his poor old eyes;
                         Nor thy fierce sister in his anointed flesh / Stick boarish fangs'.
Shakespeare makes use of animal imagery to emphasise the barbarity and inhumanity of Goneril and Regan. The comparison of the characters' vicious behaviour with animal savagery, points to the vileness that humanity is capable of. Animal imagery is employed, not to illustrate how humans are similar to animals but rather to distinguish between them. Goneril and Regan's behaviour invites the audience approbation and recognition of its unnaturalness. The animal imagery heightened my awareness of this idea.

Shakespeare also uses animal imagery to represent the characters' attempts to understand humanity's place in the chain of being. It provokes the question: what is a man and where is his place in the natural order? As Lear's pride is toppled during the storm scene, he comes to see humanity as having no greater significance than an animal. He declares that 'man is no more but such a poor bare, forked animal'. This is prompted by the spectacle of Poor Tom's suffering. At this point of the play Lear fails to see the dignity that comes with being human.

Echoing this, Gloucester says that the unfortunate sight of Poor Tom 'made [him] think a man a worm'. Gloucester despairs that next to the gods, humanity is as insignificant and feeble as a fly: 'As flies to wanton boys, are we to the gods. / They kill us for their sport'.

Both Lear and Gloucester try to make sense of their own suffering. Through this process they initially fail to differentiate between the status of humanity and animals. However, as they grow in wisdom, both characters come to understand the dignity of being human. Gloucester appreciates humanity's capacity to endure suffering as he accepts Edgar's view that 'Men must endure / Their going hence, even as their coming hither; / Ripeness is all.' Lear too comes to see the value of humanity. He draws on animal imagery as he recognises the true value of life and the dignity that comes with being human. As he pitifully grieves over Cordelia's body he cries, 'Why should a dog, a horse, a rat, have life / And thou no breath at all?' Lear has come to see that a human's life is more important than an animal's; he now appreciates humanity's greater status in the chain of being.

Animal imagery in 'King Lear' heightens the audience's understanding of some of the play's central themes. Shakespeare uses it to explore the value of human life and to condemn human villainy.

Like the play's animal imagery, images of blindness and seeing offer powerful metaphors that enrich the exploration of key themes. Blindness is present through the language but also, in the harrowing spectacle of the eye-gouging scene.

Shakespeare uses blindness imagery to highlight the moral blindness of the characters, principally Lear and Gloucester. At the start of the play, Lear is presented as a man blinded by his inflated pride. In his short-sightedness Lear abdicates his royal responsibilities but still retains the title of King. Just as he is blind to his own folly, Lear fails to recognise the true natures of his daughters: he is fooled by Goneril and Regan's empty flattery of him and misunderstands Cordelia's plain spoken words. The imagery in this scene stresses the idea of Lear's blind judgement. When Lear disowns Cordelia he shouts, 'Out of my sight!' Perceptively, Kent recognises Lear's inability to see his daughters' true natures and says, 'See better, Lear'.

As Lear starts to understand his own flaws and recognises the emptiness of his inflated pride, the imagery changes to one of seeing. Amidst his 'madness', Lear recognises Gloucester: 'I remember thine eyes well enough' and, 'If thou wilt weep my fortunes, take my eyes. / I know thee well enough, thy name is Gloucester'. Lear says that 'A man may see how this world goes with no eyes'. The imagery of seeing echoes Lear's attainment of insight. As the fog of his moral blindness lifts, Lear can now recognise his own folly and flawed humanity.

Gloucester too is morally blind at the start of the play. Shakespeare shows that Gloucester does not see the significance of his lust that produced Edmund. Gloucester is also blind to the true natures of his own sons as he lacks the insight to recognise Edmund as a scheming villain. There is great irony when he is presented with a forged letter by Edmund, only to comment that he will not need 'spectacles' to read it. Gloucester also is initially unable to see Edgar for who he really is. Instead he disowns him, branding him a villain: 'O villain, villain! His very opinion in the letter! Abhorred villain! Unnatural, detested, brutish villain! Worse than brutish…Abominable villain!'

Gloucester is punished in a very literal way for his moral blindness: his eyes are gouged out. As Edgar says to Edmund: 'The dark and vicious place where thee he got / Cost him his eyes.' The dramatic spectacle of Gloucester being blinded is intensified by the other characters' language. Goneril cries, 'Pluck out his eyes' and Cornwall cruelly says, 'Out, vile jelly! / Where is thy lustre now?'

Ironically, after he is blinded, Gloucester develops moral vision. He starts to see his own folly, 'I stumbled when I saw' and tells Lear that now he is blinded he understands the world at a deeper emotional level: 'I see it feelingly'.

The imagery of blindness and seeing is continued as Gloucester comes to see Edgar's true nature: 'O dear son Edgar, / The food of thy abused father's wrath! /
                    Might I but live to see thee in my touch, / I'd say I had eyes again!'

As with Lear, the fog of Gloucester's spiritual blindness lifts as he grows in insight. Both men see their own flawed humanity and accept ownership of their own fates. Empathising with the suffering of others, they grow in compassion. Importantly, both men see their children's true natures, recognising the depth of love in their loyal children (Cordelia and Edgar). These ideas are brought together in the play through the imagery of blindness and seeing.

Shakespeare's motifs in 'King Lear' are not confined to animal and blindness imagery. The rich tapestry of his writing makes use of many extended metaphors and recurring images. However, I feel that the images I have discussed here, enriched my experience of the play and heightened my understanding of many of the key themes.